CW01249928

Medieval ring brooches in Ireland

Medieval ring brooches in Ireland

A study of jewellery, dress and society

Mary B. Deevy

Wordwell

Monograph Series No. 1

First published in 1998
Wordwell Ltd
PO Box 69, Bray, Co. Wicklow

Copyright © Wordwell 1998.

All rights reserved. No part of this book may be reprinted or reproduced or utilised in any electronic, mechanical or other means, now known or hereafter invented, including photocopying and recording, or otherwise without either the prior written consent of the publishers or a licence permitting restricted copying in Ireland issued by the Irish Copyright Licensing Agency Ltd, The Writers' Centre, 19 Parnell Square, Dublin 1.

ISBN 1 869857 24 0

British Library Cataloguing-in-Publication Data.
A catalogue record for this book is available from the British Library.

Editor: Emer Condit
Cover design: Catherine MacConville

Typeset in Ireland by Wordwell Ltd.
Origination by Wordwell Ltd and the Type Bureau.

Printed by Brookfield Printing Company.

CONTENTS

List of figures	vi
List of plates	vii
Acknowledgements	ix
I Introduction	1
II Classification, chronology and comparative material	5
III Distribution and provenances	29
IV Medieval metalworking and the manufacture of ring brooches	39
V Medieval dress and the wearing of ring brooches	53
VI Jewellery and society in medieval Ireland	63
References	75
Catalogue of ring brooches	87
Glossary	141

LIST OF FIGURES

1. Terminology.
2. Diameters of ring brooch frames.
3. Metals used in the manufacture of ring brooches.
4. Classes of ring brooch.
5. Representative examples of classes of ring brooch.
6. Mid–late fourteenth-century gunmetal ring brooch, London (after Egan 1991c, 249, cat. no. 1307).
7. Copper-alloy ring brooch, Glenluce, Scotland (after Jope *et al.* 1960).
8. Mid-thirteenth-century gunmetal ring brooch, London (after Egan 1991c, 249, cat. no. 1310).
9. Late thirteenth/early fourteenth-century copper-alloy ring brooch, Winchester (after Biddle and Hinton 1990, 642, cat. no. 2025).
10. Mid-thirteenth-century gunmetal ring brooch, London (after Egan 1991c, 249, cat. no. 1309).
11. Mid–late fourteenth-century bronze ring brooch with traces of gilding, London (after Egan 1991c, 251, cat. no. 1319).
12. Late thirteenth/mid-fourteenth-century gunmetal ring brooch, London (after Egan 1991c, 254, cat. no. 1335).
13. Early thirteenth-century pewter ring brooch, London (after Egan 1991c, 253, cat. no. 1323).
14. Late thirteenth/mid-fourteenth-century pewter ring brooch, London (after Egan 1991c, 253, cat. no. 1328).
15. Distribution of medieval ring brooches in Ireland.
16. Distribution of medieval ring brooches in Dublin. (Map: Aidan O'Sullivan.)
17. Regional distribution of medieval ring brooch classes in Ireland.
18. Provenance of ring brooches.
19. Means of recovery of ring brooches.
20. Clay ring brooch mould from Ashill, Norfolk, England (after Anon. 1808).
21. Thirteenth-century stone effigy of Queen Berengaria, Espan, France (after Stothard 1876).
22. Late fourteenth-century stone effigy from Wales, depicting paternosters with ring brooches and other jewellery attached (after Gresham 1968).
23. Late fourteenth-century stone effigy from Wales, depicting paternosters with ring brooches and other jewellery attached (after Gresham 1968).
24. Late thirteenth-century stone sculpture of a young male musician, Maison des Musiciens, Rheims, France (after Musée du Louvre 1968).
25. Late thirteenth-century stone sculpture of a young male harper, Maison des Musiciens, Rheims, France (after Evans 1952).

LIST OF PLATES

1. RB 25: unprovenanced copper-alloy ring brooch (Class 1).
2. RB 16, 22 and 27: unprovenanced silver ring brooches (Class 1).
3. RB 34 and 60: copper-alloy ring brooch, Ardara, Co. Donegal, and unprovenanced silver ring brooch (Class 2).
4. RB 65: unprovenanced silver ring brooch (Class 2).
5. RB 48: copper-alloy ring brooch, Knowth, Co. Meath (Class 2).
6. RB 80 (obverse): silver ring brooch, Trim, Co. Meath (Class 2).
7. RB 80 (reverse): silver ring brooch, Trim, Co. Meath (Class 2).
8. RB 85 and 86: unprovenanced silver and gold ring brooches (Class 2).
9. RB 91, 92 and 97: silver ring brooch, Killeigh, Co. Offaly; copper-alloy ring brooch, Co. Roscommon; and unprovenanced silver ring brooch (Class 3).
10. RB 98: unprovenanced silver ring brooch (Class 3).
11. RB 103 and 104: silver ring brooch, Trim, Co. Meath, and unprovenanced silver ring brooch (Class 3).
12. RB 106: silver ring brooch, Athlone, Co. Meath (Class 4).
13. RB 108: silver ring brooch, Dysart, Co. Westmeath (Class 5).
14. RB 110: gold ring brooch, Marlboro Street, Dublin (Class 6).
15. RB 112: unprovenanced silver ring brooch (Class 6).
16. RB 116: copper-alloy ring brooch, Cornmarket/Francis Street, Dublin (Class 6).
17. RB 117: gold ring brooch, Bakehouse Lane, Waterford (Class 6).
18. RB 118: gold ring brooch, Enniscorthy, Co. Wexford (Class 6).
19. RB 121, 122, 123 and 125: gold ring brooches—Ballinrea, Co. Cork; County Kilkenny; Trim, Co. Meath; unprovenanced (Class 7).
20. RB 124: unprovenanced gold ring brooch (Class 7).
21. RB 132 and 134: lead-alloy ring brooches, Wood Quay, Dublin (Class 8).
22. RB 140: unprovenanced silver ring brooch (Class 9).
23. Late thirteenth/early fourteenth-century (K. Campbell, pers. comm.) pottery sherd with ring brooch excavated at South Quay, James Street, Drogheda, Co. Louth.
24. Late thirteenth/early fourteenth-century stone effigy of a woman, church of St John the Baptist, Cashel, Co. Tipperary.
25. Late thirteenth-century (Barry 1987) stone carving of a man, label stop on the porch of St Canice's Cathedral, Kilkenny.
26. Late thirteenth-century (Barry 1987) stone carving of a woman, label stop on the porch of St Canice's Cathedral, Kilkenny.
27. Early sixteenth-century (Hunt 1974) stone carving of Christ showing his five wounds, on the tomb-chest of a Butler knight in Gowran, Co. Kilkenny.
28. Sixteenth-century (Hunt 1974) stone carving of St Margaret of Antioch, on a tomb-chest at Jerpoint Abbey.
29. Sixteenth-century (Hunt 1974) stone carving of St Andrew, on a tomb-chest at Jerpoint Abbey.
30. Fifteenth-century (MacLeod 1945) wooden sculpture of St Catherine, Kilcorban,

Co. Galway (after Mahr 1976).
31. Thirteenth-century mural depicting *Largesce* and *Covoitise*, originally in the chamber of Westminster, London. (By permission of the Society of Antiquaries of London.)
32. Fourteenth-century French manuscript illustration of a woman working at a forge, from *Le Roman de la Rose* by Guillaume de Lorris and Jean de Meun, MS 1126, folio 115. (By permission of La Bibliothèque Sainte-Geneviève, Paris.)
33. Fourteenth-century English manuscript illustration of a blacksmith, from BL Egerton MS 1894, f. 2vo. (By permission of the British Library.)
34. Fourteenth-century German illustration on parchment of St Hedwig of Silesia

The author is indebted to many people and organisations who have generously allowed her to reproduce photographs of items in their collections. I wish to thank the following (many of whom also retain the copyright): Director Patrick Wallace and the National Museum of Ireland; John Cherry and the British Museum; the British Library; the Society of Antiquaries of London; La Bibliothèque Sainte-Geneviève, Paris; Eamonn McEneaney and Waterford Corporation; the Office of Public Works; St Canice's Cathedral, Kilkenny; Kieran Campbell; Dr George Eogan and Alan Hayden.

ACKNOWLEDGEMENTS

This book is based on an M.A. thesis submitted to the Department of Archaeology, University College Dublin, in 1995. I would firstly like to thank Dr George Eogan, then head of the department, and John Bradley, my supervisor, for advice and encouragement throughout the writing of the thesis. The staff of a number of museums not only allowed me access to their collections but were also very helpful with my enquiries, for which I am most grateful: Dr Patrick Wallace and the staff of the National Museum of Ireland (Paul Mullarky was particularly helpful, with comments on many of the brooches and advice on metalworking in general); John Cherry of the British Museum, London; Julia Nicholson of the Pitt Rivers Museum, Oxford; Cormac Bourke of the Ulster Museum, Belfast; Stella Cherry of the Cork Public Museum; Mairéad Dunlevy, then director of the Hunt Museum, Limerick; Daire O'Rourke, then archaeologist in 'Dublinia'; Orla Scully and the Town Clerk of Waterford Corporation, who allowed me access to the Waterford Heritage Centre out of season; and Christopher Chippindale of the Cambridge University Museum, who sent me information on Irish artifacts.

I would also like to thank a number of individuals who kindly allowed me access to artifacts in their care and/or provided me with information in advance of their own publications: Kieran Campbell, Rose Cleary, Dr George Eogan, Alan Hayden, Jim Higgins, Brian Hodkinson and the St Mary's Restoration Project Committee, Maurice Hurley, Dr Ann Lynch, Dr Betty O'Brien, Raghnall Ó Floinn, Dr Mark Redknap, Helen Roche, Lesley Simpson, Linzi Simpson, Dr Patrick Wallace and Claire Walsh.

A number of individuals also generously provided me with slides: Dr Ann Lynch, Lesley Simpson, Dr George Eogan, Eamonn McEneaney and John Cherry. I would like to thank David Jennings, who photographed many of the brooches. Christine Baker very kindly allowed me to read her M.A. thesis on Irish medieval finger-rings, and Sarah Cross supplied the original backdrop maps of Ireland.

I am indebted to many people who assisted me in my enquiries on various aspects of the research. These include Dr Terry Barry, John Cherry, Dr Philomena Connolly, Professor Christine Meek, Dr Kieran O'Connor and Seamus Taaffe.

I am especially grateful to Dr Gabriel Cooney, John Cherry and Dr Terry Barry, who all gave freely of their valuable time to read and comment on drafts of the book. They saved me from many errors and omissions and improved the text enormously. Where mistakes remain, they are, of course, my own.

I would like to thank Miriam McAlinney for her assistance with my fieldwork, and Mary and Paddy McAlinney for their generous hospitality. I owe the greatest debt of gratitude to Aidan O'Sullivan for his advice, constant encouragement, and endless proof-reading and comments on the thesis. He is also responsible for the excellent production of the artifact drawings and distribution maps for both the thesis and the final publication. Finally I would like to acknowledge the work of Jen Brady, Emer Condit and Nick Maxwell of Wordwell Ltd in the production of this book.

Dedicated to the memory of Andrew Deevy (1939–91).

I. INTRODUCTION

Introduction

The study of medieval jewellery can introduce us to many aspects of life in the Middle Ages, including aesthetic perceptions of art and beauty, concepts of wealth and worth, and occasionally the complexity of spiritual beliefs. Ring brooches were one of the most common items of medieval jewellery. This study examines the corpus of Irish medieval ring brooches to enable investigation into these and other aspects of medieval Irish society.

The origin of medieval ring brooches is unclear. Ring brooches have been compared to penannular and annular brooches, which date from the sixth to the tenth century AD. While these brooches were also primarily practical dress-fasteners they functioned in a completely different way. Medieval ring brooches have more in common with Anglo-Saxon annular brooches dating from the fifth to the seventh century AD. These dress-fasteners functioned in exactly the same way but were worn in a different position on the costume. Some types of Anglo-Saxon annular brooches are quite distinctive, with a wide flat frame and rows of ring and dot ornament. However, others are very similar to some of the simply decorated medieval brooches. Annular brooches are known as early as the first century AD from Scandinavia and northern Germany, and the Anglo-Saxon types may have derived from these (Hirst 1985, 56). The earliest date for the occurrence of ring brooches in Ireland is in the late twelfth century. This agrees with the dating for the popular wearing of ring brooches throughout Europe, including Britain. While the introduction of the ring brooch to Ireland was probably largely a result of the Anglo-Norman invasions, it can also be viewed as a consequence of the commercial and cultural contacts with Britain and continental Europe that existed long before 1171.

Ring brooches and annular buckles

A distinction has been made in this study between annular buckles and ring brooches. There are many similarities between annular buckles and the simpler ring brooches so that the differences are not always immediately clear. It could be pointed out that the similarities in form between annular buckles and ring brooches may also have been reflected in their respective uses in the Middle Ages. Nevertheless it has been proposed (Egan 1991b, 65) that a frame with a constriction or hole which limits the movement of the pin can be classified as a ring brooch. Similarly, a frame without a constriction or perforation limiting the movement of the pin around the circumference of the frame is an annular buckle. This is a general rule, and some exceptions and occasional ambiguous artifacts do occur, such as circular frames without a constriction but made of precious metal and highly decorated (e.g. Egan 1991b, 65, fig. 39:211 and 213). There are three such exceptions in this study, i.e. three artifacts which do not have constrictions but which are identical in their decoration to ring brooches; these are included here as ring brooches.

Nomenclature

There are many inconsistencies in the nomenclature of early medieval and medieval jewellery. Traditionally the brooches examined in this study are known as 'ring brooches'. In Britain the term 'ring brooch' is preferred by many archaeologists and jewellery historians (Cherry 1985; 1987; 1988; Murdoch 1991; Lightbown 1992), while the term 'annular brooch' is now more commonly employed by British archaeologists in excavation reports. Both terms are used by Irish archaeologists. However, in both Ireland and Britain various types of Early Christian brooches and brooch pins have been called 'ring brooches' in both nineteenth-century and more recent literature (Ryan 1983, 146–7, nos 64–5; M.G. Welch 1989; Brown 1977). Using the term 'annular brooch' does not circumvent the possible confusion generated by the term 'ring brooch'. What have previously been referred to as 'pseudo-penannular brooches' and 'pseudo-penannular brooch pins' have also recently been called 'annular brooches' (Youngs 1990, 91–107). Fanning (1994) termed some of his ringed pins 'penannular ring-brooches' and 'pseudo-penannular ring-brooches' in order to distinguish them from the classic 'ringed pin', as he explained that they would have functioned in a similar way to penannular or pseudo-penannular brooches. It is desirable, however, to distinguish penannular brooches from ring brooches. In this study of a medieval brooch type the term 'ring brooch' is employed throughout.

History of research

The earliest publication of an Irish ring brooch was in 1854 in the *Journal of the Archaeological Institute of Great Britain and Ireland* (Anon. 1854, 285). This was a description and drawing of an inscribed gold ring brooch found near the ruins of Donaghmoyne or Mannin Castle in Monaghan. Similar antiquarian publications of stray finds included an inscribed silver ring brooch found near Carrickfergus Castle (Anon. 1857), a copper-alloy ring brooch from Castleskreen Castle, Co. Down (Anon. 1862, 233), and a silver ring brooch found at Killeigh, Co. Offaly (Anon. 1874, 81–2). Two silver ring brooches were listed as acquired by the Royal Irish Academy from the collection of the late Rev. Richard Butler in 1864 (Anon. 1864).

Four gold ring brooches were listed by William Wilde in a section on breast pins and brooches in his *A descriptive catalogue of the antiquities of gold in the museum of the Royal Irish Academy* (Wilde 1862, 44). Antiquarian excavations at the turn of the century also led to the discovery and publication of several brooches. A silver ring brooch was recovered during excavation of a mound at Patrickstown, Co. Meath (Crofton Rotheram 1898), while a copper-alloy ring brooch was found in a midden at Rosapenna, Co. Donegal (R. Welch 1902, 227). In 1915 Armstrong concluded and published a catalogue, begun by William Wilde, of the silver and ecclesiastical antiquities in the collection of the Royal Irish Academy. In a section on brooches he described 23 silver ring brooches and included drawings of two (Armstrong 1915, 294–5, pl. 26).

With the development of archaeological excavation, the number of published brooches increased. A copper-alloy ring brooch, described as 'a small bronze penannular brooch', was recovered from excavations at Nendrum, Co. Down (Lawlor 1925, pl. 11, no. 85), and another copper-alloy ring brooch was recovered from an excavation at Clonroad More, Ennis, Co. Clare (Hunt 1946, 205, fig. 3:6). A copper-alloy ring brooch found in a field in Kilkenny College, Kilkenny, was published in the list of the archaeological acquisitions of the National Museum of Ireland for the year 1959 (NMI 1961, 101, fig. 23:e). More recently, in 1976, a copper-alloy ring brooch was published in a paper entitled 'A descriptive catalogue of some ancient Irish metalwork in the collections of the Royal Ontario Museum, Toronto' (Pryor 1976, 88, fig. 33:84).

A number of ring brooches have been found during more recent archaeological investigations. A copper-alloy ring brooch was recovered during excavation of a medieval settlement site in Jerpointchurch townland, Co. Kilkenny (Foley 1989, 95, fig. 12:3644). A photograph of a ring brooch was published in a summary report of the Carrickfergus excavations (Simpson and Brannon 1988, 65). A photograph of the gold Waterford brooch was published in *The illustrated archaeology of Ireland* (Ryan 1991, 161). Lightbown (1992, 147–8) also mentioned this brooch in his study of medieval European jewellery. A ring brooch was among the finds described in the recent publication of Linzi Simpson's excavations at Essex Street West, in Temple Bar in Dublin (Johnson 1995, 75). The most recent publication of a number of Irish ring brooches was by Lightbown (1997) in his fascinating discussion of the jewellery from the Waterford City excavations.

The first actual discussion of Irish ring brooches is to be found in a preliminary survey of medieval jewellery from Ireland by Cherry (1988). This ground-breaking paper focuses on a number of items, including four ring brooches, which had been acquired by the British Museum in the nineteenth century. Cherry also discusses the three brooches from Tom Delaney's excavations at Carrickfergus and a small number of the brooches in the National Museum of Ireland's collection. More recently, the author has briefly discussed the distribution, use and symbolism of ring brooches in medieval Ireland (Deevy 1996).

There is no corpus of British or continental European ring brooches. There is, however, a paper on ring brooches in the National Museum of Antiquities of Scotland by James Graham Callender (1924). Recent publications of excavations in Winchester (Biddle 1990; Biddle and Hinton 1990) and London (Egan and Pritchard 1991) have been invaluable in providing comparative material with good archaeological dating and discussion. Recent publications of stray finds and brooches recovered from other excavations in Britain have also been valuable.

There are also a number of general histories of jewellery, such as those by Evans (1970), Steingraber (1957) and, more recently, Scarisbrick (1994), which have included chapters on medieval jewellery, and a number of catalogues of museum exhibitions which have included ring brooches (Cherry 1976; NMAS 1982). In 1992 Lightbown published the first 'full-length book on medieval jewellery' in Europe, in which he interwove 'social, economic, religious and political history with the history of fashion, style and iconography'. This important publication included a number of chapters on brooch types and a catalogue of the Victoria and Albert Museum's collection of jewellery.

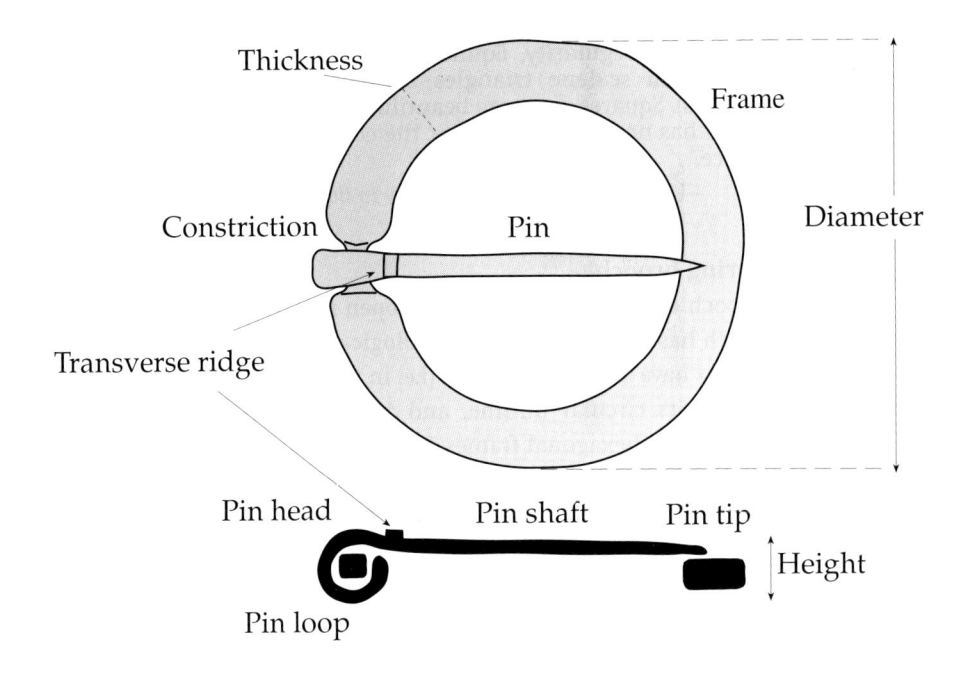

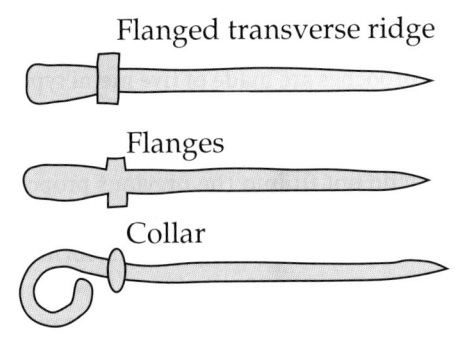

Fig. 1—Terminology.

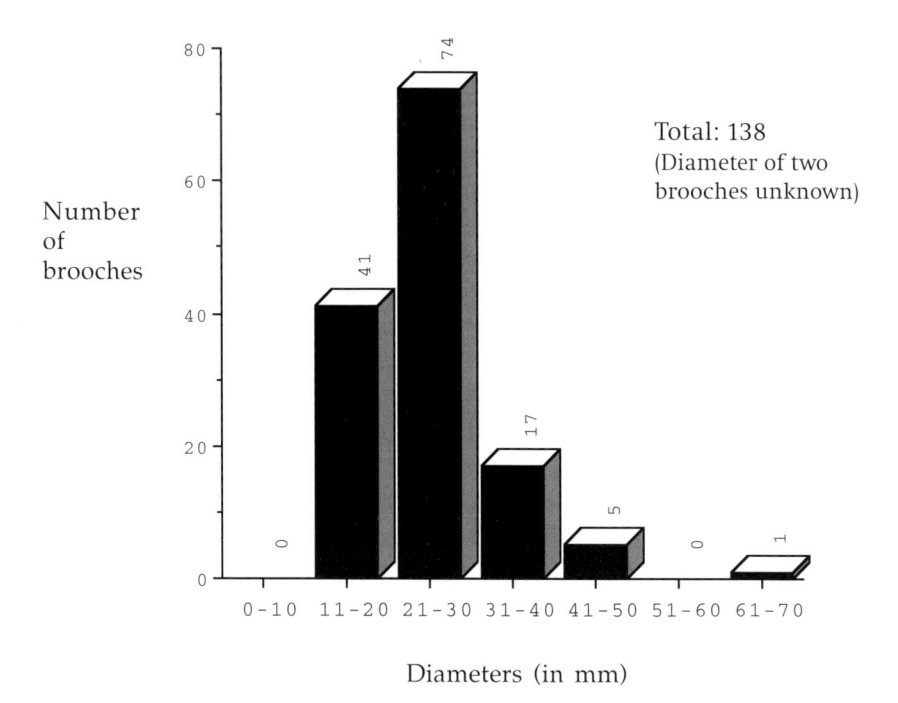

Fig. 2—Diameters of ring brooch frames.

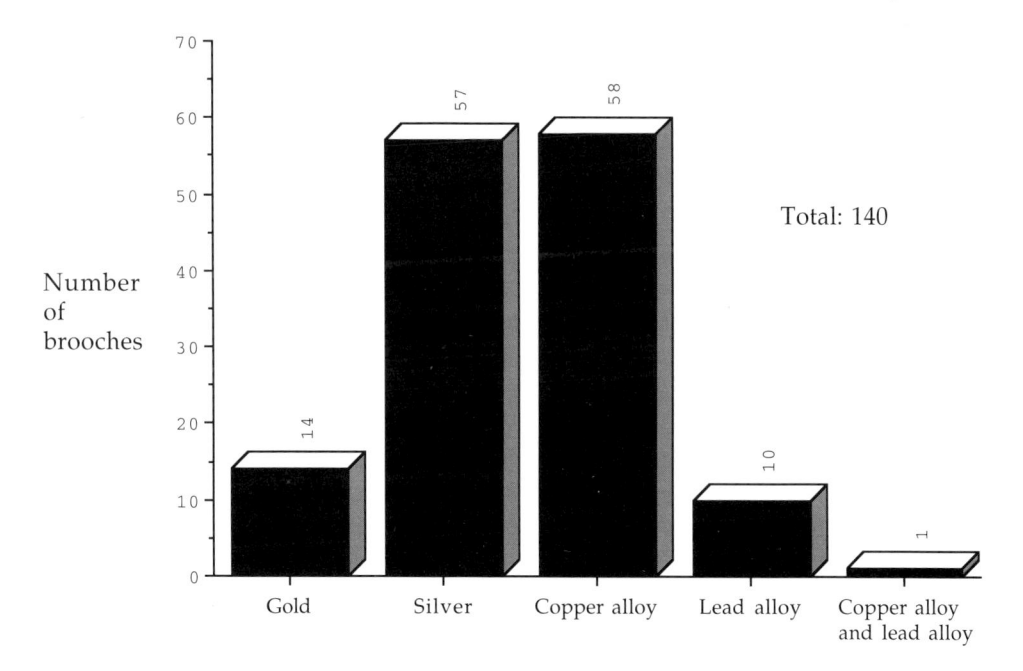

Fig. 3—Metals used in the manufacture of ring brooches.

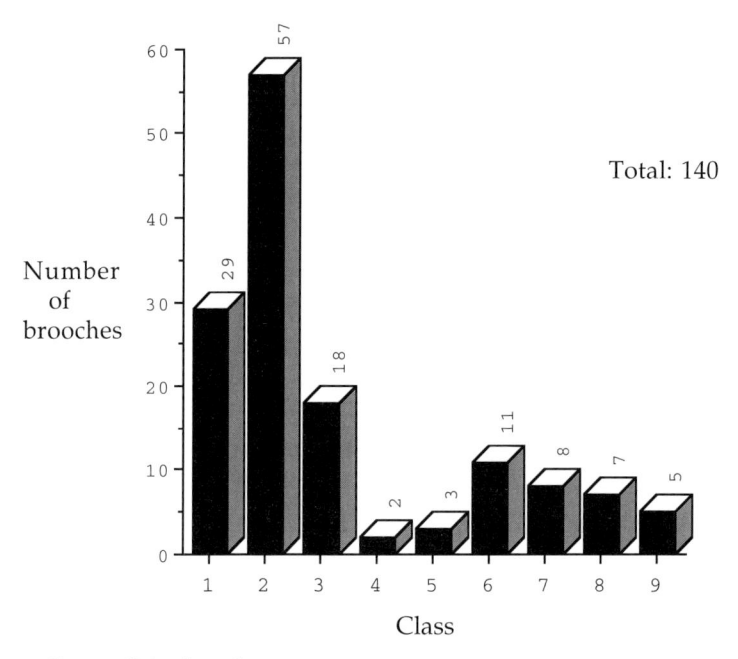

Fig. 4—Classes of ring brooch.

and the basis of this subdivision is discussed. Descriptions of examples of brooches from each class are used to establish the features of each class. Brooches are referred to by the letters 'RB' followed by their catalogue number (e.g. RB 1).

CLASS 1: undecorated ring brooches (RB 1–29)

There are 29 ring brooches in this class. Fifteen are made of silver, thirteen of copper alloy, and one of a combination of copper alloy and lead alloy. They measure between 12mm and 45mm in diameter, with an average of 22.5mm. Class 1 ring brooches have plain undecorated frames. They are all circular in outline and simple in form. They may have a flat, curved or bifaceted front face. The frame of the majority of Class 1 brooches narrows at one point to restrict the pin; however, nine have a small circular or D-shaped perforation which performs the same function. The pins may have a circular, plano-convex or rectangular cross-section. They may also have transverse ridges, flanges or collars. A ring brooch from Wood Quay, RB 8, is an unusual Class 1 brooch. Its frame is composed of two rings, an upper ring of copper alloy formed of sheet metal with a convex cross-section and a lower ring of lead with a rectangular cross-section. The lead ring may have added weight to what might otherwise have been quite a lightweight brooch.

Classification, chronology and comparative material

Class 1
Undecorated (RB1–29)

Class 2a

Class 2b

Class 2
With engraved and/or false relief decoration (RB 30–86)

Class 3a

Class 3b

Class 3
With cable decoration (RB 87–104)

Class 4
With applied plates (RB 105–6)

Class 5
Brooches with projecting elements
(RB 107–9)

Class 6a

Class 6b

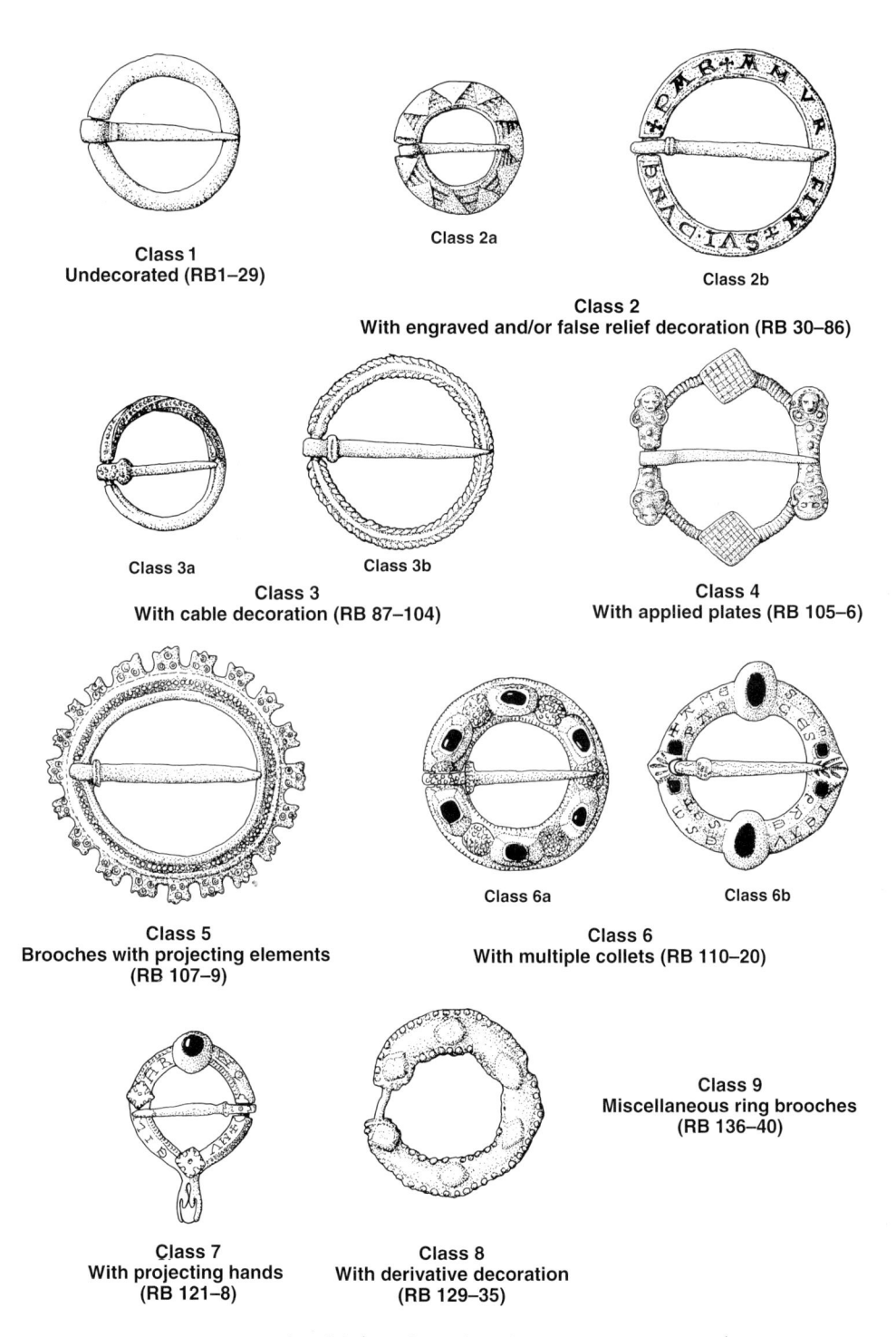

Class 6
With multiple collets (RB 110–20)

Class 7
With projecting hands
(RB 121–8)

Class 8
With derivative decoration
(RB 129–35)

Class 9
Miscellaneous ring brooches
(RB 136–40)

Fig. 5—Representative examples of classes of ring brooch.

Chronology and comparative material

Six of the 29 Class 1 brooches are contextually dated. RB 4, from High Street, Dublin, is contextually dated to the thirteenth century (A. Halpin, pers. comm.). Another brooch from High Street, Dublin, RB 5, is dated to the late twelfth/thirteenth century (A. Halpin, pers. comm.). RB 7, from Ross Road/Christchurch Place, Dublin, is dated to the first quarter of the thirteenth century (Walsh, forthcoming). Two brooches from Wood Quay, RB 8 and 9, are dated to the thirteenth century (A. Halpin, pers. comm.), and RB 12, from Bakehouse Lane, Waterford, is dated to between the mid-thirteenth and early seventeenth centuries (Lightbown 1997, 522). RB 3 was an unstratified find from St Mochaoi's monastery, Nendrum (Lawlor 1925, pl. 11, no. 85). This was essentially an early medieval monastery but a chancel was added to the church in the late twelfth century, when a Benedictine cell was established there (Barry 1987, 158). This was abandoned shortly afterwards, and it seems likely that the brooch may date from this late twelfth- to early thirteenth-century period.

These simple undecorated ring brooches are also common in England (e.g. Roach Smith 1857, pl. 28, no. 6; Ward-Perkins 1940), Scotland (e.g. Callendar 1924, 181, fig. 6:4; Jope *et al.* 1960, 269–70, fig. 95:1), Wales (Redknap 1996) and France (Coutil 1938, 106, nos 1–2). Many of these parallels are almost identical to the Irish Class 1 brooches. The evidence of contemporary depictions confirms the archaeological evidence that this type of simple undecorated ring brooch was worn throughout western and northern Europe.

Two copper-alloy examples, one from London (Fig. 6) (Egan 1991c, 248, fig. 160:1307) and one from Bramber Castle, Sussex (Barton and Holden 1977, 58–9), are dated to the mid- to late fourteenth century and the fourteenth century respectively. Two other copper-alloy brooches, one from Deddington Castle, Oxfordshire (Jope *et al.* 1960, 269–70, fig. 95:2), and one from Rumney Castle, South Glamorgan, Wales (Lightfoot 1992, 141, fig. 10), are dated to the late thirteenth century. A further copper-alloy example from Exeter is dated to the late fourteenth/early fifteenth century (Goodall 1984, 339, fig. 190:55). Three copper-alloy brooches from Winchester are dated to the fourteenth century (Hinton 1990, 523, no. 1242, fig. 134:1239 and 1241). A thin sheet-metal brooch from London, with an angled cross-section similar to unprovenanced brooch RB 28, is contextually dated to the late thirteenth to early fourteenth century (Egan 1991c, 248, fig. 160:1305).

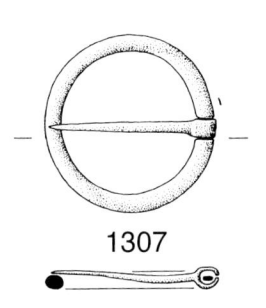

Fig. 6—Mid–late fourteenth-century gunmetal ring brooch, London (after Egan 1991c, 249, cat. no. 1307).

Conclusion

The large number of close parallels for the Irish Class 1 brooches from Britain and France and the range of depictions from elsewhere suggest that this type of brooch was being worn throughout western and northern Europe. Interestingly, many of these parallels are almost identical to Irish examples. Five of the Irish Class 1 ring brooches are contextually dated to the late twelfth to thirteenth century. Analysis of the provenances of two of the brooches suggests a similar date for them. The archaeological evidence from Britain appears to suggest a slightly later date for this type of brooch, from the late thirteenth century to the fourteenth and fifteenth centuries. However, this does not necessarily mean that this type was in use in Ireland earlier than in Britain. Rather, it supports the evidence of contemporary British depictions from the twelfth to the fifteenth century. The combination of evidence suggests that these brooches were worn from the twelfth century but were more common in the thirteenth century. They were still in use in the fourteenth century but became rarer in the fifteenth century. While there is some evidence that ring brooches were still worn in Ireland on a limited basis into the sixteenth century, it seems more likely that the Waterford brooch, RB 12, belongs to the earlier years of its possible date range.

CLASS 2: ring brooches with engraved and/or false relief decoration (RB 30–86)

There are 57 ring brooches in this class. Three are made of gold, 22 of silver, 31 of copper alloy, and one of lead alloy. They measure between 14mm and 67mm in diameter, with an average of 24.5mm. They are circular in outline and simple in form. Class 2 ring brooches are similar in their simple form to Class 1 ring brooches but are distinguished by being decorated. This decoration takes the form of a great variety of incised, engraved or false relief motifs. These brooches are subdivided into two classes. Class 2a are decorated with mainly abstract motifs while Class 2b are decorated with inscriptions.

Class 2a

Class 2a contains 49 ring brooches (RB 30–78). Seventeen are made of silver, 31 of copper alloy and one of lead alloy. They measure between 14mm and 67mm in diameter, with an average of 24.5mm. Class 2a ring brooches are decorated with a range of motifs such as concentric and radial lines, either used singly or combined in a variety of ways. Another common motif is the chevron, incised or deeply engraved in a continuous line on the whole or on only half of the front face. Chevron and line motifs may also be combined. The resulting inner or outer triangular spaces of the continuous chevrons may be filled with incised decoration such as rocked tracer ornament or single or multiple concentric or radial lines. Other examples have slightly more unusual, simply worked decoration. This includes incised rosettes and quatrefoils, concentric rows of beading, and evenly spaced, slightly swollen segments which are either plain or decorated with punched circles. When the design is in false relief, the surrounding cutaway areas are often roughly cross-hatched. This was probably intended as a key to hold niello or enamel, much of which is now missing from the brooches.

Class 2a: chronology and comparative material

Nine of the 49 Class 2a brooches are contextually dated. RB 30, from High Street in Carrickfergus, Co. Antrim, is dated to the sixteenth century, while RB 31, from Joymount in Carrickfergus, is dated to the early thirteenth century (Lesley Simpson, pers. comm.). Two brooches from High Street, RB 38 and 39, are dated to between the mid-twelfth and early fourteenth centuries, and another from the same site, RB 41, is dated to the late twelfth–early thirteenth century (A. Halpin, pers. comm.). RB 43 and 44, from Wood Quay, Dublin, are dated to the thirteenth century (A. Halpin, pers. comm.). RB 47, from St Mary's Cathedral, Limerick, is dated to the mid–late thirteenth century (Hodkinson, forthcoming). RB 52, from Bakehouse Lane, Waterford, is dated to between the mid-thirteenth and early seventeenth centuries (Lightbown 1997, 523).

Several of the brooches have some possible dating associations. RB 46 was recovered during excavations at Jerpointchurch townland, Co. Kilkenny. This site, interpreted as a possible medieval grange or manor house, produced such thirteenth-century artifacts as a copper-alloy finger-ring, two bone gaming-pieces, and Saintonge and Ham Green ware pottery. Although the brooch was unstratified it may date from the thirteenth century (Foley 1989). RB 48 was recovered during excavations at Knowth, Co. Meath. Anglo-Norman occupation on the main passage tomb mound was associated with pottery dating from the twelfth, thirteenth and fourteenth centuries (Eogan 1984, 7; O'Kelly 1978, 91; H. Roche, pers. comm.). The rocked tracer ornament on this brooch was used to decorate artifacts in the twelfth century and earlier, but it is most characteristic of thirteenth- to fifteenth-century metalwork (Biddle 1990, 690; Egan 1991a, 31). The Knowth brooch therefore probably dates from the twelfth- to fourteenth-century period of occupation.

Ring brooches with decorative motifs comparable to the Irish Class 2a are common in England, Scotland, Wales and France (Coutil 1938, 106). A close parallel for the continuous chevron decoration of RB 33 from County Donegal, RB 36 from County Down, RB 49 from County Meath and RB 53 from County Westmeath is found on a copper-alloy brooch from the Hamel, Oxford, which is dated to the late fourteenth century (Palmer 1981, 183, fig. 23:5). Another copper-alloy brooch decorated with continuous chevrons, from Winchester, is dated to the mid-thirteenth century (Biddle and Hinton 1990, 641, fig. 172:2019). A copper-alloy brooch from Winchester with incised concentric lines around its inner and outer edges, similar to unprovenanced brooch RB 72, is dated to the early thirteenth century (Biddle and Hinton 1990, 640, fig. 172:2018). A close parallel for the spaced groupings of radial lines around the frames of RB 30 from County Antrim, RB 45 from County Kildare and the unprovenanced RB 77 is supplied by a silver brooch from Cambridgeshire (Hattatt 1987, 332, fig. 107:1338).

A close parallel for RB 34 from County Donegal, RB 42 from Winetavern Street, Dublin, and the unprovenanced RB 67 with decoration in the form of continuous chevrons combined with concentric lines in the outer spaces is provided by a copper-alloy brooch from Rattray, Aberdeenshire, Scotland (Goodall 1993, 190). A brooch from the Isle of Wight has chevron decoration along its pin shaft similar to that on RB 34 (Anon. 1852, 110). This brooch is contextually dated to between the fourteenth and sixteenth centuries. Two copper-alloy brooches from Winchester have similar concentric rings of beading to the unprovenanced RB 71 (Biddle and Hinton 1990, 641, fig. 172:2020 and 2023). Both are contextually dated to the thirteenth century. A close parallel for the unprovenanced RB 74 is a brooch from Glenluce sand-dunes, which has similar radial lines surrounding a square-like outline (Fig. 7) (Jope et al. 1960, 270, fig. 95:3).

A brooch from London with a similar robust bevelled frame to that of the unprovenanced RB 73 is dated to the late twelfth century (Egan 1991c, 248, fig. 160:1308). No close parallels for RB 32 from Christchurch, Cork, RB 35 from County Donegal and RB 38 from High Street, Dublin, with the combined features of a lozenge cross-section and continuous zigzag decoration are known. However, there are parallels for the lozenge cross-section but with different decoration. A copper-alloy brooch with punched line decoration from Winchester is contextually dated to the thirteenth century (Biddle and Hinton 1990, 641, fig. 172:2021). There is also a silver brooch from Cliffe Hill, Lewes, with an inscription in Lombardic lettering which can be stylistically dated to the thirteenth to early fourteenth century (Cherry 1981). A gilt copper-alloy brooch with a mock inscription from Winchester is contextually dated to the thirteenth–fourteenth century (Biddle and Hinton 1990, 643, fig. 173:2038). A copper-alloy brooch from Winchester with quatrefoil decoration comparable to that on the unprovenanced RB 57 is contextually dated to between the mid-fifteenth and early sixteenth centuries (Biddle and Hinton 1990, 643, fig. 173:2033).

Fig. 7—Copper-alloy ring brooch, Glenluce, Scotland (after Jope et al. 1960).

Class 2b

There are eight ring brooches in this class (RB 79–86). Three are made of gold and five of silver. They measure between 19mm and 29.5mm in diameter, with an average of 24mm. Class 2b ring brooches are similar in form to many Class 2a brooches in that they also have engraved or raised decoration. However, this decoration is always in the form of an inscription, on one or both faces. The inscriptions are either in Lombardic or Black Letter script, and the language used is either Latin or French.

Class 2b: chronology and comparative material

Class 2b brooches are a distinctive type decorated with incised inscriptions. None of the eight Irish examples are contextually dated. However, medieval inscriptions can be broadly dated according to the style of lettering used. The majority of the inscriptions on these Class 2b brooches are in the Lombardic style, which was in use during the thirteenth–early fourteenth century (Alexander and Binski 1987, 543). One brooch is inscribed in Black Letter script, which replaced Lombardic and was used extensively in the late fourteenth and fifteenth centuries (Cherry 1994, 25).

Ring brooches inscribed in Lombardic script are very common from England, Scotland and continental Europe. There are many parallels for the inscription 'AVE MARIA GxP III' on the brooch from Carrickfergus, RB 79. Callander has described ten silver and three gold inscribed brooches from various parts of Scotland, three of which are inscribed 'AVE MARIA' (1924, 169–70, nos 3, 12 and 13). There are also a number of lead-alloy examples from London with versions of the 'AVE MARIA' legend. These include a pewter brooch contextually dated to the mid-thirteenth century and a silver brooch dated to the mid- to late fourteenth century (Egan 1991c, 255, fig. 164:1336). There are a number of unprovenanced inscribed ring brooches in the Victoria and

Albert Museum, London, including one gold brooch with the inscription 'AVE MARIA GRAC' for which Lightbown (1992, 491, no. 2) has suggested a thirteenth-century date. Other examples with this legend include a silver brooch from near Winchester (Hattatt 1987, 384–5, fig. 125:1429) and a copper-alloy brooch found near Corbridge, Glamorganshire (Anon. 1853, 248).

Two silver brooches with niello inlay from Cluny, France, are inscribed 'AVE MARIA G[racia]' and 'AMOR G[?] I G[?] IOM', possibly a version of 'Amor Vincit Omnia' as on the unprovenanced RB 82. A thirteenth-century date has been suggested for both these brooches (Taburet-Delahaye 1989, 223). A ring brooch of unspecified metal type from London is also inscribed 'AMOR VINCIT OMNIA' (Roach Smith 1857, 109, pl. 28). RB 82, 85 and 86 with a plano-concave cross-section also have close parallels in Scotland and England. There are three silver examples from Scotland (Callender 1924, 170–1, nos 14–16) and one gold example in the Victoria and Albert Museum (Lightbown 1992, 492, no. 6).

The inscription on the silver brooch from Trim, RB 80, is in Black Letter script, used in the late fourteenth and fifteenth centuries when it replaced Lombardic script (Alexander and Binski 1987, 541; Cowen 1937, 203). Comparable to RB 80 is a copper-alloy brooch found in Norfolk, which bears an inscription with the names of the three Magi and the Virgin, 'CASPAR + MELCHIOR + BALTHASAR + MARIA' (Hattatt 1987, 334, fig. 108:1347). As on RB 80, the inscription is in relief and in Black Letter script. Similar examples include one illustrated in the *Archaeological Journal* (Anon. 1846, 78), and they are also known from France (Coutil 1938, 106–7).

Conclusion

The wide range of comparable brooches with incised, engraved and punched decoration, especially in the form of inscriptions, from other parts of Europe shows that this type of brooch was worn throughout western Europe. Four of the Class 2 brooches are contextually dated to the thirteenth century. One is contextually dated to between the late twelfth and thirteenth centuries while two more are contextually dated to between the mid-twelfth and early fourteenth centuries. One brooch is contextually dated to the sixteenth century, while another may date to any time between the mid-thirteenth and early seventeenth centuries. Analysis of the provenances of two other brooches suggests a thirteenth-century date for one and a twelfth- to fourteenth-century date range for the other. The contextual dating evidence of British parallels suggests a mainly thirteenth- to fourteenth-century date range, with one example having a fourteenth- to sixteenth-century range. The epigraphical evidence of Class 2b brooches indicates a thirteenth- to mid-fourteenth-century date range for those with Lombardic script, and a mid-fourteenth- to fifteenth-century date range for those with Black Letter script.

The combined results of this dating evidence for Class 2 brooches suggests a twelfth- to fifteenth-century date range, although clearly they were more common in the thirteenth century. There is some evidence that they may have lingered in use in Ireland on a very limited basis until the sixteenth century. However, I would tentatively suggest that the sixteenth-century copper-alloy brooch from Carrickfergus may have been an import from Scotland, where ring brooches continued in use into the post-medieval period, and indeed up to the nineteenth century (NMAS 1979).

CLASS 3: ring brooches with cable decoration (RB 87–104)

Eighteen ring brooches have been assigned to this class. Ten are made of silver, six of copper alloy and two of lead alloy. They measure between 14mm and 39mm in diameter, with an average of 23.5mm. Class 3 ring brooches are decorated with a variety of 'cable' motifs. Cabling is when the frame is twisted for decorative effect. Class 3 also includes brooches that are incised or cast to give the appearance of twisting. The cable motif provides a subtle variation in the circular outline of the frame of each brooch. The manipulation of the frame by twisting also gives the decoration of the frame greater plasticity than the engraved or false relief decoration of Class 2 brooches. Class 3 brooches are divided into two subtypes in order to distinguish two brooches which combine cabled rings to form what could be called a laurel wreath.

Class 3a

This class contains sixteen ring brooches (RB 87–102). Eight are made of silver, six of copper alloy and two of lead alloy. They measure between 15.5mm and 39mm in diameter, with an average of 23.5mm. Class 3a brooches may have cabling on the whole or on only half of their frame. A number of brooches are plain and circular-sectioned for half the circumference of the frame, and twisted and square-sectioned for the other half. The spiralling bands of the twisted square half are often decorated with 'beading'.

Class 3a: chronology and comparative material

Six of the sixteen Class 3 brooches are contextually dated. RB 87 from Cornmarket, Dublin, is dated to the late thirteenth century (Hayden, forthcoming). RB 88 from Wood Quay, Dublin, is dated to the thirteenth century (A. Halpin, pers. comm.). One brooch from Arundel Square, Waterford, RB 94, is dated to the mid-twelfth century, while a second brooch from that excavation, RB 93, is dated to the thirteenth century (Lightbown 1997, 522–3). RB 95 from Bakehouse Lane, Waterford, is dated to between the mid-thirteenth and early seventeenth centuries (Lightbown 1997, 523). RB 96 from Tintern Abbey, Co. Wexford, is dated to the thirteenth century (Lynch, forthcoming). RB 90 was recovered from a motte at Patrickstown, Co. Meath (Crofton Rotheram 1898). While this brooch is not contextually dated, it may possibly be associated with the period when the motte was occupied. The construction and initial occupation of mottes is generally believed to date to the twelfth–thirteenth century (Barry 1987, 71). Class 3 brooches are a distinctive type, common in England, Scotland and Wales. Similarities with foreign parallels may help to clarify their chronology.

Close parallels for RB 89 from Kilkenny city, RB 91 from County Offaly and the unprovenanced brooches RB 97, RB 101 and RB 102 are provided by three copper-alloy brooches from London. These are decorated with double lines of opposed punched triangles or continuous zigzags instead of beading, and one of them (Fig. 8) (Egan 1991c, 249, fig. 160:1310) is contextually dated to the mid-thirteenth century (Goodall 1981, 69, fig. 68:3; Murdoch 1991, 107, no. 192). Two close parallels but without any punched

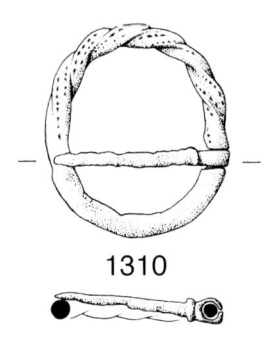

Fig. 8—Mid-thirteenth-century gunmetal ring brooch, London (after Egan 1991c, 249, cat. no. 1310).

decoration are a copper-alloy brooch from Bedford, which has a suggested date in the fourteenth century (Baker et al. 1979, 280, fig. 174:1372), and an unstratified copper-alloy brooch from Oxford (Goodall 1991, 223, fig. 60:3). Another copper-alloy example from Carmarthen Greyfriars, Wales, is dated to the late thirteenth–early fourteenth century (James, forthcoming, cited in Redknap 1996, 106). Redknap also cites two copper-alloy examples found at Caerleon, Wales (1996, 105–6). Two similar copper-alloy examples from a moated house excavation at Wintringham, Huntingdonshire, England, are dated to the late thirteenth–early fourteenth century (Beresford 1977). A silver example from Middlebie, Dumfriesshire, Scotland, which is much larger than the Irish examples, has zigzag ornament on its spiralling bands (Callender 1924, 175, fig. 5:5). A distinct difference is that all the English and Welsh parallels are of copper alloy, while four of the six Irish examples cited above are made of silver and only two are of copper alloy. Only the single example from Scotland which is much larger than the Irish brooches is also of silver.

A close parallel for the 'rilling' in the spiralling bands of RB 92 from County Roscommon is provided by a copper-alloy brooch from Gloucestershire (Hassall and Rhodes 1974, 66, fig. 26:6). A brooch with decoration comparable to the incised cable motif of RB 96 from County Wexford and the unprovenanced RB 98 is a silver brooch found at Coventry in a coin hoard deposited c. 1286 (Anon. 1937; Cherry 1976, 142, no. 321). Two short sections of either side of the frame are decorated with this motif instead of one half of the frame as in the Irish examples. A parallel for the transverse ridges and grooves or 'ribbing' of the unprovenanced RB 100 is supplied by a pewter brooch from London, contextually dated to the early thirteenth century (Egan 1991c, 252, fig. 163:1322). A silver brooch from London whose complete frame has a twisted square cross-section, similar to RB 93 from Waterford city but with beading along the spirals, is contextually dated to the early thirteenth century (Egan 1991c, 255, fig. 163:1334).

Class 3b

There are two ring brooches in this class (RB 103–4). Both are made of silver and they measure 14mm and 27mm respectively in diameter. These brooches are decorated in the form of what could be called a laurel wreath. They incorporate two rings of twisted wire attached to each other with the twists facing in opposite directions, creating the impression of leaves. A central 'stalk' is attached between the two twisted rings.

Class 3b: chronology and comparative material

Neither of the two Class 3b brooches are contextually dated. A close parallel for an unprovenanced silver brooch in the National Museum of Ireland, RB 103, is provided by a silver brooch from the Cubin Sands, Scotland, for which a fourteenth-century date has been suggested (Callander 1924, 179, fig. 6:2). At present there do not appear to be any parallels from England, Wales or continental Europe.

Conclusion

The evidence of comparative material suggests that brooches with simple cable decoration were commonly worn in Ireland, England, Scotland and Wales. Five Class 3 brooches are contextually dated to either the twelfth or the thirteenth century. An analysis of the provenancing of one of the brooches suggests a similar date for it. Contextual dating of comparative material from Britain suggests an early thirteenth- to fourteenth-century date range. The combined results of this dating evidence suggest that these brooches were worn from the twelfth century, were more common in the thirteenth century and were still worn in the fourteenth century. Again, while there is some evidence that ring brooches were still worn in Ireland on a limited basis into the sixteenth century, it seems more likely that the Waterford brooch, RB 95, belongs to the earlier years of its possible date range.

Class 4: ring brooches with applied plates (RB 105–6)

There are two ring brooches in this class. RB 105 is made of copper alloy and RB 106 of silver. They measure 32mm and 34mm respectively in diameter. Class 4 brooches are decorated with one or more pairs of plates and/or plaques applied to their frames. The plates may be triangular or lozenge-shaped and are usually decorated with an incised motif. The plaques may represent stylised animals or humans. In the previous decorated types the development of the decoration has been towards providing greater surface detail, which is increasingly plastic in effect. The plates of Class 4 brooches achieve this in combination with elaborating the circular outline of the frame.

Chronology and comparative material

One of the two Class 4 brooches, RB 105, from Essex Street West, Dublin, is contextually dated to the thirteenth century (Linzi Simpson, pers. comm.). The application of plates and plaques to wire ring brooches is also known from other parts of Europe. There are a number of parallels for RB 105 from Scotland. Two silver wire brooches with six applied lozenge-shaped plates were found at Canonbie and at Langhope (Callender 1924, 173–4, fig. 5:3 and 4). A fourteenth-century date has been suggested for a copper-alloy example with three remaining lozenge-shaped plates engraved with lattice decoration (Margeson 1985, 204, fig. 35:5). A copper-alloy brooch which would originally have had four plates, from Aberdeen, Scotland, has a suggested date of the late thirteenth–early fourteenth century (Goodall 1982, 186–7, fig. 107:51). Another copper-alloy example from Aberdeenshire, Scotland, is contextually dated to the fourteenth–sixteenth century (Goodall 1993, fig. 40:182).

There are no parallels for RB 106 from Athlone, Co. Westmeath. While the engraved lattice design on the lozenge-shaped plates on the silver brooch from Langhope mentioned above are very similar to those on RB 106, its hourglass-shaped plates are very unusual and are unknown from any Scottish or English ring brooches. The decoration of ring brooches with human-head plates is, however, quite common on brooches from Germany and Scandinavia (Lightbown 1992, 149–51, figs 64–6, 68–9). The use of these motifs dates from the fourteenth century, but John Cherry (pers. comm.) has suggested that this brooch is probably late medieval, possibly sixteenth- or even seventeenth-century.

Conclusion

The application of plates is particularly common on Scottish brooches and may suggest a Scottish influence or even origin for these brooches. However, the application of human-head plaques to RB 106 may suggest a Scandinavian or German influence or origin. The combination of dating evidence suggests a thirteenth- to sixteenth- or even seventeenth-century date range for Class 4 brooches.

Class 5: composite ring brooches with projecting elements (RB 107–9)

There are three ring brooches in this class. They are all made of silver and measure 12.5mm, 16mm and 35mm respectively in diameter. Class 5 ring brooches have unusual composite frames formed of three circular rings, one 'ribbed' ring between two cylindrical rings, each slightly smaller and arranged on top of each other at an oblique angle. This construction lends the brooch greater height and width. The brooches are further widened and elaborated with additional elements projecting out from the lower ring, such as small joined spheres, tubular collets set with red glass 'stones' alternating with conical cups 'set' with metal studs, or multiple flat projections with scalloped edges and punched decoration. In each of these brooches a small section is cut from the middle 'ribbed' ring to provide a rectangular hole for the pin loop. The projections from the frames of Class 5 brooches achieve a similar effect to the plates of Class 4 brooches in elaborating the circular outline of the frame. These projections, combined with the oblique height of the frames and the surface intricacy of the alternating plain and ribbed rings, achieve a more 'three-dimensional' or sculptural effect than the decoration of the previous types.

Chronology and comparative material

None of the three Class 5 brooches are contextually dated. RB 107 was an unstratified find from an excavation at Ballynarry Rath, Co. Down (Davison 1961–2), a motte (raised over an earlier ringfort) with occupation material dating to the early thirteenth century (Barry 1987, 99). Although the brooch was unstratified it may be dated to this period. There are no comparable brooches of this type from any other part of Europe.

Conclusion

Despite the lack of systematic study of ring brooches from other parts of Europe it has been possible to discuss comparative material for most of the other types. This type of brooch, however, appears to be unique to Ireland at present. No contextual dating or comparative dating evidence is available, although RB 107 might possibly be dated to the thirteenth century. While the overall decoration of these brooches is unique, the decorative elements themselves—such as ribbed wire, punched circles and collets—are very common on other brooches. In the absence of more precise dating evidence it is nevertheless possible to suggest a broad medieval, probably thirteenth- to fifteenth-century, date for these brooches.

Class 6: ring brooches with multiple collets (RB 110–20)

There are eleven ring brooches in this class. Five are made of gold, two of silver and four of copper alloy. They measure between 26mm and 47.5mm in diameter, with an average of 31mm. Class 6 ring brooches have a frame which would originally have been decorated with 'gems', although often only the collets in which they were set remain. While many of the precious-metal brooches were set with gems, it is likely that all the copper-alloy brooches were set with glass 'stones'. Occasionally the pin may also be decorated with a gem set in a collet. The collets may be low or high, tubular or tapering, with a circular or oval shape. The majority of brooches have circular frames, but one example has a lozenge-shaped outline. Class 6 ring brooches are divided into two subtypes on the basis of their decoration. Class 6a are decorated with multiple collets, generally alternating with bosses. Class 6b are also decorated with multiple collets, but instead of bosses they have a variety of other types of additional decoration. Class 6 brooches are highly decorative. The high tapering and tubular collets combined with hemispherical bosses and other motifs further accentuate the sculptural effects achieved by Class 5 brooches.

Class 6a

Six ring brooches are assigned to Class 6a (RB 110–15). One is made of gold, two of silver and three of copper alloy. They measure between 26mm and 47.5mm in diameter, with an average of 33mm. Class 6a brooches were originally decorated with gems, either four, six, eight or ten, set into collets and evenly spaced around the frame. The collets are all high and tapering. They alternate with an equal number of bosses, usually hemispherical in shape and decorated with rows of punched circles. The pin is attached around a constriction created through one of the bosses and its tip rests on a boss on the opposite side of the frame. Two of the Class 6a brooches are somewhat simpler than the other four. They are both made of copper alloy and have six collets with shallow swellings or flat spaces between the collets rather than bosses.

Class 6a: chronology and comparative material

None of the six brooches are contextually dated. Ring brooches decorated with alternating collets and punched bosses are also known from Scotland, England, France and Denmark. Similarities to dated examples can help to clarify the chronology of the Irish brooches. A close parallel for this type, especially for the Marlboro Street brooch, RB 110, is the silver brooch fragment from a coin hoard found in Dumfries, Scotland (Callender 1924, 160–2, fig. 1:5). This brooch was set with red stones, possibly alternating with blue stones. McDonald's analysis of the coins (in Callender 1924, 162 and 163) suggests that the hoard was deposited about 1310. Another brooch with collets and punched bosses (although the bosses are also surmounted by an open fruit pod) is the Manchester gold brooch for which Cherry

(1983) has suggested a thirteenth- to fourteenth-century date. A gold brooch in the Victoria and Albert Museum has collets alternating with punched bosses and pairs of miniature tubular collets for which Lightbown (1992, 499, no. 28) has suggested a fifteenth-century date.

Included among the six brooches which the Metropolitan Museum of Art acquired for the Cloisters Collection from John Hunt in 1957 was an unprovenanced silver brooch with eight collets alternating with ten punched bosses for which Katherine Reynolds Brown (1992, 411–12, fig. 5) has suggested a probable late thirteenth-century date. A close parallel for the unprovenanced copper-alloy brooch RB 113 is a copper-alloy brooch found in London which also has eight faceted collets alternating with eight bosses, through one of which the pin is attached to the frame (Roach Smith 1857, 111). Roach Smith suggests a fourteenth-century date for this brooch. A parallel for the collet on the pin of the unprovenanced silver brooch RB 112 is provided by a gold brooch in the British Museum which has eight collets set with rubies alternating with sapphires (Cherry 1976, 264), although the intervals between the collets were decorated with an inscription and engraved quatrefoils instead of bosses. A small unprovenanced gold brooch in the National Museum of Denmark has four (now empty) collets alternating with four bosses, as RB 115 would originally have had.

Neither of the two Class 6a copper-alloy brooches, which both have six collets alternating with flat spaces or very shallow swellings, are contextually dated. Similar brooches are very common in England (Ward-Perkins 1940, 276, pl. 28:1; Oswald and Taylor 1964, 73, fig. 4:17; Murdoch 1991, 156, no. 409; Goodall 1984, 339, fig. 190:51; Cherry 1985, 24, fig. 19) and France (Coutil 1938) and generally date to the thirteenth–fourteenth century. A very close parallel for the subtle swellings between the six collets of RB 114 can be found on a brooch from Little Avebury for which a thirteenth- to fourteenth-century date has been suggested (Grant King 1969). A close parallel for the high pyramidal faceted collets alternating with plain spaces and serrated edge decoration on RB 120 is provided by an example from Maidstone (Cuming 1862, 227) and an unprovenanced brooch, formerly in the Hunt collection and now in the Metropolitan Museum of Art Cloisters Collection, for which Reynolds Brown (1992, 412, fig. 7) suggests a fourteenth-century date.

Class 6b

There are five ring brooches in this class (RB 116–20). Four are of gold and one of copper alloy. They measure between 26mm and 37mm in diameter, with an average of 29mm. Class 6b brooches have a variety of decoration incorporating what would originally have been multiple gems set into collets. The collets may be high and tapering or tubular. There may be collets of different shapes and sizes on the one brooch. The frame may also be decorated with an inscription, blind holes, filigree, or rosettes and diagonal foliate struts. One unusual unprovenanced brooch, RB 119, is formed of sixteen cups, each holding one tiny tubular collet set with an emerald *en cabochon* (Cherry 1988).

Class 6b: chronology and comparative material

One of the five Class 6b ring brooches, RB 116, from Cornmarket/Francis St., Dublin, is contextually dated to the mid- to late thirteenth century (Hayden, forthcoming). Gold brooches, such as the example from Enniscorthy, RB 118, decorated with two opposing collets combined with a pair of smaller collets at either end of the pin are a distinctive type also known from England and France (Cherry 1988). A very close parallel for RB 118 is provided by a stray find from Sydling in Dorset (now in the Dorchester Museum), which has sapphires and carbuncles set alternately, a Lombardic inscription (but on a flat rather than a bifaceted frame), and a small triangular projection on the frame under the pin tip (Anon. 1859, 181). A number of very similar brooches have been assigned thirteenth-century dates (Cherry 1969; Ellis 1916; Lightbown 1992, 492, cat. no. 4). Lightbown has suggested a thirteenth-century date for an unprovenanced gold brooch in the Victoria and Albert Museum which has two collets set with a ruby and a sapphire and a Lombardic inscription on a flat frame (1992, 492, cat. no. 5).

Copper-alloy parallels for the opposing collets of brooch RB 118 include a brooch from Winchester contextually dated to the late thirteenth–early fourteenth century (Fig. 9) (Biddle and Hinton 1990, 641, fig. 172:2025), one from London contextually dated to the mid-thirteenth century (Fig. 10) (Egan 1991c, 249, fig. 160:1309), and a fragment of one from Perth, Scotland, dated to the early to mid-fourteenth century (Ford 1987, 123, fig. 59:1). Cherry (1988, 145) also cites two copper-alloy examples, one from London, now in a private collection, and an unprovenanced example in the Ashmolean Museum, Oxford.

The combination of foliage decoration and collets is also known on brooches from England, France and Denmark. There are a number of close parallels for the foliate struts of the unprovenanced brooch RB 120. One example is a French gold brooch with collets surrounded by diagonal foliate struts in the Victoria and Albert

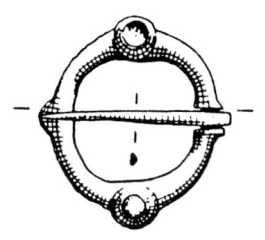

Fig. 9—Late thirteenth/early fourteenth-century copper-alloy ring brooch, Winchester (after Biddle and Hinton 1990, 642, cat. no. 2025).

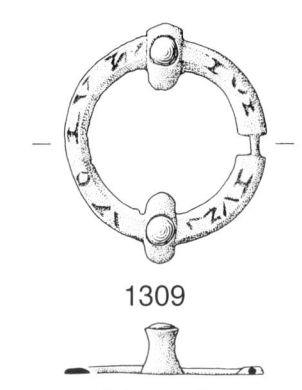

Fig. 10—Mid-thirteenth-century gunmetal ring brooch, London (after Egan 1991c, 249, cat. no. 1309).

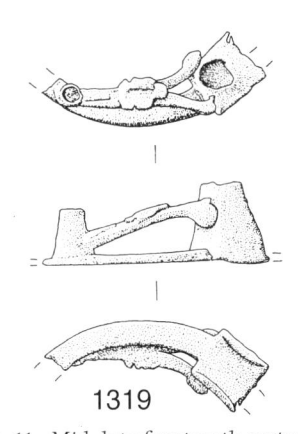

Fig. 11—Mid–late fourteenth-century bronze ring brooch with traces of gilding, London (after Egan 1991c, 251, cat. no. 1319).

Museum, London, for which Lightbown (1992, 493, fig. 9) has suggested a late thirteenth- to early fourteenth-century date. Egan (1991c, 252, fig. 162:1319) describes a fragment of an example in copper alloy contextually dated to the mid- to late fourteenth century (Fig. 11), and cites an unstratified similar silver-gilt example set with amethysts, both from London. The very large Scottish Glenlyon brooch also has an arrangement of struts and collets, and has two conflicting suggested dates of the late fourteenth century (Lightbown 1992, 425, pl. 32) and c. 1500 (NMAS 1982, 90, E71). A large gold brooch in the National Museum of Denmark from Sonder Lem, near Ringkobing, has four large collets alternating with four small collets each set with a red, blue or green stone and surrounded by diagonal foliate struts. Another large gold brooch in the Danish collection, from Bringstrup near Ringsted, has ten collets set with emeralds alternating with garnets surrounded by diagonal foliate struts. A slightly different combination of foliage, in the form of stylised vine-leaves and bunches of grapes, and collets occurs on another French gold brooch in the Victoria and Albert Museum, London, for which Lightbown (1992, 493, cat. no. 8) has suggested a thirteenth-century date. A more delicate foliate wreath surrounds a possibly French silver-gilt brooch in the Museo Nazionale del Bargello, Florence, dated to the early thirteenth century (Lightbown 1992, 424, pl. 29).

A parallel for the Waterford brooch RB 117 might be provided by a silver-gilt brooch from Laverstock (Musty *et al.* 1969, 147, fig. 28). This brooch does not have tubular collets but it does have a very similar arrangement of gold filigree and granules on a flat frame with raised edges. It also has a hole instead of a constriction to secure the pin. A date in the early thirteenth century was suggested for this brooch. A brooch 'enriched with delicate gold filigree' from Northampton was exhibited at the Archaeological Institute of London (Anon. 1852). The gold brooch from County Wexford, RB 119, formed of sixteen cups set with tiny collets with emeralds *en cabochon,* appears to be quite unique within the Irish corpus, and indeed there do not appear to be any comparable brooches from any other part of Europe. The use of rivets on this brooch is paralleled on a brooch from Oxwich, Wales (Lewis 1982, 128; Redknap 1996, 100). The lozenge-shaped brooch from Cornmarket/Francis Street, Dublin, RB 116, is also unique within the Irish corpus, and while there are no close parallels for it there are lozenge-shaped ring brooches from Norfolk and Dorset (Hattatt 1987, 333, fig. 108:1342–3) and one from London which is contextually dated to the late thirteenth–early fourteenth century (Egan 1991c, 256–7, fig. 165:1344). A female effigy from Darlington, England (Tummers 1980, pl. 159), and the Queen of Sheba on the west front of Wells Cathedral, England, which dates from the thirteenth century (Tudor-Craig 1975), are also depicted wearing lozenge-shaped ring brooches.

Conclusion

The decoration of ring brooches with gemstones set in multiple collets is also common on ring brooches from England, Scotland, Wales, France and Denmark. The combination of these multiple collets with other elements such as bosses or diagonal struts is also paralleled on European brooches. However, certain brooches within this class, such as RB 119, do not have any close parallels. The combination of dating evidence suggests a thirteenth- to fourteenth-century date for Class 6 brooches, with limited use into the fifteenth century.

Class 7: ring brooches with projecting hands (RB 121-8)

Eight ring brooches are grouped as Class 7 brooches. Six are made of gold, one is of silver and one is possibly of gilded silver. They measure between 10mm and 20mm in width, with an average of 16.5mm, and have an average length of 25.5mm. Class 7 brooches have a frame which is usually of pointed oval shape, less often circular, with a pair of hands projecting out from the lower edge. The decorative feature opposite the projecting hands on the frame may be a raised collet, a four-petalled rosette, or a pair of clasped hands. Most of these brooches also have a four-petalled rosette on the left of the frame, and another on the right of the frame incorporated into the pin head and constriction shoulders. The projecting hands are usually joined 'in prayer' or they may clasp a gemstone or a collet. Most of these brooches also have a bifaceted front face decorated with a Lombardic inscription in French or Latin or an incised chevron motif.

While previous types of brooches have had projecting elements, they have always retained an essentially circular outline. The majority of Class 7 brooches have a pointed oval frame, with the point culminating in the tip of the projecting pair of hands. The projecting hands are not so much an additional decorative feature that happens to project from the frame as the defining feature of these brooches. They do, however, share decorative features of previous types, such as inscriptions, incised motifs and the use of high collets to accentuate the beauty of precious gemstones.

Chronology and comparative material

None of the eight Irish examples are contextually dated. However, the Lombardic inscriptions of RB 123 from County Meath and the unprovenanced brooches RB 124 and RB 125 can date these brooches to the thirteenth and fourteenth centuries. Projecting-hands brooches are also known from England, Scotland and, probably, France. There are two unprovenanced gold examples in the Victoria and Albert Museum for which Lightbown (1992, 494-5, figs 13-14) has suggested a French and an English origin and a fourteenth-century date. One unprovenanced gold example in the National Museum of Scotland has a suggested fourteenth-century date (NMAS 1892, 359; 1979, pl. 17a). A gold stray find from Canterbury, whose present location is unknown, has a suggested date of c. 1400 (Anon. 1878). Cherry (1988, 145) cites two further unprovenanced gold examples in the British Museum. Lightbown (1992, 434, pl. 57) suggests a thirteenth-century date for an unprovenanced gold example in Walters Art Gallery, Baltimore, Maryland, America.

Somewhat cruder copper-alloy versions of this type are also known from England. One from London, with a collet opposite stylised hands, is contextually dated to the late thirteenth to mid-fourteenth century (Fig. 12) (Egan 1991c, 255, fig. 164:1335). A similar example was found in Wiltshire (Hattatt 1987, 331, fig. 107:1334). Cherry (1988, 145) cites a further example from Lyveden. A brooch from Ixworth, now in the Ashmolean Museum, Oxford, has a human head opposite the joined hands and the frame of the brooch is shaped like arms, so that the whole brooch becomes anthropomorphic (Roach

Smith, no date). Scarisbrick (1994, 39) cites a further example from Felixstowe, Suffolk, now in the Norwich Castle Museum collection.

Conclusion

The comparative evidence shows that this type of brooch was also worn in Scotland, England and France. What may be contemporary references to these types of brooches occur in English and French wills of the fourteenth century. The will of Philippa, Countess of March, mentions '*un fermayl bleu avec deux maings tenang un diamant*' ('a blue brooch with two hands holding a diamond'), and an inventory of the goods of King Charles V lists a '*fermillit d'or, azure, a deux mains qui s'entretiennent*' ('gold and azure brooch with two clasping hands') (Evans 1970, 58; trans. Professor Christine Meek). The Irish projecting-hands brooches are the largest surviving group of this type of brooch in precious metal from any one country, perhaps suggesting that this was an Irish brooch type. The combination of dating evidence suggests a thirteenth- to fourteenth-century date for Class 7 brooches.

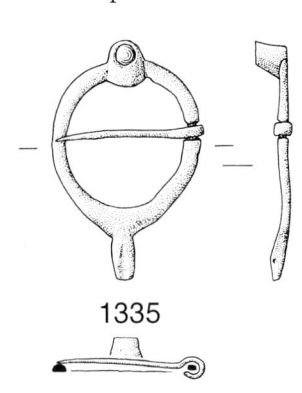

Fig. 12—Late thirteenth/mid-fourteenth-century gunmetal ring brooch, London (after Egan 1991c, 254, cat. no. 1335).

Class 8: ring brooches with derivative decoration (RB 129–35)

There are seven ring brooches in this class. Six are made of lead alloy and one is of copper alloy. They measure between 13mm and 37.5mm in diameter, with an average of 24.5mm. Class 8 ring brooches are cast with a variety of raised decoration that is imitative of the decoration of previous types. This most often takes the form of 'collets' and raised bosses of a variety of shapes. These collets may originally have been filled with glass paste, and similarly the bosses may have been painted to imitate precious gems. These brooches develop and borrow from the decoration of a number of previous brooch types without elaborating that decoration.

Chronology and comparative material

Five of the seven examples of this type are contextually dated. RB 130, from High Street, Dublin, is dated to the late twelfth–early thirteenth century, while RB 132, 133 and 134 from Wood Quay, Dublin, and RB 131 from High Street all date from the thirteenth century (A. Halpin, pers. comm.). This type of brooch is also known from England. Three lead-alloy brooches decorated with bosses within circles, one of which also has a beaded border like RB 130, are dated to the early thirteenth century, late thirteenth to mid-fourteenth century and the late fourteenth century respectively (Figs 13 and 14) (Egan 1991c, 252–4, fig. 163:1323, 1328 and 1332). These bosses may have been intended to imitate stones and might perhaps originally have been painted (Egan 1991c, 271). Cast lead-alloy brooches such as RB 131, with knops which appear to imitate those decorating many silver Scottish and northern English brooches (Callender 1924;

Cherry 1985, 21; Brewis 1930), are also known in England. There are a number from London, including one dated to the late fourteenth century (Egan 1991c, 253–4, fig. 163:1330).

Conclusion

Class 8 brooches were also worn in England. There do not appear to be any parallels for these brooches from other parts of Europe; however, it should be noted that the limited publications of European collections of ring brooches have tended not to include brooches of non-precious metals. The combination of contextual dating of Irish brooches and comparable brooches suggests a late twelfth- to fourteenth-century date for Class 8 brooches. Another version of this classification could include some of these brooches within the types they imitate—e.g. RB 129 and 135 could have been included in Class 2a. However, while elements of this class clearly overlap with other classes, there are also aspects which distinguish them, including their cheap metal composition and their low-quality production. It will be suggested below that these brooches may have satisfied the needs and desires of a particular element of Irish society.

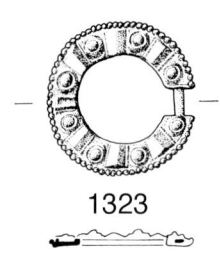

Fig. 13—Early thirteenth-century pewter ring brooch, London (after Egan 1991c, 253, cat. no. 1323).

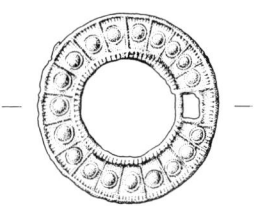

Fig. 14—Late thirteenth/mid-fourteenth-century pewter ring brooch, London (after Egan 1991c, 253, cat. no. 1328).

Class 9: miscellaneous ring brooches (RB 136–40)

There are five ring brooches in this class. This group is comprised of brooches which are unique within the Irish corpus and do not fit into any of the previous eight classes. They will therefore be considered individually.

RB 136 is a silver-gilt ring brooch from Carrickfergus, Co. Antrim. It has an eight-lobed outline and measures 25mm in diameter. Its frame is formed of four ovoid bosses alternating with four D-shaped open rings. Both the bosses and the rings are decorated with beading. RB 136 is dated to the early thirteenth century (Simpson and Dickson 1981). There are no parallels for this brooch from the rest of Europe.

RB 137 is a lead-alloy circular ring brooch from High Street, Dublin, measuring 22.5mm in diameter. Its frame has cast openwork decoration. It is contextually dated to the late twelfth–early thirteenth century (A. Halpin, pers. comm.). There are no close parallels for this brooch from the rest of Europe, but lead-alloy brooches cast with openwork decoration are known from excavations at London and are dated to the thirteenth–fourteenth century (Egan 1991c, 257, fig. 166:1345 and 1348).

RB 138 is an unprovenanced copper-alloy ring brooch, slightly D-shaped in outline. Its front face and outer edge are decorated with deep radial grooves and incised lines. The outer edge is decorated with brambling (i.e. it is deeply scored in a grid pattern, leaving upstanding knobs somewhat like the surface of a blackberry). RB 138 is not contextually dated. There are no parallels for this brooch from any other part of Europe.

RB 139 is an unprovenanced copper-alloy circular ring brooch, 25mm in diameter. It is decorated with three alternating rows of blind holes on its curved front face. There is also a faintly incised foliate design in lozenge shapes surrounding the holes. RB 139 is not contextually dated. There are no parallels for this brooch from England, Scotland or Wales. There is, however, an identical brooch from Rouen in Normandy, for which a late thirteenth–early fourteenth-century date has been suggested (Coutil 1938, 106). Although there are no British parallels for this brooch, the occurrence of blind holes on copper-alloy ring brooches is known from a number of English brooches, such as one from Laverstock with a suggested thirteenth-century date (Musty *et al*. 1969, 147–8) and one from London dated to the late thirteenth–early fourteenth century (Egan 1991c, 251–2, fig. 162:1317).

RB 140 is an unprovenanced silver ring brooch, 39mm in diameter. Its frame has a sexfoil outline created by six lion-heads. It is not contextually dated. There do not appear to be any parallels for this brooch from any other part of Europe. Decoration in the form of stylised lions is found on some Swedish ring brooches, which were intended to display princely might (Lightbown 1992, 151, fig. 69). However, the lions on Swedish brooches are whole lions rather than lion-heads, and these brooches cannot be compared with the Irish brooch.

Conclusion

The majority of ring brooches in Ireland have been shown to date from the twelfth to the thirteenth century. It is interesting that most of the types established have each produced examples from this period. An important conclusion is the fact that to a large extent both the simplest and the most ornate brooches were being worn at the same time. Epigraphical dating evidence and contextual dating of comparative material suggest that ring brooches were still worn in the fourteenth century, and to a lesser extent in the fifteenth century.

It should be noted that some Irish contemporary depictions of ring brooches date right up to the sixteenth and early seventeenth centuries (Hunt 1974, 159, 165, 169, 176–7, 192–3, 233). On the whole, the archaeological dating evidence does not confirm this; however, one brooch from Carrickfergus dates from the sixteenth century and some of the Waterford ring brooches were archaeologically recovered from burial fill with broad dating possibilities, spanning the years between the thirteenth century and the early seventeenth century. As mentioned above, certain types of ring brooches continued in use up to the nineteenth century in some parts of Europe, including Scotland (NMAS 1979), Norway and parts of eastern Europe. Indeed, the manufacture and use of ring brooches were adopted from Scottish settlers by the Iroquois and other native peoples of Canada in the seventeenth and eighteenth centuries (Lyford 1945, 67–70; Karklins 1992). It is possible that the occurrence of one brooch of sixteenth-century date, in County Antrim, may reflect Antrim's close links with Scotland at this period rather than the continued manufacture of ring brooches in Ireland.

In conclusion, the chronological and comparative analysis of Irish ring brooches suggests that they were first worn in the twelfth century, became more popular in the thirteenth century, and continued in use into the fourteenth and fifteenth centuries on a more limited basis. This was a period of profound social and cultural change in Ireland, witnessing, among other events, the advent, growth and expansion of Anglo-Norman colonisation and the resulting Gaelic response. The following chapter will explore in more detail, through analysis of the distribution and precise provenancing of Irish ring brooches, their relationship with these historical developments and resulting settlement patterns in medieval Ireland.

III. DISTRIBUTION AND PROVENANCES

'Tradition has long connected it [the motte] with the Danes, and it would be a matter of no small difficulty to persuade some of the peasants living in the neighbourhood that dwarf-like men have not been known to vanish mysteriously into the interior . . . so widespread was this idea that the owner was induced to excavate and so settle the question . . . the remains of a fire yielded several rusted fragments of iron, probably the blade of a knife and a silver buckle or brooch.'

—E. Crofton Rotheram, 'The Moat of Patrickstown' (1898)

Distribution

Of the 140 ring brooches examined in this study, 74 (52.9%) can be provenanced to either general or precise locations within Ireland (Fig. 15). The brooches have a biased distribution, being generally found in the north-east, east and south of the island. However, within this broad pattern a number of concentrations can be noted. There are particular clusters in urban centres: 26 (18.6%) from Dublin (Fig. 16), six (4.3%) from Waterford, four (2.9%) from Carrickfergus, and one (0.7%) from Cork. There is also a notable concentration of sixteen brooches (11.4%) in the north Leinster/midlands region, mainly in counties Meath and Westmeath, with one each from Kildare and Offaly. Six brooches (4.3%) come from the south Kilkenny and south Wexford region. Smaller concentrations include three (2.1%) from the east of County Down, three (2.1%) with a Donegal coastal distribution and two (1.4%) from the River Blackwater in Ulster, on the Tyrone/Armagh border. Seven single isolated examples (5%) include a brooch from an unknown location in County Antrim, one from Ennis, Co. Clare, one from Ballinrea, Co. Cork, one from County Leitrim, one from Limerick city, one from County Monaghan, and one from County Roscommon. The predominant patterns, then, show that most of the brooches come from east Ulster, north Leinster and south-east Ireland.

The distribution can also be analysed in regional terms (Fig. 17). The largest number of brooches, 48 examples (34.3%), are from Leinster. There are fourteen brooches (10%) from Ulster, ten (7.1%) from Munster and only two (1.4%) from Connacht. In terms of classes represented, Leinster has examples of all nine classes of brooches, while Munster, Ulster and Connacht have progressively more limited ranges of classes.

Provenances

The provenances of ring brooches can also provide useful insights into their wider social and economic context. In particular, those recovered from known types of medieval settlement provide some indications as to their date and cultural background. As shown above, 74 brooches (52.9%) can be provenanced to locations within Ireland (Fig. 15). A number of these can only be generally located to either counties, townlands or places (e.g. 'a field' or river dredgings) with no known archaeological context. More precise provenances and archaeological contexts for 60 brooches (42.9%) can be

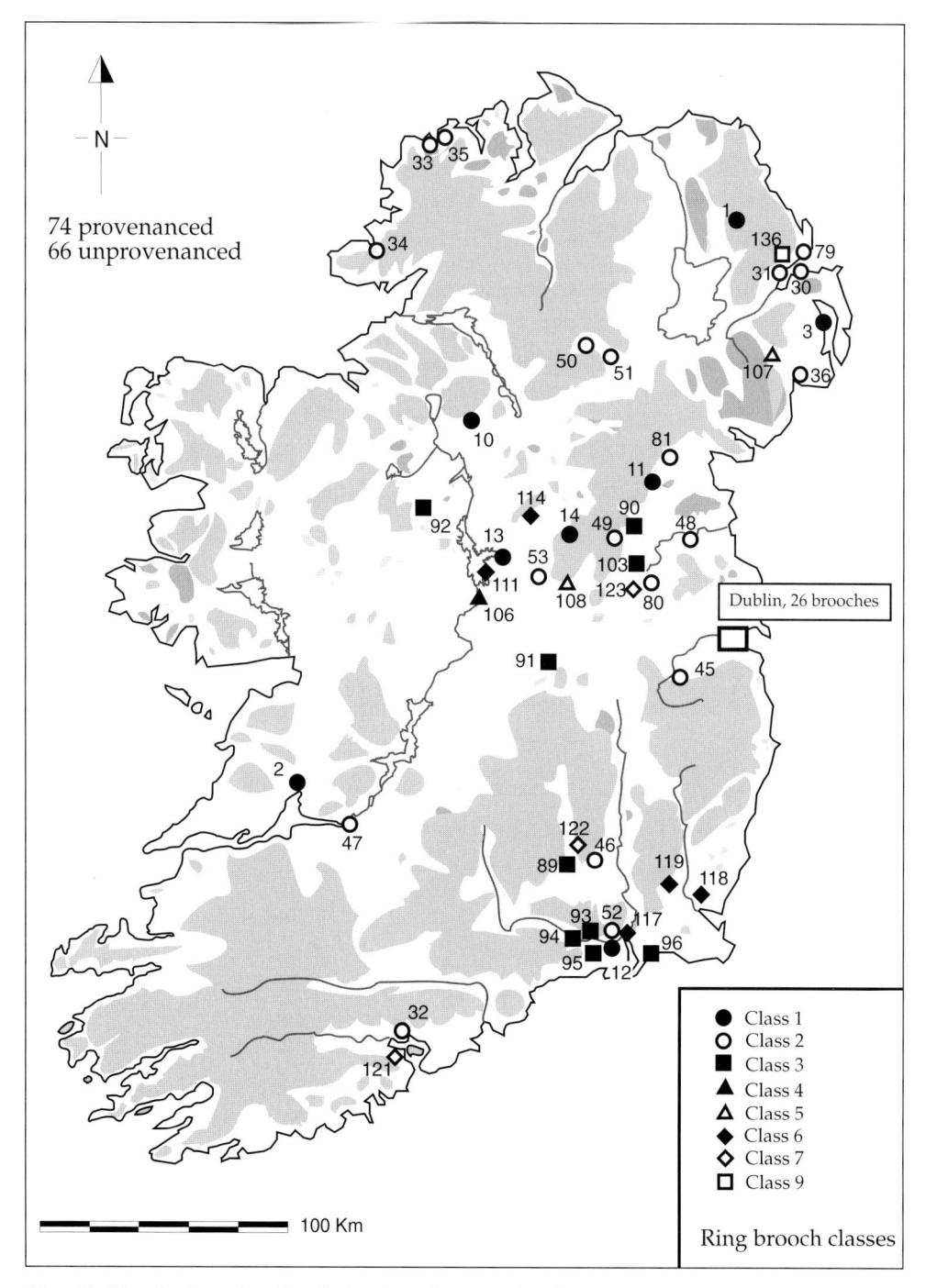

Fig. 15—Distribution of medieval ring brooches in Ireland.

identified (Fig. 18). These provenances have been classified according to medieval settlement types to enable interpretation. Forty-two brooches (30%) came from medieval towns, one (0.7%) from a rural nucleated settlement, six (4.3%) from on or near rural fortifications, four (2.9%) from rural ecclesiastical foundations, three (2.1%) from coastal middens, and four (2.9%) from crannogs. The provenances of 66 brooches (47.1%) are unknown.

Medieval towns

The largest number of ring brooches with a known provenance have been recovered from medieval urban settlements. Towns which have produced ring brooches include Dublin, Waterford, Cork, Carrickfergus, Trim, Kilkenny, Limerick and Naas. By the twelfth century, towns in Ireland were already fulfilling the role of market-places for an increasingly manorial society (Bradley 1995, 14). They served as the centres for the production and exchange of a range of products, which no doubt included jewellery. The earliest urban activities of the Anglo-Normans in Ireland involved both the expansion of existing towns such as Dublin, Limerick, Kilkenny, Waterford and Cork and the establishment of several new towns (Bradley 1995, 14; 1991, 177). Three of these new towns—Carrickfergus, Naas and Trim—have produced ring brooches. Ring brooches were undoubtedly one element in the cosmopolitan nature of medieval town life. Urban merchants and craftworkers would have been involved in the widespread trade of high-status goods in the Middle Ages (Bradley 1991), of which jewellery was probably a part.

Rural fortifications

Ring brooches from rural fortified sites include RB 2 from Clonroad More, Co. Clare (Hunt 1946), RB 36 from Castleskreen, Co. Down (Anon. 1862, 233), RB 48 from Knowth, Co. Meath (H. Roche, pers. comm.), RB 107 from Ballynarry 'Rath', Co. Down (Davison 1961–2), RB 81, found near Donaghmoyne or Mannin Castle in County Monaghan (Anon. 1854, 285), and RB 90 from Patrickstown, Co. Meath (Crofton Rotheram 1898). The Patrickstown ring brooch was recovered during an antiquarian excavation of a motte carried out in the last century. The published account indicates that it was found in occupation material in the upper layers, with a probable iron knife (*ibid*., 63). More recent excavations of a motte which had been raised over an earlier ringfort at Ballynarry Rath produced a single unstratified brooch (Davison 1961–2, 62). Occupation material from the motte included thirteenth-century Downpatrick glazed pottery (Barry 1987, 99; Davison 1961–2, 62–71). That ring brooches have been recovered from mottes is interesting. Mottes (flat-topped earthen mounds which originally carried wooden buildings and defences and sometimes had defensive enclosures, known as baileys, at their bases) were an important element in the initial military expansion of Anglo-Norman settlement in Ireland. Mottes tend to be found in the eastern part of the country, within areas controlled by the Anglo-Normans. However, it has also been pointed out that several mottes may be the result of Gaelic settlement activities. They are generally dated to between the late twelfth and thirteenth centuries (Sweetman 1991; 1995, 5–7). RB 48 was an unstratified find from the excavations at Knowth, Co. Meath. There is evidence that the main passage tomb mound may have been adapted

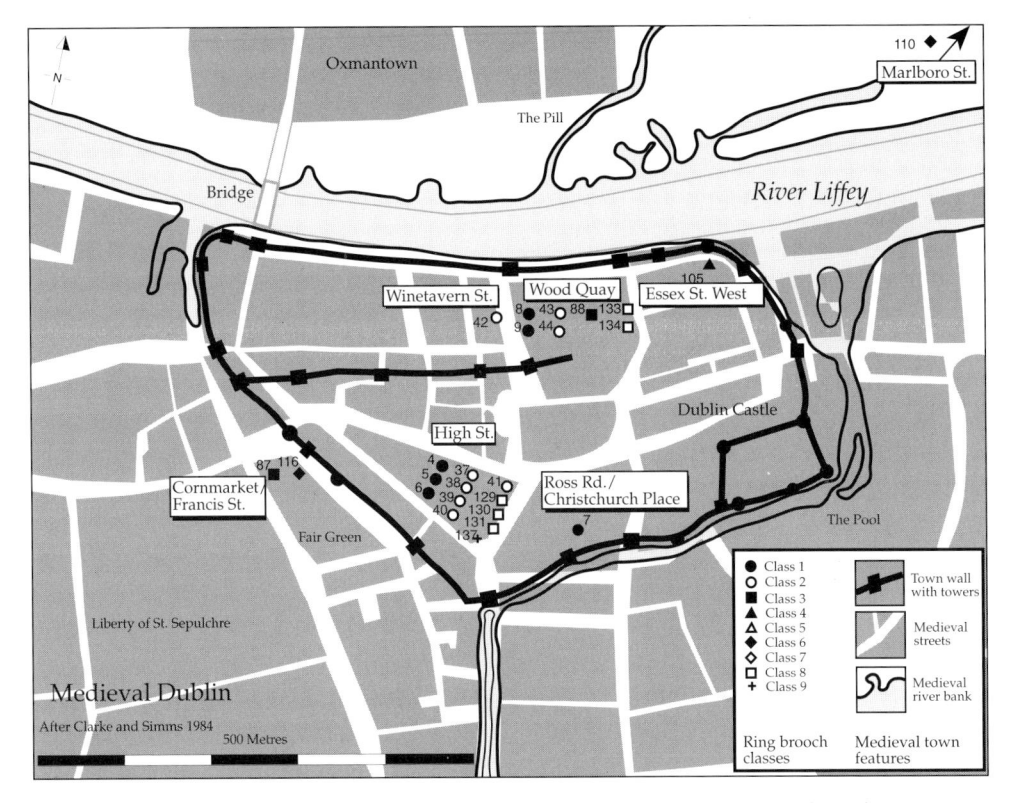

Fig. 16—Distribution of medieval ring brooches in Dublin. (Map: Aidan O'Sullivan.)

for use as a motte in the twelfth century. By the thirteenth century a large rectangular stone structure was in use on the summit. Abundant Anglo-Norman occupation material and pottery indicate a continuity of settlement until the early fourteenth century (O'Kelly 1978, 90–3; Eogan 1984, 7). RB 48 might be associated with any of these medieval phases of activity at Knowth.

RB 81 was a nineteenth-century stray find from near Donaghmoyne/Mannin Castle. Donaghmoyne began as a motte and bailey in the last decade of the twelfth century, became a stone castle in 1244 and was abandoned in the fifteenth century (Harbison 1970, 200; Brindley 1986, 90–1). RB 36 was also an antiquarian stray find from what was probably a Gaelic tower-house (K. O'Connor, pers. comm.) at Castleskreen. Excavations at Castleskreen in the 1950s suggested a fifteenth-century date for the tower-house (Dickinson and Waterman 1960, 67).

The recovery of a number of medieval artifacts, including brooch RB 2 and high-quality imported pottery, during excavations at Clonroad More, Ennis, Co. Clare, led the excavator tentatively to suggest that they may have been associated with the Gaelic lordly residence *Cluain Ramhfhada* (Hunt 1946, 208). In the thirteenth century, Clonroad became the new capital of the O'Brien lordship (Lydon 1993, 252). The *Caithreim Thoirdealbhaigh* records a 'residence with open smooth-grassed lawn, wide roadways, regal treasures, and great opulence' at Clonroad in 1311 (Hunt 1946, 195). The exact location of this 'palace' is unclear and no actual structural remains were found during this excavation. However, while RB 2 was not actually recovered from within this high-status Gaelic residence, it is very possible that it is associated with it. At the very least it provides tentative evidence that the Gaelic Irish were also wearing ring brooches.

Rural nucleated settlements

One ring brooch (RB 46) was recovered from the excavation of a rural nucleated settlement site at Jerpointchurch townland, Co. Kilkenny (Foley 1989, 95–6). The expansion and consolidation of the Anglo-Norman colony in Ireland in the thirteenth and early fourteenth centuries led to the introduction of a network of rural nucleated settlements, typically grouped around a manor house and church (Barry 1987, 72–95). These could be regarded as primarily Anglo-Norman settlements, probably of relatively high social and economic status.

The remains of two substantial stone buildings excavated at Jerpointchurch, Co. Kilkenny, very close to the site of Newtown Jerpoint, a deserted medieval town, possibly represent a medieval grange or manor house. The excavated finds from the settlement included jewellery, gaming-pieces, and native and imported pottery. The structures and finds indicate both a high standard of living and wider trading links (Foley 1989; Barry 1987, 76).

Rural ecclesiastical foundations

Ring brooches from probable rural ecclesiastical sites include RB 14 from Portloman Abbey, Lough Owel, Co. Westmeath, RB 3 from Nendrum, Co. Down (Lawlor 1925), RB 96 from Tintern Abbey, Co. Wexford (Lynch, forthcoming), and RB 118 from Enniscorthy Abbey, Co. Wexford (Cherry 1988). The medieval period was one of profound change and reform in the Irish church (Watt 1972). European religious orders such as the Cistercians, Augustinians, Dominicans and Franciscans, as well as several smaller orders, were establishing abbeys and friaries throughout Ireland. This expansion was especially vibrant in the period between 1150 and 1250, and saw a revival in the fifteenth century. The brooch from Tintern Abbey, Co. Wexford, was recovered from the main drain south of the cloister, which was constructed in the second half of the thirteenth century and continued in use until the late fourteenth century (Barry 1987, 148; Lynch, forthcoming). While Nendrum was ostensibly an early medieval monastery, a Benedictine cell was established there in the late twelfth century and abandoned shortly afterwards (Barry 1987, 158).

Coastal middens

Ring brooches from coastal middens include RB 33 from Dunfanaghy, RB 34 from Magheramore, near Ardara (Ó Floinn 1996, 87, pl. 41), and RB 35 from Rosapenna on the Rosguil peninsula (Welch 1902), all along the Donegal coastline (Lacy 1983, 55–8, fig. 24, pls 5 and 6). The role of shell middens in medieval settlement has yet to be satisfactorily explained. They are typically interpreted in terms of the local seasonal use of coastal resources (Wilson 1995, 24; McCormick 1995, 12). However, the discovery of ring brooches at several sites may allow alternative explanations. The north-west and west coasts of Ireland and the north Atlantic were important fisheries in the medieval

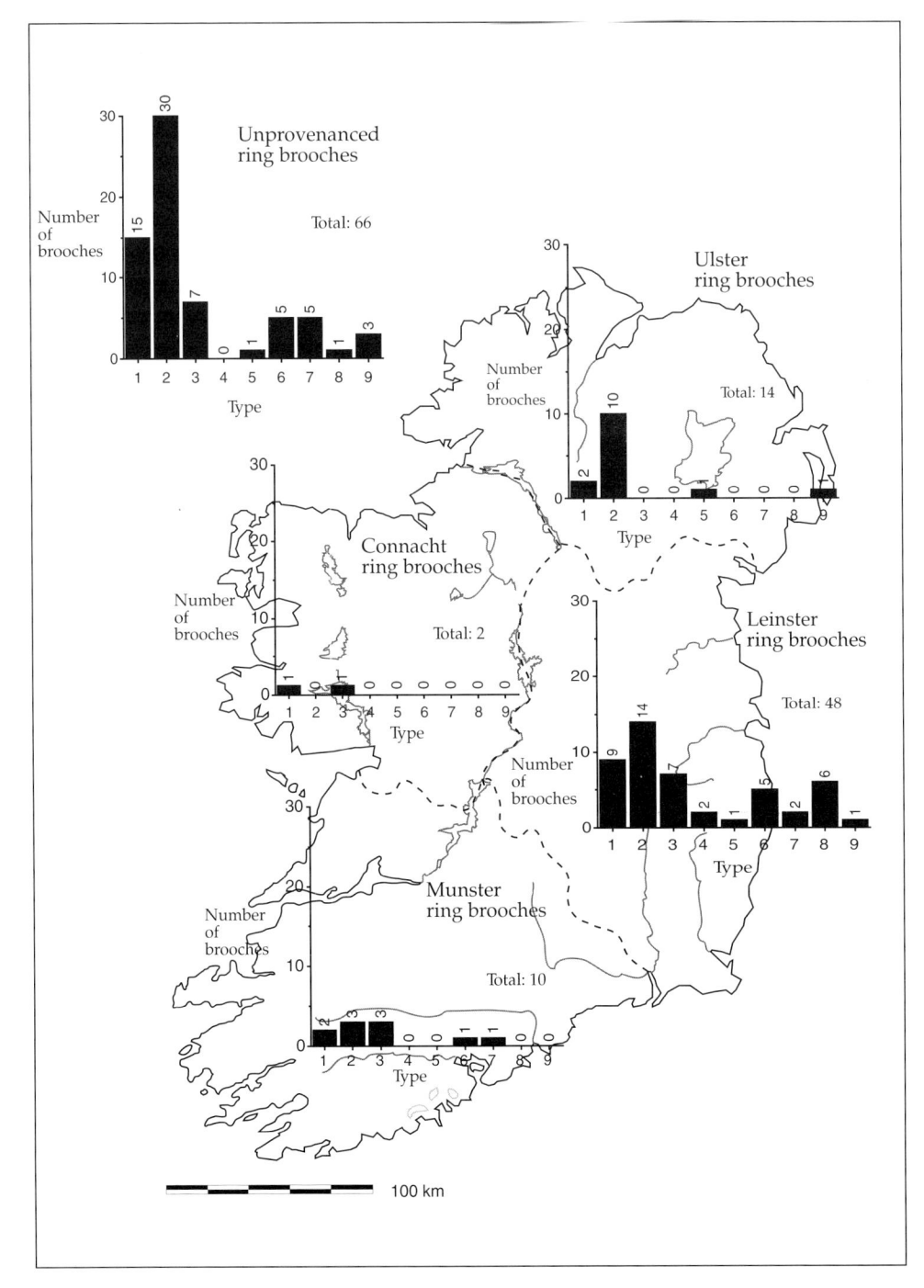

Fig. 17—Regional distribution of medieval ring brooch classes in Ireland.

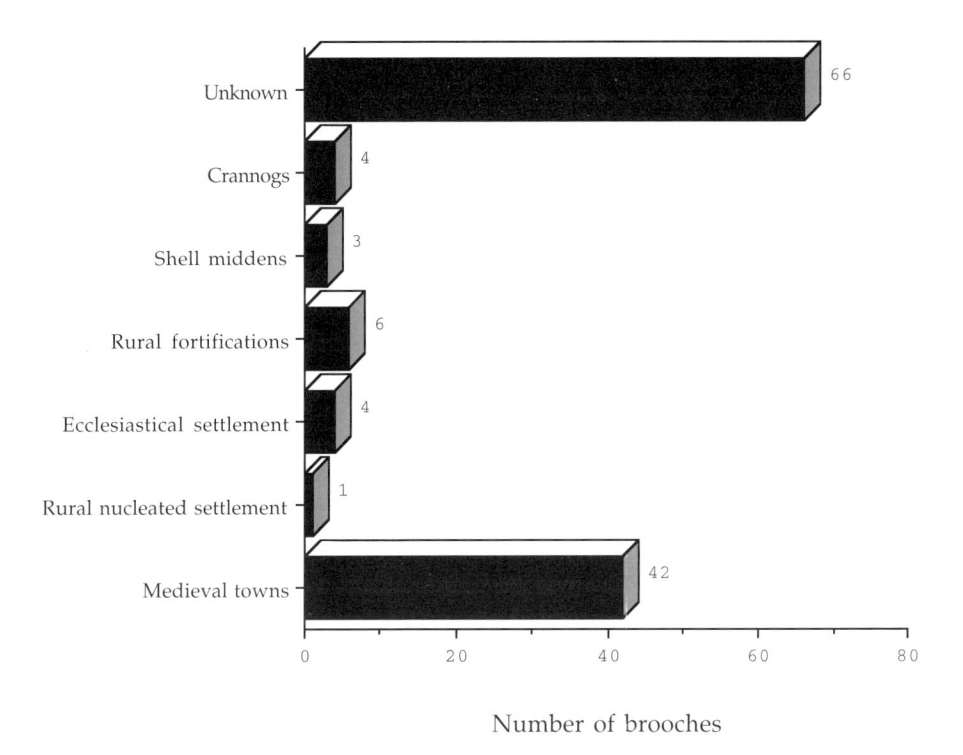

Fig. 18—Provenance of ring brooches.

Provenance	Number of brooches
Unknown	66
Crannogs	4
Shell middens	3
Rural fortifications	6
Ecclesiastical settlement	4
Rural nucleated settlement	1
Medieval towns	42

period. English and other foreign fishing fleets caught herring, cod and other fish offshore and used the bays and shorelines as anchorages and locations for processing the catch (O'Neill 1987, 33). It might be suggested that these middens represent the activities of English fishing fleets (A. O'Sullivan, pers. comm.). However, it should also be considered that the deposition of these ring brooches in middens may be a result of native Irish settlement.

Crannogs

Several ring brooches have been found on sites that could be considered as a classic form of early medieval Gaelic habitation. Ring brooches from crannogs include RB 11 from Lake Ervey, Co. Meath, RB 10 from Lake MacHugh, Co. Leitrim, RB 53 from Newtownlow, Co. Westmeath, and RB 92 from Lough na hIncha, Co. Roscommon. It should be pointed out that all these brooches were recovered as a result of the activities of metal-detectorists and the identification of their provenances as crannogs may not be entirely accurate. However, there is evidence from the midlands and south Ulster that some crannogs continued in use well into the later medieval period. Crannogs were constructed in County Fermanagh in the medieval period, while at Deredis Upper, Co. Cavan, artifacts from a rebuilt crannog suggest a fourteenth-century occupation. In addition, fourteenth-century castles and tower-houses were placed on crannogs at Cro-Inis, Co. Westmeath, Island MacHugh, Co. Tyrone, and possibly Clough Oughter, Co. Cavan (E. P. Kelly 1991, 122). The ring brooches from crannog sites, especially those from

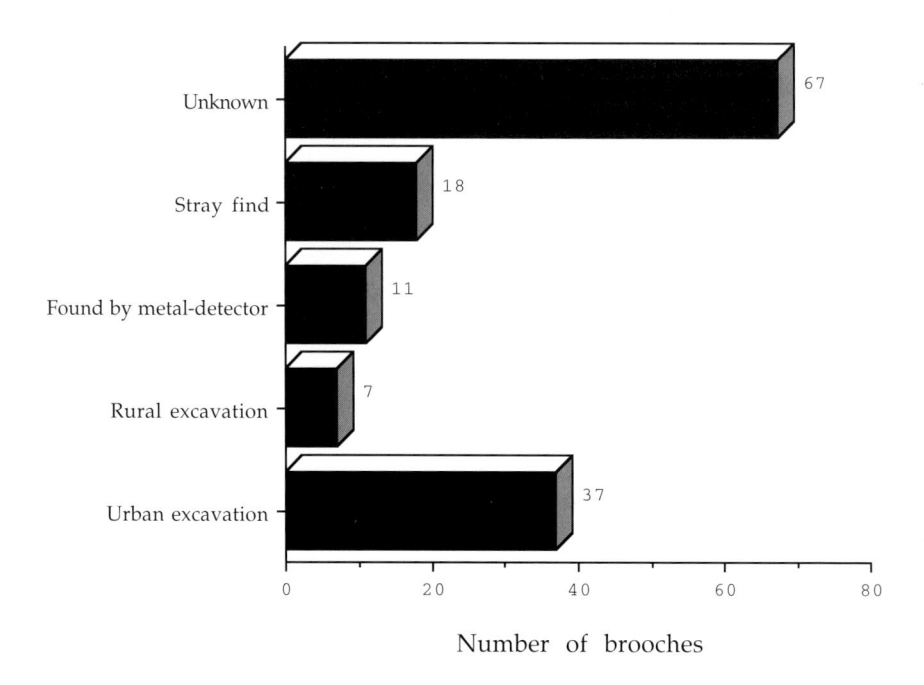

Fig. 19—Means of recovery of ring brooches.

the north-west, are the strongest indication that the Gaelic Irish had adopted the use of this form of jewellery, probably through contact with Anglo-Norman colonists or through trading contacts with France, Spain and Britain.

Means of recovery

The various means of recovery of Irish medieval ring brooches have had an effect on their distribution and provenances (Fig. 19). Forty-four ring brooches (31.4%) were recovered through archaeological excavation. Thirty-seven (26.4%) of these were from urban excavations and seven (5%) from rural excavations. Eleven (7.9%) ring brooches were recovered through metal-detecting. Two of these were recovered from dredgings of the River Blackwater in counties Tyrone/Armagh. The remaining nine are associated with the illegal targeting by metal-detectorists of suspected Early Christian sites (E. Kelly, pers. comm.), many of which are actually known medieval sites in the midlands. These activities have certainly contributed to a concentration in the north Leinster/midlands region. Ironically, a benefit to this study of these activities is that, although stratigraphic dating is not available, provenances have been provided in most cases. Eighteen (12.9%) brooches were stray finds. The means of recovery of 67 brooches (47.9%) is unknown. The majority of these were originally collected by antiquarians in an era when context was not considered paramount.

Conclusion

The distribution of ring brooches shows a striking concentration in the areas controlled by the Anglo-Normans from the late twelfth to the fourteenth century (Barry 1987; Richter 1988; Glasscock 1993; Bradley 1995). By the late twelfth century, the main urban centres, south Leinster, Meath and east Ulster had all been colonised. Ring brooches are especially common in these areas. In contrast, although such Connacht towns as Galway and Sligo were important Anglo-Norman port settlements, they have yet to produce a single ring brooch. The provenances of the majority of ring brooches also emphasise strong Anglo-Norman associations, with examples from towns, rural fortifications, manorial settlements and the ecclesiastical foundations of the new religious orders. While many of these could be considered relatively high-status settlements, it is important to remember that ring brooches could have been worn by individuals across the social spectrum, whether noble, merchant or artisan. It is difficult to examine the relationship between high-status ring brooches and high-status sites, as only five of the fourteen gold ring brooches have relatively precise provenances (one rural fortification, one ecclesiastical site, two towns, and what has been recorded as an open field). Finally, considering the complex social and economic links between Anglo-Norman and Gaelic communities, it is unsurprising that there is also evidence of their use amongst the Gaelic Irish.

IV. MEDIEVAL METALWORKING AND THE MANUFACTURE OF RING BROOCHES

> 'The words of the Lord are unalloyed:
> silver refined in a crucible,
> gold purified seven times over.'
> —Psalm 12, verse 6 (Cherry 1992, 5)

Introduction

It is more than likely that some Irish ring brooches were manufactured in Britain or France or another part of Europe and imported into Ireland in the Middle Ages. Certainly gemstones such as rubies and sapphires which originate in India and Burma had to be imported, probably via merchants from cities across Europe, especially Italy (Campbell 1991, 115). They were often already set into a jewel rather than in a loose form which could later be broken up for refashioning (*ibid*.). Historical records attest to the quantity of luxury goods, including jewellery, being imported and exported around Europe. For example, an entry in the *Calendar of justiciary rolls of Ireland* in 1306 refers to 'a ship called the Nicholas of Doun in Ulster, laden with wine and other merchandise', including coffers with jewels, furs, clothes, etc., which 'was by severe tempest of the sea wreaked in the parts of Portmarnok near Molaghyde' in Dublin Bay (Mills 1914, 507). The account books of a fourteenth-century Italian merchant, Francesco Datini, who traded in jewellery and other luxury items across Europe indicate that his partner, Baldassare degli Ubriachi, planned to visit Ireland while Richard II was there in the hope of selling him jewels (Scarisbrick 1994, 11). Scarisbrick illustrates 'the intricacies of the . . . international jewellery trade' with Ubriachi's comments that the best time for business in England was at New Year and at royal weddings, when the demand for jewels sent prices up (*ibid*.).

It has been shown that Irish ring brooches range from classic European forms to what might be distinctively Irish types. In the Middle Ages substantially the same types of clothing and jewellery were worn throughout Europe, but with regional variations and local expressions of the same broad themes. Ring brooches are part of this pan-European phenomenon—a fact illustrated by their occurrence in countries as diverse and far apart as Norway, Italy, Ireland and Hungary (Héjj-Détári 1965). Metalworkers in Ireland would have been heavily influenced by the work of their European contemporaries, especially those in England and France. Therefore it is not surprising that the decoration of ring brooches from Ireland, England and France can often be compared very closely. It has been shown that there are no specifically Irish types of finger-rings (Baker 1994, 77). In contrast, while metalworkers in Ireland made ring brooches identical to British and French forms, it appears that they may also have developed indigenous forms of ring brooches. In comparison to medieval finger-rings in Ireland (*ibid.*) there are a number of European ring brooch types which are not found in the Irish corpus. Clearly the Irish ring brooch collection is one example of a regional expression of medieval European jewellery.

Metals and their sources in medieval Ireland
Metal types

In the Middle Ages, precious metals were held in the same high regard as they were in biblical times, when their fineness was compared in the Psalms to the purity of the word of God (Cherry 1992, 5). They were considered to be symbols of divinity and nobility, and this regard is reflected in the many medieval sumptuary laws that were enacted in an attempt to restrict their use to the aristocracy. However, in contrast to 'the words of the Lord', many of the Irish ring brooches examined in this study are of alloyed metals. Many of these are of intentionally 'gold-coloured' copper alloys, while others may originally have been gilded. Five metal types—gold, silver, copper alloy, lead alloy and iron—were identified in this study (Fig. 3). Fourteen (10%) brooches were made of gold, 57 (40.71%) were of silver, 58 (41.43%) were of copper alloy, and ten (7.14%) were of lead alloy. One composite brooch was formed of both copper alloy and lead alloy (0.71%). Two brooches, one of copper alloy and one of lead alloy, had iron pins (probably replacements).

Gold

Gold has long been valued for its rarity and because of its superior metallurgical properties which, for example, allow it to be hammered without annealing (Tylecote 1962, 2). Above all these qualities gold is valued for its intrinsic beauty and has long been used to make decorative and symbolic ornaments (Eogan 1994, 1). The source of gold for the production of both prehistoric and early medieval Irish metalwork has been the subject of academic debate (e.g. Eogan 1994; Whitfield 1993). Whitfield has suggested three possible gold sources in Ireland in the Early Christian period. It may have been melted down from older artifacts, as gold can be and is repeatedly recycled; it may have been imported; or it may have been produced in Ireland. While much of the gold and silver used by medieval goldsmiths was not new but consisted of old plate, most gold used by British goldsmiths in the twelfth and thirteenth centuries was imported in the form of coins, either as besants from Byzantium or as *obols de musc*, Alomohade dinars, from Moslem Spain or North Africa (Campbell 1991, 108).

The importation of gold into Ireland in the twelfth century was mentioned by Giraldus Cambrensis, who commented that the Irish were 'very desirous of gold' and entered into dealings with 'traders that search the ocean for gain'. Giraldus also provides evidence for the use of native gold in the *Topographia Hibernica*, where he referred to gifts of Irish gold to Henry II (O'Meara 1982). In his *Expugnatio Hibernica* ('Conquest of Ireland') he advised King John to tax the Irish in gold, and he argued that the availability of gold in Ireland made the country too valuable to be lost by the Normans (Scott and Martin 1978, 262–3). It would appear that his advice was heeded, as revenue in the form of gold and silver ingots was collected on 16 October 1203

(Whitfield 1993, 23).

In the 1430s the prospect of great mineral wealth in Ireland was held out to the English in a poem attempting to show the political and commercial advantages of building up the English navy. This poem, *The Libelle of Englysche Polyce*, suggested that gold was one reason for the English crown to retain control of Ireland (Down 1993, 489):

> 'For of sylvere and golde there is the oore
> Among the wylde Yrishe, though they be poore,
> For thye ar rude and thereone no skylle;
> So that if we had there pese and gode wylle
> to myne and fyne and metall for to pure
> In wylde Yrishe myght fynde the cure'.

It is uncertain to what extent this perception of vast Irish gold resources was hearsay and wishful thinking. In fact it may have been largely exaggerated as an inducement to the English crown to maintain its interests in the colony at the time of the Gaelic resurgence (Down 1993, 490).

Silver and lead

Local and imported old metal and coinage would have provided an important source of silver for goldsmiths (Lightbown 1978, 98). *The Libelle of Englysche Polyce* quoted above also held out the possibility of large deposits of silver available in Ireland. Mining for silver, which occurs in argentiferous lead ores (Homer 1991, 57), in County Tipperary and County Waterford is indicated in a number of medieval sources. In 1296 the English king made payments of 30s. as 'part payment of the wages of Wm. de Borham, the borer, going to Ireland with four miners . . . to open and work mines', and a payment of five marks to R. de Saham, Baron of the Exchequer, 'going to Waterford and Munster with the above borer and miners to place them in mining works and raise their expenses' (Sweetman 1881, 164). In the late thirteenth century mines in the Silvermines area of County Tipperary were developed and worked by a colony of Florentine and Genoese merchants, to whom there are many references in contemporary state papers (Gleeson 1937, 103; Sweetman 1880, 230, 322). The Italian miners may have departed as a result of a combination of local opposition and financial difficulties. In 1303 there were reports of miners coming into conflict with 'the men of the country' (Gleeson 1937, 105), and it was reported in 1304 that 'the Merchants of Florence were harassed by debts' (Sweetman 1881, 87).

In 1375 the Butlers of Ormond asked for and were granted the right to all lead and half the silver found in their territory (Curtis 1932, 287–9). In 1503 there is further reference in *The Red Book of the Earls of Kildare* (Mac Niocaill 1964, 12–13) to mining for gold and silver: 'There is in the Erl of Desmonds country a mine of goold . . . and in Ormond a myndis of silver'. In the 1540s an attempt was made to provide the royal mint with silver from Bannow in County Wexford; however, the high costs far exceeded the value of the results and the enterprise was abandoned shortly afterwards (Cowman 1988, 97).

Copper alloy

In the Middle Ages copper was rarely used on its own but was alloyed with varying proportions of one or more other metals, such as tin, zinc and lead, to produce a range of copper alloys with varied properties (Bayley 1991, 13). For wrought (cold-worked) material the copper alloy contained small amounts of tin and zinc, while cast material required an alloy of copper and zinc with small quantities of lead and tin to lend greater fluidity to the molten metal (Goodall 1981, 63). In modern usage *bronze* is an alloy mainly of copper and tin and *brass* an alloy mainly of copper and zinc; however, medieval terminology and alloys were much more variable (Blair and Blair 1991, 81). It is nearly impossible to distinguish between copper alloys by non-scientific means, and in the absence of such scientific compositional analysis it is more accurate to use the term copper alloy rather than bronze or brass, etc. (Blair and Blair 1991, 81; Goodall 1981, 63).

The source of copper used in Irish artifacts in the Middle Ages has not been established. As well as the deliberate addition of one or more of the elements tin, zinc and lead, copper alloys contain low levels of other elements. These would have occurred as accidental inclusions which were not removed during the smelting process. Trace elements have been used to suggest sources or geographical areas of use for metals in the Bronze Age. However, this possibility has been largely unexplored for medieval metal sources (Bayley 1991, 13). Although Ireland had substantial quantities of native copper, the evidence for copper-mining in Ireland in the medieval period has not been examined. There are medieval references to copper-mining, such as a description in 1557 of 'the setting forth of the King and Queen's majesties' mines in Barristoune by Claymyne, in the County of Waxfforthe' in the Carew manuscripts (Jackson 1980, 9–10), but we do not know to what extent these attempts were successful.

It is possible that copper, tin, zinc and lead were imported into Ireland. Britain was one of the main producers of medieval Europe's tin supply and we know that lead was produced in abundance throughout Europe, so much so that the market was frequently saturated (Homer 1991, 57). Certainly quantities of iron were imported into Ireland from Brittany and Spain (O'Neill 1987, 90) and via Bristol (Down 1993, 490), although there is also some evidence for the production of iron from native ore at Carrickfergus, Co. Antrim (Barry 1987, 109). While these contemporary references show that Ireland was considered to have substantial reserves of metals (*ibid.*, 108) and that many attempts were made to exploit them, it is less clear to what extent these attempts were successful. Indeed, the output of many of these mines appears to have been minimal (Down 1993, 490; Cowman 1988, 97). Despite indications of the presence of ore deposits in Ireland, it may be that the bulk of Ireland's metal requirements were imported (Down 1993, 489–90).

The organisation of metalworkers
Goldsmiths, bronzesmiths and pewterers

It is important to stress that medieval craftsmen who made jewellery and plate in both gold and silver were known as goldsmiths rather than jewellers (Campbell 1991, 107; Lightbown 1992, 41). It is only towards the end of the fourteenth century that we find goldsmiths so specialised in jewellery that they were termed jewellers (Lightbown 1992, 49). However, the evidence of wills and personal names has been used to suggest that in the thirteenth century some goldsmiths did specialise in smaller items such as brooches and finger-rings (Campbell 1991, 148). Bronzesmiths may have been responsible for the production of copper-alloy ring brooches, although it is likely that goldsmiths who specialised in jewellery would not have worked exclusively with precious metals (J. Harvey 1975, 175). A number of the Irish copper-alloy brooches do not merely imitate but are almost identical to brooches of precious metal. Lead-alloy brooches would have been made by pewterers.

Anglo-Norman metalworkers, clients and guilds

Medieval goldsmiths worked for a range of clients. Ecclesiastical authorities were a major source of patronage because of the demand for gold and silver objects, such as chalices, candlesticks, shrines, reliquaries and crosses, for use in church services (Cherry 1992, 7). Some goldsmiths worked exclusively for kings and aristocratic courts; however, many others were based in growing urban centres like London, Florence and Paris, as described in the 1220s by Jean de Garlande in his *Dictionarius* (Lightbown 1978, 4):

> 'The goldsmiths sit before their furnaces and tables on the Grand-Pont and make hanaps of gold and silver and brooches and pins and buttons, and choose garnets and jasper, sapphires and emeralds for rings. The skill of the goldsmith hammers out gold and silver sheets with slender hammers on iron anvils. It sets precious gems in the bezels of rings that barons and noblemen wear.'

Indeed, most of the products of the medieval goldsmith were secular objects such as silver bowls, cups, fittings for knives and belts, silver and gold finger-rings and brooches. This explains why the symbol of the goldsmith's craft on personal seals and arms was more likely to be a secular object such as a covered cup or a brooch than a chalice (Cherry 1992, 36).

Secular goldsmiths and other craftspeople were organised into guilds—mutual benefit associations which flourished in the towns and cities of western Europe from the eleventh century. Craft or trade guilds were formed to set standards of workmanship and to teach apprentices the mysteries of their craft. Guild members had the exclusive right to practise a craft within the franchises (boundaries) of the city of Dublin. The *guild merchant* or merchant guild was the most important as it was responsible for the regulation of commerce, but initially it included artisans as well as merchants (Clark and Refaussé 1993, 7, 11). In the *Dublin Guild Merchant Roll* for the years 1190–1265 at least twenty 'aurifabri'—goldsmiths—are listed (Connolly and Martin 1992). The Dublin goldsmiths were first incorporated by charter shortly before 1557 (Clark and Refaussé 1993, 21) and it is the only guild which still exists in Dublin today.

There are many references to goldsmiths in contemporary Irish archival sources, such as the Dublin guild merchant roll mentioned above. In 1344 the Priory of the

Holy Trinity in Dublin considered its pewter tableware sufficiently valuable to employ Walter the goldsmith to mark it for 9d. (Mills 1891, 90). Goldsmiths were not only based in the large coastal urban centres. In the *Calendar of documents relating to Ireland* there are a number of references to goldsmiths in towns around the country. We know of Thomas the goldsmith of Tipperary, mentioned in 1296 (Sweetman 1881, 137), Berkhoc the goldsmith, possibly of Kildare, mentioned in 1297 (*ibid.*, 180), and Nicholas the goldsmith of Kilkenny, mentioned in 1301 (Sweetman and Handcock 1886, 7).

Gaelic Irish metalworkers

While Anglo-Norman craftsmen would appear to be the main candidates for the production of ring brooches, it is also possible that metalworkers trained in the native tradition were involved. In Ireland the achievements of metalworkers in the early Middle Ages are well known (Youngs 1990; Ó Floinn 1991). In Gaelic medieval Ireland the main source of patronage for skilled metalworkers were the upper classes. A resurgence of some of the native Irish chieftains in the fourteenth century led to such work as the refurbishment of the Shrine of the Stowe Missal between 1371 and 1381, and the gilt silver plates added to the Domnach Airgid book-shrine by the goldsmith John O'Barrdain in the mid-fourteenth century (Ó Floinn 1983, 70). The Limerick crozier and mitre were commissioned in 1418 for Conor O'Dea, bishop of Limerick, from the goldsmith Thomas O'Carryd (O'Neill 1987, 95). The privileged position of Gaelic goldsmiths is emphasised by the recording in the annals of the death in 1471 of Matthew O Maelruanaigh, 'ollamh' in metalwork to the Mag Uidhir of Fermanagh (Nicholls 1993, 418).

Gaelic Irish were officially excluded from admission to guilds. In Dublin no one was admitted 'without he be of English name and blood, of honest conversion and also free citizen of the city' (Lydon 1972, 94–5). However, there is evidence that this exclusivity was not always maintained. Indeed, it has been suggested that goldsmithing was one craft which bridged the ethnic barriers in medieval Ireland (O'Neill 1987, 95). For example, Gaelic apprentices were admitted in Dundalk in the mid-fourteenth century (Lydon 1972, 95). One Gaelic goldsmith, Dermot Lynchy, was admitted to the franchise of Dublin in 1473 (O'Neill 1987, 95), and another, Donal Oge O'Vollaghan, was made a freeman of Galway in 1500 (F. Kelly 1895, 383).

Irish archaeological evidence for metalworking

Archaeological evidence for the working of copper alloys in the medieval period suggests work on a domestic scale rather than an organised industry (Goodall 1981, 63). Recent excavations in Dublin (Ó Ríordáin 1971; Wallace 1985; Hayden 1992; Hayden, forthcoming), Waterford (Hurley *et al.* 1997) and Cork (Hurley 1990) have produced evidence for metalworking. The working of copper alloys is represented by clay crucibles and heating trays, the waste product slag and the artifacts themselves—ring brooches, buckles and stick-pins (Wallace 1985, 399, 403). The ironworker's craft is mainly represented by the numerous finds of iron objects such as ships' nails and roves, padlocks and keys, and also by the waste product slag.

There is also archaeological evidence for a thirteenth-century metalworking area at the west of the Anglo-Norman town of Dublin. Recent excavations at Cornmarket, between Francis Street and Lamb Alley, recovered waste from a thirteenth-century bronze workshop among the fills of the thirteenth-century town ditch (Hayden 1992, 21; forthcoming). This waste included ash, charcoal, burnt clay, tuyères, a buckle mould, rings, buckles, brooches and unfinished pins. The workshop itself was uncovered outside the ditch. In this area a post-and-wattle building survived which had been refloored on numerous occasions, and on each floor a thick deposit of charcoal had accumulated. One of the deposits contained a large quantity of liquid mercury, probably used in 'fire' gilding. Research into the contemporary archival sources dealing with this part of the town reveal that Waltei Bukeler and Patricii le buckeler (the buckle-makers) were resident in Bertram Court in 1278-9 and 1280-2 respectively (Brooks 1936, 77-8, 85, 119; Linzi Simpson in Hayden, forthcoming). Significantly, artifacts recovered from the site included a copper-alloy annular buckle, a lozenge-shaped copper-alloy ring brooch decorated with collets and blind holes, RB 116, and a ribbed copper-alloy ring brooch, RB 87.

Production techniques

The primary methods of producing ring brooches from all metals were the casting of molten metal and forging (cold/wrought work) with a hammer of sheet metal and wire. Much of our information about the techniques used to produce ring brooches comes from contemporary literature. These archival sources can be combined with the archaeological evidence to elucidate the techniques employed by the manufacturers of ring brooches. One of the best written sources for information about medieval metalworking is the manual *De diversis artibus*, written in the early twelfth century by a German metalworker known as Theophilus who was probably also a Benedictine monk (Hawthorne and Stanley Smith 1979, xv). His manual was written in three parts: the first is concerned with painting, the second with glass-making and the third with metalworking. While Theophilus was concerned with the production and decoration of objects such as chalices, candlesticks, crosses, shrines and reliquaries, the techniques and tools he describes in detail are of enormous benefit in understanding how secular goldsmiths would have decorated items of personal ornament such as ring brooches.

Metalworking tools

Contemporary archival material is also a valuable source of evidence for metalworking tools, many of which have not been recovered or identified in the archaeological record. An English goldsmith, Alexander Neckham (1157–1217), described some of the equipment a goldsmith should have (Cherry 1992, 24; Holmes 1964, 142):

> 'The goldsmith should have a **furnace** with a hole at the top so that smoke can get out ... Let him have an **anvil** of extreme hardness on which the iron or gold may be laid and softened and may take the required form. They can be stretched and pulled with the **tongs** and the **hammer**. There should also be a hammer for making gold leaf, as

well as sheets of silver, tin, brass, iron or copper . . . He should have a **touchstone** for testing, and one for distinguishing steel from iron. He must have a **rabbit's foot** for smoothing, polishing and wiping the surface of gold and silver . . . He must have . . . a toothed **saw** and **file** for gold as well as gold and silver wire . . . He must know how to distinguish pure gold from latten and copper, lest he buy latten for pure gold. For it is difficult to escape the wiliness of the fraudulent merchant.'

An inventory of the workshop of a York goldsmith, John Colan, in 1490 similarly lists a variety of hammers, anvils and tongs, as well as equipment for enamelling, a small 'tryblett' (taper mandrels on which finger-rings were made), several punches and stamps, and 'pattrones', probably wooden patterns from which clay moulds were made (Campbell 1991, 122).

Assaying

A goldsmith's touchstone was an important piece of equipment used to assay the purity of gold and silver. The gold or silver was rubbed onto the surface of the touchstone (a fine-grained black stone) and the resulting colour was compared with marks produced by alloys of known composition in the form of touch-needles (Campbell 1991, 113). At the beginning of the fourteenth century the leopard's-head mark was introduced as a guarantee that silver had been assayed and found good. None of the Irish silver brooches are marked; however, this is only to be expected as jewels were usually exempted from marking because of the small amount of metal used in them.

Forging

To forge metal, an ingot was hammered into sheet metal of suitable thickness, cut to size and raised (hammered) into shape. Frequent annealing (heating and then cooling) was necessary to prevent hardening. The object was then given a smooth surface by planishing with hammers followed by polishing (Campbell 1991, 117–18).

Casting

Casting would have been the most versatile of manufacturing techniques (Goodall 1981, 63). Ring brooches and annular buckles were cast in either open (one-piece) or two-piece moulds. Many of these moulds were slabs of stone with a matrix carved out of one face. Fired clay moulds were also used. The following description of the construction and use of clay two-piece moulds, based on eighth-century moulds found at Orkney for casting penannular brooches (Craddock 1990, 170), is probably almost identical to that for medieval clay two-piece moulds.

Two balls of prepared clay were pressed against a board to create a perfectly flat surface. A template of the brooch or buckle to be cast was made in wax, lead or wood, and then one side of this was pressed into the soft clay of one of the flat faces. A funnel-shaped template for the pouring channel was also pressed into the clay. When the first half had dried, the flat surface of the second piece was pressed against the first so that the impression of the reverse of the artifact could be taken. The two pieces of the mould were then parted and the template carefully removed. The mould was then refitted together, fired and the metal poured in. After casting, the metal shape formed in the pouring funnel, called the casting sprue, would be removed and the brooch would require filing, scraping and polishing. A thirteenth-century copper-alloy ring brooch from Ludgate Hill, London, was still attached to its casting sprue. The presence of the casting sprue on a brooch otherwise nearly finished might be explained by its being used to hold the work firmly while the pin was being fitted and the gems/stones set into collets (Murdoch 1991, 156, no. 409).

One difference between early medieval and medieval clay moulds is that early medieval moulds had a number of triangular keys formed up with a knife on the first piece. When the second piece of the mould was pressed against the first, a series of corresponding depressions would be formed. These keys ensured that the two pieces of the mould would be fitted together properly for firing. Both sides of medieval clay and stone moulds were drilled with tapered keying-holes. Wooden or iron dowels would have been slotted into the corresponding holes in both pieces of the mould to ensure accurate registration. On a stone ring brooch mould from Rochester, England, the matrix is linked by tiny incisions to a vent to let out air and gases. The loop of the pin of this brooch would have been cast around a core possibly of wood; a groove to receive this core runs from the edge of the mould and across the top of the pin (Spencer 1968, 102). Medieval moulds can have a number of matrices on one face. Stone moulds often had matrices on both sides of the block, and these would have been used interchangeably as one half of two different two-piece moulds.

A mould for making ring brooches has yet to be found in Ireland. However, the discovery of a mid-twelfth-century finger-ring mould from Backhouse Lane, Waterford, shows that jewellery was being cast in Ireland in the Middle Ages (Hurley *et al.* 1997, 405). This is a two-piece stone mould with matrices for casting three finger-rings. Very few ring brooch moulds have been found in Britain, but those that have provide us with useful information about how Irish ring brooches would have been cast. A thirteenth- to fifteenth-century mudstone mould from Hungate, York, was used to cast undecorated circular ring brooch frames (Richardson 1961, fig. 28:10). The matrix on one face would have produced flat rectangular ring brooch frames, and the other would have produced ring brooch frames with a faceted front face. This mould is probably identical to the types of moulds used to produce Irish Class 1 ring brooches. The resulting brooches could also have been decorated after casting, as in the Irish Class 2 brooches.

A thirteenth-century stone mould from High Street, Perth, Scotland, has matrices for two plain circular ring brooch frames and their pins (Bogdan and Wordsworth 1978, 23). Brooches produced from the Perth mould or from a similar limestone mould from Rochester would be identical to Irish Class 1 brooches (Spencer 1968, 102–3, fig. 18:4a, pl. iv). A clay mould from Norfolk with matrices for producing two circular ring brooches and their pins would have produced ring brooches with rectangular cross-sections, decorated with raised inscriptions (Fig. 20) (Anon. 1808). The inscriptions were variants of the 'AVE MARIA' legend, as seen on the Irish Class 2b brooch RB 79 from Carrickfergus.

The metal for casting was melted in small ceramic or stone crucibles. Different types

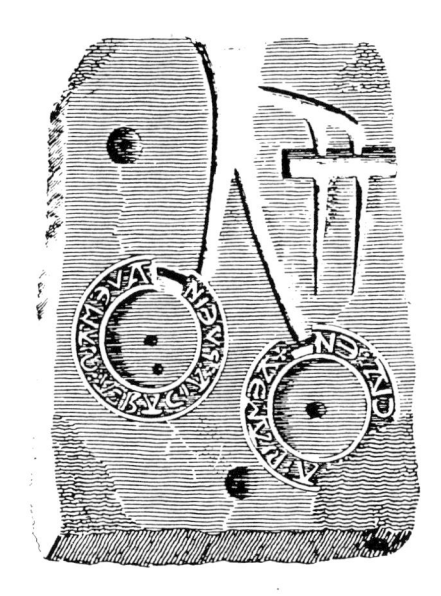

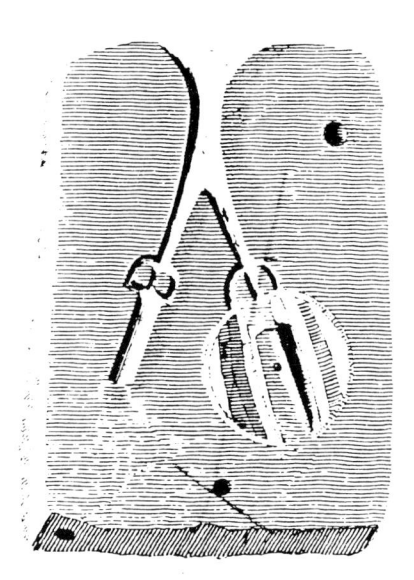

Fig. 20—Clay ring brooch mould from Ashill, Norfolk, England (after Anon. 1808).

of crucibles were used for different metal types, as each has its own requirements: for example, zinc tends to evaporate rapidly from molten brass and so a lidded crucible is necessary (Craddock 1990, 171).

Joining

Some ring brooches were assembled from a number of pieces. Two joining techniques, soldering and riveting, were recognised on the Irish ring brooches. The tiny tubular collets of the unusual ring brooch from County Wexford, RB 119, are joined onto their cups by tiny rivets, visible on the undersurface of each cup. The collets and bosses of the unprovenanced ring brooch RB 115, which originally had four alternating collets and bosses, were soldered to the baseplate of the frame.

Decoration
Cast decoration

The decoration of ring brooches could be cast integrally to the frame or could be applied after casting or forging of the frame. Parts of some of the more elaborate brooches could have been cast separately and subsequently soldered together. The decoration of many of the ring brooches probably involved a combination of these techniques. It is not always possible to identify whether a brooch was cast or forged as the signs left by both these processes were usually filed and polished away. It is often only possible to specify when castings are left very rough or are crudely executed. A copper-alloy brooch from County Roscommon, RB 92, was cast in a mould whose two sides were not aligned properly as the design is slightly out of kilter where the front and reverse meet. Similarly a casting seam is visible on a lead-alloy brooch from Waterford, RB 94, which the pewterer did not file smooth. It may be that such objects merely represent cheap copies of the precious-metal examples worn by the wealthy and were not intended to be viewed closely (Goodall 1981, 64).

Incised, engraved and punched decoration

Decorative motifs, such as the continuous chevrons, lines and inscriptions seen on Class 2 and other ring brooches, are incised or engraved onto the surface of the artifact. Incising involves cutting a design, with a tracer, into the artifact without removing any metal: the metal is merely pushed aside. Engraving involves removing a thin strip of metal from the surface of the artifact as the design is cut. Theophilus describes how gravers are made of solid steel, 'as long as the middle finger, as thick as a straw, though thicker in the middle, and square or round in section with the tang put into a handle' (Hawthorne and Stanley Smith 1979, 91).

On a number of the Irish brooches (e.g. RB 42, 59, 66 and 67) the incised lines were not cleanly cut but were probably made by repeated pecking using a fine punch and hammer (Goodall 1981, 63). Another type of incised decoration, seen on RB 48 from Knowth and on RB 105 from Essex Street West, Dublin, is 'rocked tracer' ornament, also known as 'rocked scorper' or 'wriggle work' (Egan 1991a, 31; Johnson 1995, 75). This was probably produced by rocking a chisel-like tool or tracer-punch from side to side as it was pushed across the surface of the metal (Goodall 1981, 63; Biddle 1990, 690). Theophilus describes various types of punches (Hawthorne and Stanley Smith 1979, 92):

> 'They are a span long, broad and headed on top, while below they are slender, round, flat, three-cornered, four-cornered, or curved back as required by the diversity of the forms in the work. They are to be struck with a hammer. A tool [a ring-punch] is also shaped in the same way but is slender at the end. A hole is impressed in the end of the punch by another even more slender tool and it is filed all around, so that a very delicate circle appears when it is struck on gold or silver or gilded copper.'

The latter ring-punch would have been used to create the beaded decoration seen on many Irish ring brooches. The hemispherical bosses which alternate with collets on the Irish Class 6a ring brooches are usually decorated with such punched circles. The rosettes which often decorate many of the Irish projecting-hands brooches (Class 7) were sometimes engraved but they were also occasionally created with a punch.

Niello

The decoration of two unprovenanced brooches, RB 63 and RB 76, is further enhanced with niello. Niello is a dense black compound of metallic sulphides which was used to inlay recesses in silver or gold, and occasionally in copper alloys (La Niece

1983, 279). These sulphides were fused onto the metal by the application of heat. The niello colours incised lines on RB 76, while on RB 63 it fills the cutaway areas surrounding the step motif. The black colour of niello provides a dramatic contrast to the brightness of the polished metal and highlights the design.

Enamelling

An enamel is a vitreous coating fused to a metallic base. It has previously been noted that no examples of medieval jewellery with enamel decoration are known from Ireland (Cherry 1988, 151). A contemporary archival source, the register of wills and inventories of the diocese of Dublin in the fifteenth century, refers to 'a gold clasp with white enamel' which the chief justice of the king's bench, John Chever, left his daughter. Cherry notes that it is also possible that the so-called Yorkist badge in Robert Day's collection was white-enamelled (*ibid.*, 151). The present location of both these objects is unknown. However, one ring brooch examined in this study has added enamelling to the range of decorative techniques employed on jewellery in medieval Ireland. A copper-alloy brooch, RB 47, recovered during excavations at St Mary's Cathedral, Limerick, is decorated with a red enamel which fills a recessed band around the frame. This brooch is dated to the mid- to late thirteenth century (Hodkinson, forthcoming). Red enamel and this enamelling technique (known as *champlevé*, where a recessed area is filled with an enamel) are common on Irish early medieval jewellery (Maryon 1971, 184; Young 1990) and were also used to decorate Irish medieval armorial pendants (Armstrong 1913). It is likely that more of the Irish brooches were originally decorated with enamel although no traces survive, e.g. RB 65 (Pl. 4) (J. Cherry, pers. comm.).

Gilding and plating

Gilding was a technique employed to colour silver and copper-alloy brooches gold. This could be achieved by applying a layer of gold leaf to the surface of the base-metal brooch after first rubbing mercury onto it. Alternatively, gold dust was mixed with mercury or fragments of gold were dissolved in boiling mercury and this amalgam was spread in a layer over the brooch, which was then heated, causing the mercury to evaporate, leaving a film of gold on the surface (Lins and Oddy 1975, 365–70). The mercury discovered in a thirteenth-century bronzesmith's workshop in Dublin may have been intended for this use (Hayden 1992, 21; forthcoming). The silver brooch from Carrickfergus, Co. Antrim, RB 136, is gilt. This method was also used to plate copper-alloy brooches with white metal. RB 5 from High Street, Dublin, is possibly plated with tin (P. Mullarky, pers. comm.). Copper-alloy brooches can be coated with a coloured layer of various shades of brown, green or black by immersing them in a solution of sulphates, chlorides or nitrates (Maryon 1971, 264–6). The result is a smooth, lacquer-like layer formed on the surface of the metal. This action imitates the natural processes of a form of corrosion that sometimes results in a brown, green or black patination. It is not possible to judge whether the ring brooches and annular buckles with patination were treated to achieve this coloured layer for decorative effect or whether it occurred naturally.

Gemstones and imitations

Many of the Irish ring brooches have collets which were intended to hold gemstones or imitation gems, but many are now empty of their original settings. Often all that remains is a white powdery substance, probably the residue of the original paste used to fix the stones in position (Lightbown 1992, 21). A collet is essentially a round band of metal that holds a gemstone in position. They are often quite high and tapering in order to display the gem in a more prominent position. Almost all the gemstones surviving on the Irish ring brooches are described as being *en cabochon*—rounded and polished rather than faceted. It is generally believed that the cutting of stones into facets began in Europe only in the early fourteenth century. There are, however, a number of thirteenth-century European jewels with faceted stones, and a ring brooch depicted on the late thirteenth-century statue of a seated king on the west front of Wells Cathedral has faceted gems (Campbell 1991, 136; Lightbown 1992, 12). RB 118 from County Wexford and the unprovenanced RB 128 are decorated with faceted stones. However, John Cherry has suggested (pers. comm.) that the emeralds in RB 118 and the opal in the hands of RB 124 are probably replacements.

False stones are also represented in the Irish corpus. While it was acceptable to use cheaper metals and false stones on jewellery to be buried with dead kings and on church plate, many medieval guild statutes either forbade or tried to regulate their use in jewellery for the living. There were many methods of manufacturing imitation gems, such as tinting crystals or making glass-paste stones. Semi-precious stones could be enhanced by being set on a gold or copper-alloy foil which caused light to be reflected back at the viewer (Lightbown 1992, 21). In order to prevent fraud, only real precious stones were to be set in gold and only inferior stones were to be set in silver and copper alloy. Despite these attempts to curtail their use, false stones were in general use throughout Europe. No stones survive in the Irish silver brooches, and all the surviving stones in the Irish copper-alloy brooches are of glass paste. Interestingly, while most of the stones in the Irish gold brooches appear to be genuine gemstones, those in the gold Waterford brooch, RB 117, are of glass paste, alternating blue and green. It is possible that in their original glory they were intended to deceive and that they are evidence of fraud on the part of an Irish goldsmith, although they may also be evidence of a general flouting of the rules laid down by goldsmiths' charters across Europe.

Filigree

Another decorative technique employed on RB 117 is filigree—a decorative pattern of fine gold or silver wires soldered onto a metal backing. These wires were often twisted or beaded. Theophilus describes how wires were made by drawing short rods of cast metal through successively diminishing holes in a draw-plate until a fine wire resulted (Hawthorne and Stanley Smith 1979, 87). Gold wire could also be made by cutting strips from gold foil (Campbell 1991, 132). The filigree on the Waterford brooch is actually achieved by using a combination of such thin strips of gold arranged on edge surmounted by beaded wire. Theophilus provides comprehensive instructions on how beaded wire was made. He describes 'an iron implement called the *organarium*' through which long cylindrical rods of gold or silver are pushed and turned while the top of the *organarium* is struck, creating round beads of various possible sizes. A file grooved on the bottom could also be used to create beaded wire (Hawthorne and Stanley Smith 1979, 90). This filigree is further enhanced on the Waterford brooch by the application of tiny spherical granules of gold at key points in the design. Furthermore, the inner and outer edges of the frame have been raised by the application of beaded wire.

V. MEDIEVAL DRESS AND THE WEARING OF RING BROOCHES

'Fleshly lust and feasts,
And furs of divers manner of beasts
The devil of hell first invented,
Clothes deliberately cut into shreds
And the pride of women's headdresses,
Have destroyed this land,
May God who wears the crown of thorns,
Destroy the pride of women's horns
For the sake of his precious passion,
And may their long trains
Which are the sails of the devil of hell,
Never be the cause of our confusion.'
—John Swayne, archbishop of Armagh, 1418–39 (trans. Bliss and Long 1993, 734)

Introduction

The study of medieval ring brooches is inextricably linked to the study of the style and development of contemporary dress. This is because ring brooches, although also serving as items of personal jewellery, primarily functioned as practical clothes-fasteners. While recent archaeological excavations have contributed much to medieval textile studies, the principal sources of evidence for medieval dress are contemporary depictions and literary descriptions. These sources are also invaluable in analysing the exact means by which ring brooches were worn and the varied functions they performed as both dress-fasteners and jewellery. The evidence from archaeological excavations of burials has been instrumental in analysing the function of annular buckles but has not yet been relevant for ring brooches.

Sources of evidence for medieval clothing and jewellery

There is a range of archaeological evidence for the forms of medieval Irish clothing. The Dublin excavations, for example, have produced a medieval dyed woollen garment from Wood Quay, gold braid and textiles from High Street, thirteenth-century cloth and silk from Winetavern Street, and a fourteenth-century wool lace from Dublin Castle (Barry 1987, 105; Ó Ríordáin 1971, 76; Wincott Heckett 1991, 13). Other examples include fragments of silk found in association with late thirteenth- or early fourteenth-century pottery at Ferns, Co. Wexford (Sweetman 1979, 239), a piece of a thirteenth-century woollen tunic from Cork, and a piece of what was probably an Irish shaggy mantle, dated to the sixteenth century, from James Street, Drogheda (Wincott Heckett 1991, 13).

Valuable information about medieval clothing and jewellery comes from contemporary depictions, which survive in a variety of forms, including stone and brass effigies, incised grave-slabs, architectural stone sculpture, wooden sculpture, decorated pottery (Pl. 23), illustrated manuscripts, frescos, oil paintings and stained glass. These serve as windows in time through which many aspects of medieval life and technology can be studied (Unger 1991).

The most important type of depictions surviving from medieval Ireland are stone effigies. Their value has already been shown in the study of the development of medieval clothes and armour (Dunlevy 1989; Hunt 1974). As far as I am aware, there are no surviving Irish medieval manuscripts containing actual depictions of ring brooches. Manuscripts from other European countries, however, have proved to be some of the most interesting sources of details, especially for some of the 'lower' classes of medieval society. In particular, medieval psalters and books of hours from Britain, France, Germany and the Low Countries typically contain, as incidental illustrated detail, a wealth of information on contemporary crafts, costume and everyday activities (e.g. Millar 1932; Backhouse 1989; 1990; Basing 1990; Collins and Davies 1991). There are no Irish medieval wall paintings illustrating the use of ring brooches, an occasional source of information in Britain. Nevertheless the recent discovery and conservation of portions of a mural at Cormac's Chapel on the Rock of Cashel, Co. Tipperary, hint that others might yet be revealed elsewhere.

Clothing in medieval Europe

There have been a number of studies of European medieval dress, based mainly on the evidence of contemporary depictions and literary descriptions (Kelly and Schwabe 1931, 17; Cunnington and Cunnington 1969; Evans 1952; Brooke 1972; Hunt 1974; Dunlevy 1989). It can be shown that dress styles were very similar throughout medieval Europe, although there were

Fig. 21—Thirteenth-century stone effigy of Queen Berengaria, Espan, France (after Stothard 1876).

certainly local variations. The following is a review of some of the main trends in the development of clothing from the twelfth to the fifteenth century.

The development of medieval dress has been said to be 'one of increasing complication and of increasing differentiation between the sexes' (Evans 1952, 1). 'Apart from the dress of war and chase', the clothes of men in the twelfth and thirteenth centuries differed little from those of women (*ibid.*, 14). Both men and women wore an underdress or kirtle under an overgown or surcoat. The kirtle had long, tight-fitting sleeves. The surcoat was often sleeveless with deep armholes, although a sleeved surcoat was also worn. Women usually wore the surcoat very long, almost covering the feet completely or occasionally trailing, while men often wore it at mid-calf length. It often had a slit or vent at the neck which could be closed by a ring brooch (Fig. 21) (*ibid.*, 17). The surcoat occasionally had vertical slits, called fitchets or placket-holes, into which the hands could be thrust for warmth or to reach items slung from a girdle worn over the kirtle (Cunnington and Cunnington 1969, 44). The girdle was more often worn around the waist or the hips over the surcoat. It was made of leather, silk, wool or linen, and was often decorated with metal mounts or embroidery. In the twelfth and thirteenth centuries the finger-ring, ring brooch and girdle buckle were the main forms of jewellery worn.

The kirtle and surcoat were supplemented in cold weather with a cloth mantle, a cloak cut as a large segment of a circle. Its edges could be clasped by a brooch at the breast, or linked by a cord which passed through two slits to ornamental bosses on the outside. This cord is often shown in contemporary depictions as being held in the hand (Pl. 24). In cold weather a hooded, sometimes fur-lined, cape was also worn. An inventory in 1322 of the effects of Roger de Mortimor, lord of Wigmore, Dunamace and Trim (Otway-Ruthven 1993, 232, 252), lists amongst the contents of the wardrobe of Lady Mortimor '*j. tunica. ij. supertunicis, j. mantell et j. capa absque furrura, de bruno panno mixto*' ('one kirtle, two overgowns, one mantle and one cape unfurred, of brown mixed cloth') (Larking 1858; translated in Hunt 1974, 37). Labourers wore a short tunic with breeches and leggings. When gentlemen went hunting they adopted a similar costume of a short belted tunic, breeches, coloured hose and a short mantle, which allowed greater freedom of movement than formal long robes. Contemporary literature, such as the *Dit de l'Eschacier*, describes hardly any difference between the peasant and the huntsman except that the huntsman's clothes were made from fine scarlet cloth instead of brown bure (Evans 1952, 9).

The fourteenth century saw the first marked differences between the clothes of men and women in the Middle Ages. This was the age in which 'tailors and dressmakers could exercise their virtuosity' (Evans 1952, 26). Men began to wear a short, fitted robe called a pourpoint. The hose, which had previously been unseen under the kirtle, were now joined to the breeches to form tight leggings, which were often brightly coloured. In more relaxed situations men wore long-sleeved overgarments such as the houppelande. The sleeves were funnel-shaped, often with a long cuff, and the skirt fell in deep tubular folds. Women began to wear gowns with a more closely fitted bodice, often tightly laced at the back and with a fuller skirt to accentuate a small waist. In the late fourteenth century the sleeves of the overgown became very long and developed into lappets. In the fifteenth century the overgown had a V-shaped vent at the neck with a wide flat collar. The vent extended down into a narrow U-shape on the abdomen and was laced. The wide skirt fell in pleated folds and was gathered high under the bust. The sleeves were gathered at the shoulders and the wrists, creating 'pudding sleeves'. The girdle was now more often worn high on the waist.

Women's head-dress

In the Middle Ages women were usually depicted wearing a head-dress. One form combined a veil and wimple. The wimple covered the throat and shoulders and was fastened under a veil worn over the head. Another form of head-dress was known as a barbette and fillet (or pill-box). This consisted of a long, narrow band of folded linen (barbette) which was worn over the head, with both ends then wrapped down around each side of the face, under the chin, and back up to be pinned on top of the head over a low, cylindrical, open-topped circlet of stiffened linen (fillet) (Dunlevy 1989, 29; Tummers 1980, 57–9). Occasionally the circlet was goffered into vertical pleats or was lengthened upwards and outwards. The hair was first centrally parted and dressed into a thick pad at the back of the neck (Hunt 1974, 35) in a knotted mesh hairnet or crespine (Pritchard 1991, 291). The barbette and fillet head-dress is more common than the veil and wimple on contemporary sculpture in Ireland (Pls 24 and 26) (Hunt 1974, 36). Several 'intermediate forms' of head-dress, combining elements of both these main types, also exist (Tummers 1980, 57–9). In the early fourteenth century plaited hair worn on each side of the face became fashionable (Pritchard 1991, 291). The ruffled, nebuly or reticulated head-dress was popular at the end of the fourteenth century. It consisted of a much-pleated veil of several layers framing the face and falling in a fantail

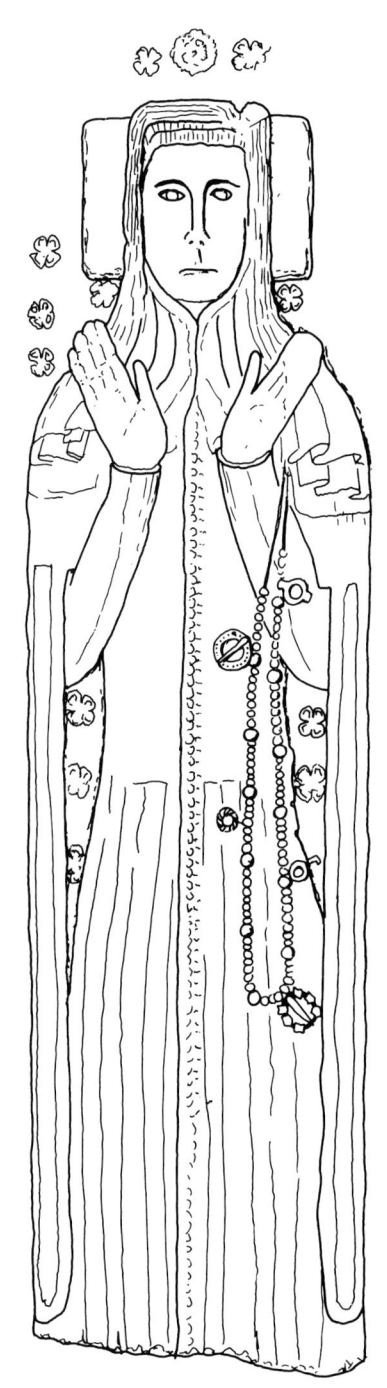

Fig. 22—Late fourteenth-century stone effigy from Wales, depicting paternosters with ring brooches and other jewellery attached (after Gresham 1968).

over the back and shoulders. These head-dresses were replaced in the fifteenth century by the horned or heart-shaped head-dress, described by the archbishop of Armagh in his satirical poem quoted at the beginning of this chapter.

Clothing in medieval Ireland

It is likely that in the twelfth and thirteenth centuries the dress of the English colonists in Ireland hardly differed from that of corresponding classes in England and France. However, in the late thirteenth, fourteenth and fifteenth centuries it would appear that their descendants were adopting the 'manners, fashion, and language of the Irish enemies' (Hardiman 1843, 3–5). Indeed, legislation was enacted to combat these trends, not necessarily with much success. The parliament of Ireland, 1297, decreed that 'all Englishmen in this land [must] wear . . . the mode and tonsure of Englishmen'. A similar statute condemned the Anglo-Irish who 'attire themselves in Irish garments and having their heads half-shaved, grow and extend the hairs from the back of the head and call them Culan, conforming themselves to the Irish as well in garb as in countenance' (Lydon 1984, 18). In 1366 the Statutes of Kilkenny ordered Englishmen to adhere to their own 'custom, fashion, mode of riding and apparel' (Hardiman 1843, 13):

> 'It is ordained and established, that every Englishman do use the English language and be named by an English name leaving off entirely the manner of naming used by the Irish; and that every Englishman use the English custom, fashion, mode of riding and apparel, according to his estate'.

Although there are frequent references to the apparent differences in costume between the English and the Gaelic Irish, relatively little is known of the actual dress and dress accessories of the Gaelic upper classes in this period. It appears that Gaelic dress in the Middle Ages was largely derived from earlier dress forms. Gaelic men and women's clothes in the tenth–twelfth centuries consisted of a long linen tunic or *léine*, worn under a large mantle or *brat*, together with a girdle called a *criss*. In the medieval period the *brat* is often referred to as the 'Irish mantle' and the *léine* as the 'saffron shirt'. The *brat* consisted of a long rectangular or semicircular piece of material wrapped around the body so that the edges overlapped in the front. The *léine* is usually described as *gel*, meaning 'bright', but the *brat* is nearly always described as being of a definite colour, or even multi-coloured. Women wore a veil on their head. The jacket or *ionar* with long or short trews seen frequently in the decorative margins of the Book of Kells (but never mentioned in Irish sagas, which were only concerned with chiefs and warriors) probably represent the clothes of labourers (McClintock 1950, 1–18).

Even less is known of the dress accessories worn by the Gaelic Irish. In the early medieval period the *brat* was occasionally fastened on the breast, near the right shoulder, with a ringed pin or penannular brooch, as worn by Christ in the depiction of the Arrest at Gethsemane on Muiredach's Cross, Monasterboice, Co. Louth. The wearing of penannular brooches, however, was dying out by the tenth century, and the latest ringed pins date from the eleventh and early twelfth centuries (Fanning 1994, 55).

Fanning (1994, 56) suggested that the stick-pin which emerged at this time may have taken over the role of dress-pin in the twelfth century and into the Anglo-Norman period.

Although the dress of the Gaelic Irish in the medieval period appears to have been largely derived from early medieval Irish dress it was also combined with English fashions and was influenced by developments in the rest of Europe. The recovery of a number of Irish ring brooches from crannogs indicates that the Gaelic Irish had adopted this accessory. In the fifteenth century similarities between Gaelic Irish and English dress prompted the enactment of the following law, passed at the parliament held in Trim in 1447 (Hardiman 1843, 13):

> 'As there is no diversity of habit between the English marchers and the Irish enemies, by colour of which the Irish enemies come into the English counties as English marchers, and rob and pillage on the high way, and destroy the common people by lodging on them by nights, and slay the husbandmen, and take their goods to the Irish: it is enacted, that he that will be taken for an Englishman shall not use a beard upon his upper lip alone, and that the said lip shall be once shaved, at least in every two weeks, the offender to be treated as an Irish enemy'.

Wearing ring brooches

In the twelfth and thirteenth centuries gowns worn by both men and women usually had a slit at the neck which enabled them to be pulled on over the head. The ring brooch served the practical purpose of closing this slit. In the fourteenth and fifteenth centuries tighter clothes fastened with buttons and laces were worn by both men and women. While the ring brooch was occasionally still worn with the looser style of dress, it was now more often seen fastening a cloak over the breast.

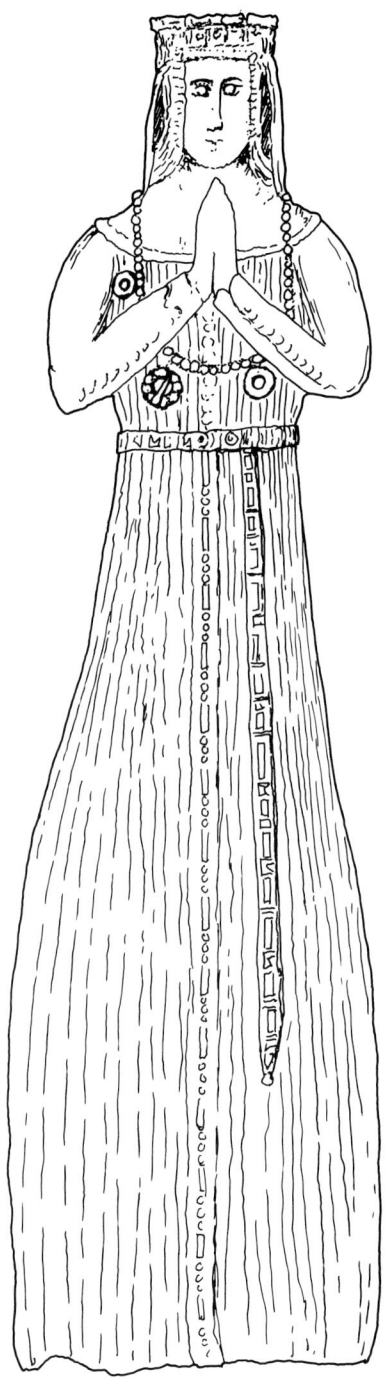

Fig. 23—Late fourteenth-century stone effigy from Wales, depicting paternosters with ring brooches and other jewellery attached (after Gresham 1968).

The exact method by which ring brooches were worn needs to be discussed, as the modern brooches that we are familiar with are provided with a clasp and function in a completely different way. The pin was thrust through the lower edges of the vertical split at the neck (Lightbown 1992, 138), which first had to be pulled slightly through the frame so that the pin could be manoeuvred through them. The result is that the pin is simply 'held in place against the opposite side of the frame by the drape of the fabric' (Egan 1991c, 247). Occasionally the opposing edges of the vent at the neck of the garment might be furnished with a sewn-on cord, a gap being left in the stitching to leave a small section free which could be lifted to insert the pin (Hattatt 1985, 223). Another option is that the pin may have been passed through two prepared slits (Ward-Perkins 1940, 274) at the edges of the vent at the neck of the garment.

Prepared slits or a sewn-on cord explain how some of the smaller brooches with more fragile pins might have functioned, and why many of these brooches have blunt-ended pins, as it was not necessary for them to pierce heavy fabric. However, we know that medieval dress styles were not always what the modern observer might consider 'sensible'. The close-fitting sleeves worn by both men and women in the thirteenth century were sometimes so tight that they necessitated being sewn closed every morning. Evans (1952, 14) cites the thirteenth-century French writer Jean Renart, who describes in his *The Romance of the Rose* or *Guillaume de Dole* how, when the emperor and his court went to the woods, they opened their sleeves to have greater freedom of action, and when they ended the chase the ladies sewed up their sleeves with threads from the pouches that hung at their girdles (Terry and Durling 1993, 22, 54, 105).

A notable feature of the Irish brooches is that many of them have severely bent pins, e.g. RB 8, 9, 19 and 25. An explanation might be that substantial pressure would have been exerted on the pin by the pull of the cloth through which it passed. This would have been enough to bend or even break a fragile pin if worn frequently with heavy cloth. Indeed, some of the Irish brooches have broken pin tips, e.g. RB 71 and RB 98, and 26 brooches have no pins remaining at all. Two brooches, RB 1 and RB 137, have iron pins which were probably replacements.

Ring brooches as dress-fasteners

A number of Irish medieval sculptures show ring brooches being worn to fasten the vent at the neck of the dress. These include four stone effigies of female figures, two from Cashel, Co. Tipperary (Pl. 24), one from Castledillon, Co. Kildare, and one from Kells, Co. Kilkenny (Hunt 1974). This use of ring brooches is also illustrated on four sculpted heads, three male and one female, which act as label stops on the porch of St Canice's Cathedral, Kilkenny (Pls 25 and 26). Another useful example is the wooden sculpture of a Madonna (missing her child) which was probably originally from the Rhineland and is now in the Hunt Museum, Limerick. Indeed, there are many European stone and wooden sculptures of the Virgin and Child in which Mary is wearing a ring brooch to fasten the slit in the neck of her gown (Aubert 1926, pl. 31; Stone 1955, 116; Vitry 1973, pl. 67). In these examples the garments would appear to have small, prepared slits at the edges of the vent through which the pins pass. All these depictions date from the twelfth–thirteenth century.

Ring brooches as cloak-fasteners

Quite a number of Irish sculptures depict ring brooches fastening the edges of cloaks over the chest, including six figures of 'Christ showing the Five Wounds'. Four of these are weepers on the side panels of tomb-chests—two from St Canice's Cathedral, Kilkenny, one from Gowran, Co. Kilkenny (Pl. 27), and one from Strade, Co. Mayo (Hunt 1974). One of these figures is carved on a tomb in the church of St Nicholas of Myra, Galway (Hunt 1974), and another, unusually, forms a panel on a baptismal font (Roe 1968, pl. 37). A further example includes a figure of St John the Baptist on a panel of a baptismal font from Kilballyowen, Co. Clare (Higgins 1995). Six further examples are also weepers on the side panels of tomb-chests. These include 'Christ as Judge' from Mothel, Co. Waterford, St Paul on the Purcell tomb, St Werburgh's, Dublin, St Catherine and St Margaret of Antioch from New Abbey, Kilcullen, Co. Kildare, and St Margaret of Antioch (Pl. 28) and St Andrew (Pl. 29) from Jerpoint Abbey, Co. Kilkenny (Hunt 1974). A wooden sculpture of St Catherine from Kilcorban, Co. Galway, similarly shows a ring brooch fastening a cloak (Pl. 30) (Mahr 1976, 167). These depictions appear to suggest that the garment—in this case a cloak—may also have had prepared slits at the edges. All the sculptures which show the use of the ring brooch to fasten the vent in the neck of the gown are dated to the twelfth–thirteenth century. However, the sculptures which illustrate the use of the ring brooch as a cloak-fastener are all dated to the fifteenth–sixteenth century.

Ring brooches as purse-fasteners

While the ring brooch was primarily used as a dress-fastener it also performed alternative or additional practical tasks. Medieval clothes did not tend to have pockets, so items such as purses, keys, paternoster beads, knives, etc., were often worn hanging from the girdle or dress, attached by brooches. The purses that hung from brooches may have held relics or gemstones for amuletic purposes as well as money. Lightbown (1992, 138–9) illustrates this use of brooches from the 1379–80 inventory of Charles V of France, which lists four brooches for purses, and that of Margaret of Burgundy in 1405, which describes a number of little gold brooches for fastening purses or keys. Contemporary depictions also provide evidence of such alternative uses for ring brooches. A thirteenth-century mural from Westminster in London illustrates the triumphant Virtue *Largesce* standing over *Covoitise* and holding a long purse in her left hand from which gold coins spill out into the glutted mouth of the Vice. *Covoitise* is laden with money-bags, one of which is attached by its strings to his dress with a simple ring brooch (Pl. 31) (Binski 1986).

Ring brooches as apron-fasteners

Another practical use for ring brooches was to fasten an apron to the dress. The medieval apron had a triangular front portion whose upper point was secured to the chest with a ring brooch. A woman working at a forge in a fourteenth-century French manuscript, *Le Roman de la Rose*, is shown wearing an apron over her dress which is pinned to her chest with a ring brooch (Pl. 32). Similar depictions of aprons fastened with ring brooches include a young painter's apprentice in the late thirteenth-century

Las Cantigas of King Alphonso the Wise of Castille (Binski 1991, 2–3) and a metalworker from a late fourteenth-century illustrated manuscript (Pl. 33). As ring brooches were essentially practical clothes-fasteners it is not surprising that they were used in this utilitarian manner.

Ring brooches and paternoster beads

Paternoster beads are the medieval equivalent of the Roman Catholic rosary beads, i.e. a string of beads used to count the number of prayers recited, initially the 'Our Father' with the 'Ave Maria' being incorporated subsequently. There are at least three thirteenth-century paternosters from Ireland, two from Waterford city (Lightbown 1992, 342; 1997) and one from Cork city (Hurley 1990, 77, ill. 4), all composed of amber. Paternoster beads were frequently worn around the neck as well as hanging from the girdle, wrist or arm. They were also worn attached to the dress with a brooch, as depicted in a fourteenth-century German manuscript illustration of St Hedwig of Silesia (Pl. 34) (Lightbown 1992, pl. 19). In the early thirteenth century paternosters were mainly worn by old women, 'preoccupied because of their age with heaven', but by the late thirteenth century they were worn by both men and women of all ages as a symbol of piety (Lightbown 1992, 341). A fourteenth-century sandstone effigy in Bangor, Wales, shows a woman with a string of paternoster beads hanging from her left hand. Attached to these beads are two large ring brooches and three smaller rings (Fig. 22) (Gresham 1968, 235, fig. 94, no. 211; Anon. 1879, 388). Another fourteenth-century stone effigy in Northop, Wales, depicts a woman wearing a long string of beads around her neck, to which are attached three ring brooches (Fig. 23) (Gresham 1968, 237–8, fig. 94, no. 212). A fifteenth-century German portrait depicts a young man, Walther von Rottkirchen, holding a coral paternoster linked by two finger-rings (Lightbown 1992, 341, pl. 111). There are also numerous contemporary references to brooches and other items of jewellery attached to paternosters. A probable Irish example is included in an inventory of the goods of Nicholas Barret of the parish of Michan, Dublin, made in 1474, which mentions 'a pair of beads with a silver ring' (Berry 1898, 69). While the presence of one brooch attached to the beads might be explained by its occasional use to attach the paternoster to the dress, it does not explain the role of multiple brooches or of finger-rings.

Although the items of jewellery depicted on the Bangor effigy are not arranged in any discernible pattern around the paternoster, it has been suggested that they may have been used to adapt the beads 'to various devotional uses; but what those uses were remains to be investigated' (Anon. 1880, 207). It has also been suggested that 'these objects have reference to pilgrimages made to celebrated shrines' (Anon. 1879, 388). Certainly in the Middle Ages it was common to attach objects of a devotional nature to paternosters, such as the jet scallop shell on the paternoster of the Duchess of York described in 1495, evidently brought back from Santiago de Compostela by a pilgrim (Maclagan and Oman 1936, 16, 22). The prioress in the Prologue to Chaucer's *Canterbury Tales*, written in the fourteenth century, had jewellery attached to her paternoster, although it is not clear whether this was for devotional reasons:

'Of small coral aboute her arm she bare
A paire of bedes, gauded al with grene.
And thereon hung a broche of gold ful shene,
On which was first i-writ a crowned A,
And after, amor vincit omnia.'

While many examples of jewellery attached to paternosters might not have been devotional aids but simply decorative pendants or souvenirs of pilgrimages, contemporary references also indicate that wedding rings were worn on paternosters for sentimental reasons (Maclagan and Oman 1936, 22). It might be concluded that both finger-rings and ring brooches, which were often intimate gifts between lovers, were also worn on paternosters for such reasons.

Pl. 1—RB 25: unprovenanced copper-alloy ring brooch (Class 1). (Photo: David Jennings.)

Pl. 2—RB 16, 22 and 27: unprovenanced silver ring brooches (Class 1). (Photo: David Jennings.)

Pl. 3—RB 34 and 60: copper-alloy ring brooch, Ardara, Co. Donegal, and unprovenanced silver ring brooch (Class 2). (Photo: David Jennings.)

Pl. 4—RB 65: unprovenanced silver ring brooch (Class 2). (Photo: David Jennings.)

Pl. 5—RB 48: copper-alloy ring brooch, Knowth, Co. Meath (Class 2). (Photo: David Jennings.)

Pl. 6—RB 80 (obverse): silver ring brooch, Trim, Co. Meath (Class 2). (Photo: David Jennings.)

Pl. 7—RB 80 (reverse): silver ring brooch, Trim, Co. Meath (Class 2). (Photo: David Jennings.)

Pl. 8—RB 85 and 86: unprovenanced silver and gold ring brooches (Class 2). (Photo: David Jennings.)

Pl. 9—RB 91, 92 and 97: silver ring brooch, Killeigh, Co. Offaly; copper-alloy ring brooch, Co. Roscommon; and unprovenanced silver ring brooch (Class 3). (Photo: David Jennings.)

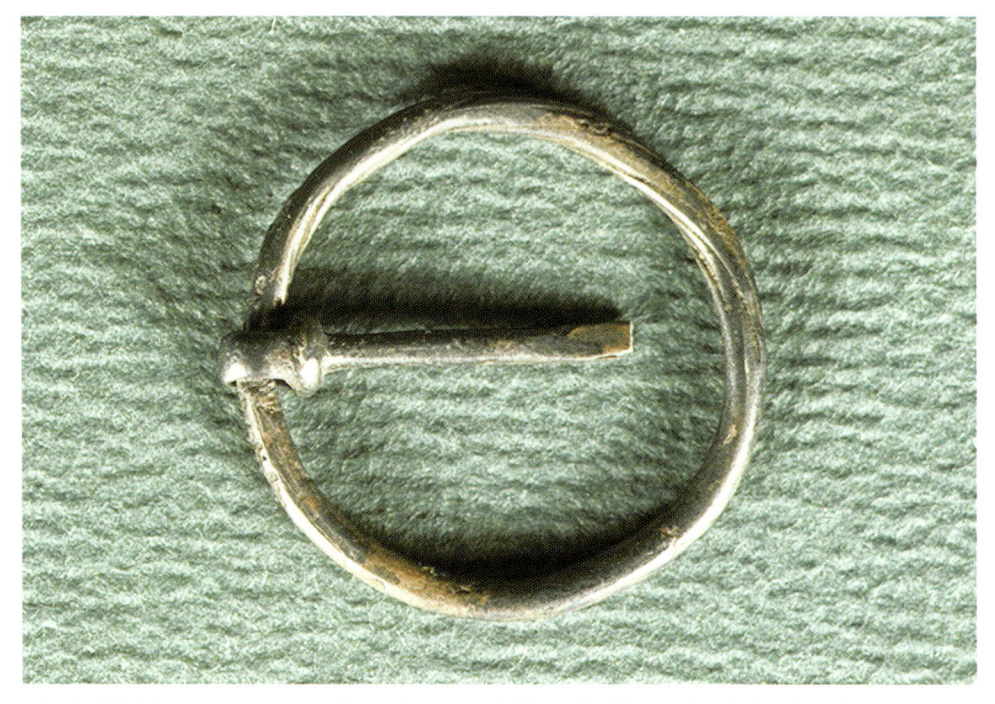

Pl. 10—RB 98: unprovenanced silver ring brooch (Class 3). (Photo: David Jennings.)

Pl. 11—RB 103 and 104: silver ring brooch, Trim, Co. Meath, and unprovenanced silver ring brooch (Class 3). (Photo: David Jennings.)

Pl. 12—RB 106: silver ring brooch, Athlone, Co. Meath (Class 4). (Photo: M.B. Deevy.)

Pl. 13—RB 108: silver ring brooch, Dysart, Co. Westmeath (Class 5). (Photo: David Jennings.)

Pl. 14—RB 110: gold ring brooch, Marlboro Street, Dublin (Class 6). (Photo: David Jennings.)

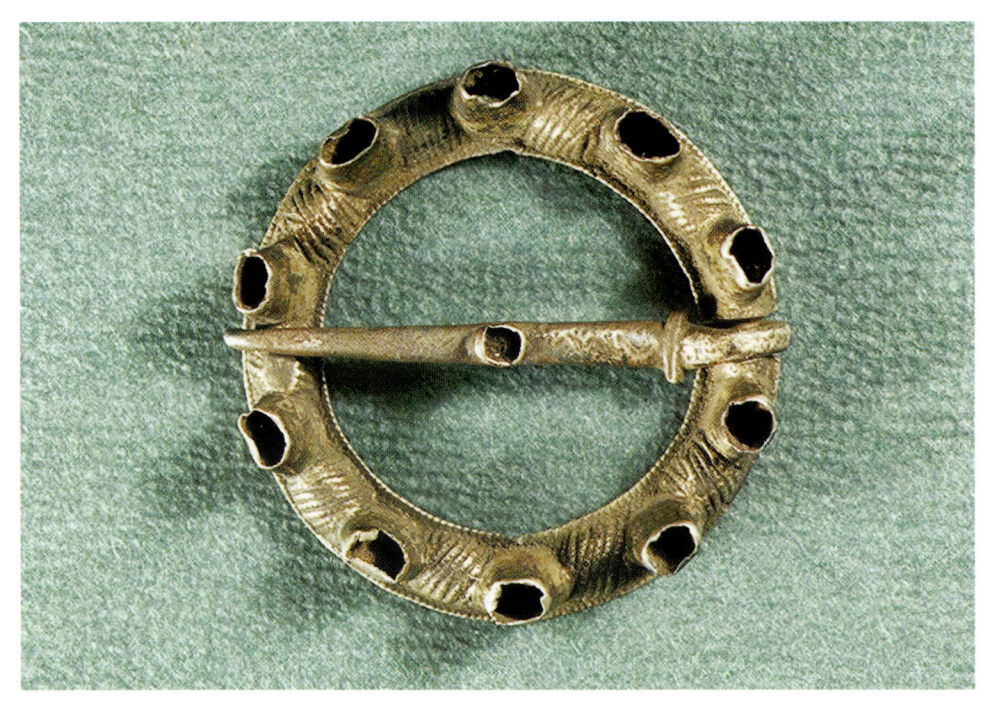

Pl. 15—RB 112: unprovenanced silver ring brooch (Class 6). (Photo: David Jennings.)

Pl. 16—RB 116: copper-alloy ring brooch, Cornmarket/Francis Street, Dublin (Class 6). (Photo: M.B. Deevy.)

Pl. 17—RB 117: gold ring brooch, Bakehouse Lane, Waterford (Class 6). (By kind permission of Waterford Corporation.)

Pl. 18—RB 118: gold ring brooch, Enniscorthy, Co. Wexford (Class 6). (By kind permission of the British Museum.)

Pl. 19—RB 121, 122, 123 and 125: gold ring brooches—Ballinrea, Co. Cork; County Kilkenny; Trim, Co. Meath; unprovenanced (Class 7). (Photo: David Jennings.)

Pl. 20—RB 124: unprovenanced gold ring brooch (Class 7). (By kind permission of the British Museum.)

Pl. 21—RB 132 and 134: lead-alloy ring brooches, Wood Quay, Dublin (Class 8). (Photo: David Jennings.)

Pl. 22—RB 140: unprovenanced silver ring brooch (Class 9). (Photo: David Jennings.)

Pl. 23—Late thirteenth/early fourteenth-century (K. Campbell, pers. comm.) pottery sherd with ring brooch excavated at South Quay, James Street, Drogheda, Co. Louth. (Photo: M.B. Deevy.)

Pl. 24—Late thirteenth/early fourteenth-century stone effigy of a woman, church of St John the Baptist, Cashel, Co. Tipperary. (Photo: M.B. Deevy.)

Top left *Pl. 25—Late thirteenth-century (Barry 1987) stone carving of a man, label stop on the porch of St Canice's Cathedral, Kilkenny. (Photo: M.B. Deevy.)*

Left *Pl. 26—Late thirteenth-century (Barry 1987) stone carving of a woman, label stop on the porch of St Canice's Cathedral, Kilkenny. (Photo: M.B. Deevy.)*

Above *Pl. 27—Early sixteenth-century (Hunt 1974) stone carving of Christ showing his five wounds, on the tomb-chest of a Butler knight in Gowran, Co. Kilkenny. (Photo: M.B. Deevy.)*

Pl. 28—Sixteenth-century (Hunt 1974) stone carving of St Margaret of Antioch, on a tomb-chest at Jerpoint Abbey. (Photo: M.B. Deevy.)

Pl. 29—Sixteenth-century (Hunt 1974) stone carving of St Andrew, on a tomb-chest at Jerpoint Abbey. (Photo: M.B. Deevy.)

Pl. 30—Fifteenth-century (MacLeod 1945) wooden sculpture of St Catherine, Kilcorban, Co. Galway (after Mahr 1976).

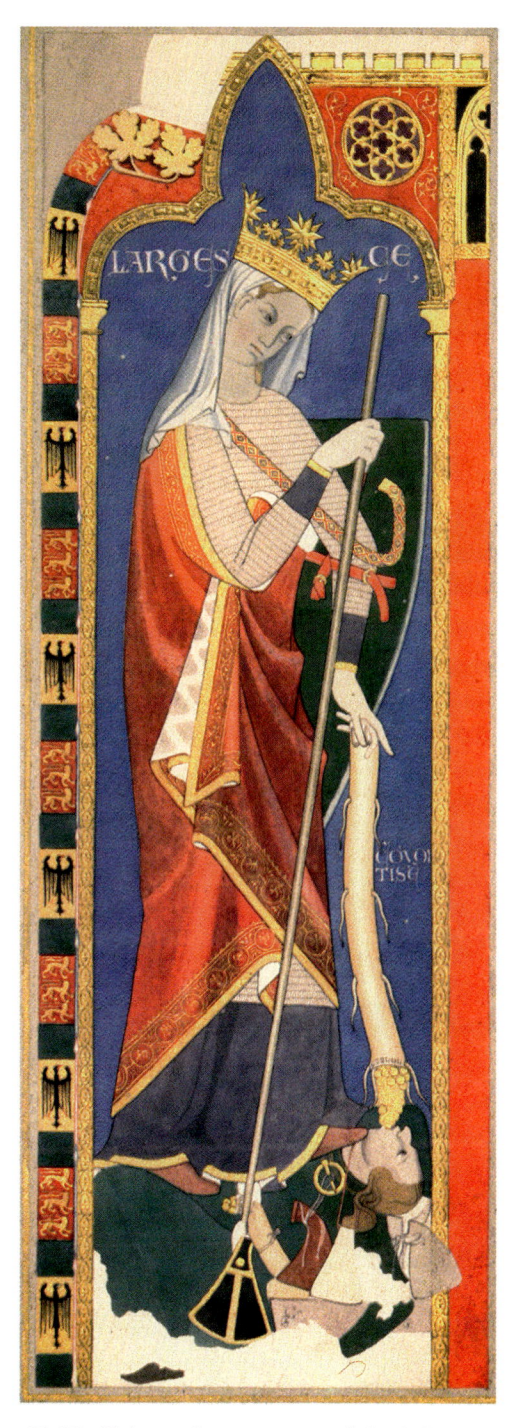

Pl. 31—Thirteenth-century mural depicting Largesce and Covoitise, originally in the chamber of Westminster, London. (By kind permission of the Society of Antiquaries of London.)

Pl. 32—Fourteenth-century French manuscript illustration of a woman working at a forge, from Le Roman de la Rose *by Guillaume de Lorris and Jean de Meun, MS 1126, folio 115. (By kind permission of La Bibliothèque Sainte-Geneviève, Paris.)*

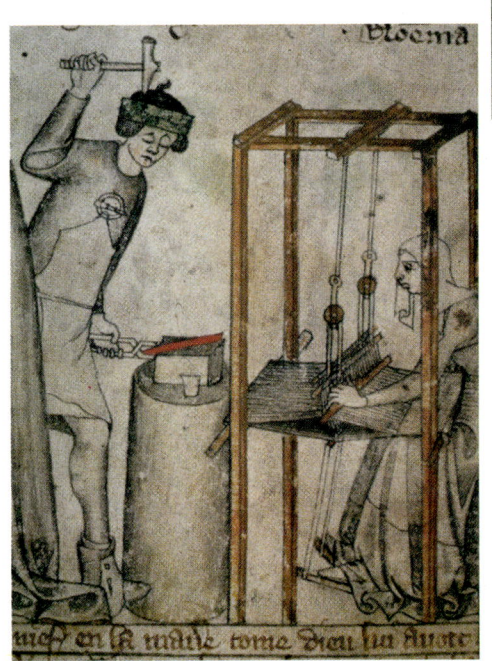

Pl. 34—Fourteenth-century German illustration on parchment of St Hedwig of Silesia (by kind permission of the J. Paul Getty Museum, Los Angeles).

Pl. 33—Fourteenth-century English manuscript illustration of a blacksmith, from BL Egerton MS 1894, f. 2vo. (By kind permission of the British Library.)

VI. JEWELLERY AND SOCIETY IN MEDIEVAL IRELAND

'To show off her neck, she closed the top of her shift with an exquisitely worked and finely made gold brooch; she placed it rather low so that an opening, one finger wide, gave a glimpse of her breasts, white as snow on the branches. This made her look even lovelier.'
—Jean Renart, *The Romance of the Rose* or *Guillaume de Dole*
(thirteenth century; Terry and Durling 1993, 77)

Introduction

By the twelfth century Ireland was already moving towards the feudal socio-economic system common throughout western Europe, and the process was accelerated by the arrival of the Anglo-Normans (O'Brien 1994). A manorial agricultural economy was established in the conquered areas, in which all land was owned by the feudal overlord but held for him by a hierarchy of nobles and peasants in return for dues in the form of money, goods, services and allegiance. Associated with European feudalism was chivalry, a series of ethical ideals representing Christian and military concepts of morality (Saul 1992, 6–7). This chapter explores what insights the study of ring brooches as jewellery can contribute to our understanding of medieval society in Ireland.

Ring brooches and jewellery as assets

'In an age without banks', collections of gold and silver coins, plate and jewellery 'represented bullion, and were assets easily realised in times of financial difficulty' (Campbell 1991, 108). Such collections are represented by British, German, French and Danish medieval coin hoards which also contained jewellery. Many coin hoards were probably deposited for safety during political unrest or from fear in economic crises. A number of hoards have been associated with the Scottish Wars of Independence (Callender 1924, 163). Two English fifteenth-century hoards from Fishpool, Nottinghamshire, and the River Thames, near Oxford, may have been associated with the Wars of the Roses (Cherry 1973, 308; Hinton 1993, 328; 1982, 21). Religious persecution may also have resulted in a number of hastily deposited hoards not being retrieved. For example, two fourteenth-century hoards, one from Colmar, France, and another from Munster, Germany, have been dated to periods when major anti-Jewish pogroms occurred in those towns (Reynolds Brown 1992, 414). However, hoards were probably also buried for safekeeping as savings in times of peace (Thompson 1956, xvi).

Many medieval Irish documentary references attest to the collection of large quantities of valuables, including jewellery and clothing, by the wealthy and of the need to safeguard them. In 1295 Silvester le Ercedekne accused Hugh Purcel, sheriff of

Tipperary, of breaking into his castle (of Dounhochil) and stealing from chests and coffers a large quantity of valuables, including money, clothes, armour, plate, gold rings, precious stones, brooches, girdles woven with silk, and other jewels (Mills 1905, 6). In the same year, in County Waterford, Leopardus de Mareys accused two men of breaking into his house and taking from a chest money, jewels, gold, silver, bonds and cloth (*ibid.*, 67). In 1297 in Waterford Milanus Petri accused four men of having broken into the house of his lord, the parson of the church of Dungaruan, of having broken open a chest and of stealing money, brooches, rings, spoons, other jewels and bonds (*ibid.*, 128). In Dublin in 1306 Alex. de Kexeby accused his serving man, Hugh de Stafford, of having broken into his coffers and stolen brooches, rings and money (Mills 1914, 498). Such references show that wealthy people accumulated their own stocks of precious metal and gemstones as well as jewellery, coins and cloth. While precious metals and stones were kept as a reserve of valuables, they were also collected in order to be converted into jewellery at a later date. When commissioning jewels, patrons were often expected to supply goldsmiths with gold, silver and gems, the raw materials of their trade (Campbell 1991, 117; Lightbown 1992, 33).

Jewellery was also pledged as security to obtain advances of money. An inventory of the belongings of Ellen Stiward in 1457 shows that she had 'a set of beads of one Agnes Broun with five rings and 1 brooch' pledged for 5s. (Berry 1898, 2). An inventory of the goods of Hugh Galliane, citizen of Dublin, in 1474 shows that he had one jewel belonging to the church of St Patrick, pledged with him for 10s. (*ibid.*, 85). In 1474 Arlandton Ussher, a merchant in Dublin, had one gold ring as security for a loan of 3s. 4d. made to John Roche (*ibid.*, 92). In Dublin in 1299 Sibilla de Fulbourne was forced to take legal action in an attempt to retrieve her jewellery, in the form of a girdle and ten gold rings, pledged as security for a loan of 40s. which she had since repaid (Mills 1905, 220).

The role of jewellery and clothing in medieval economics might also be reflected in some of the varied motives inspiring contemporary sumptuary laws. Baldwin (1926, 10) has suggested that while these laws endeavoured 'to encourage home industries and to discourage the buying of foreign goods', they were also an 'attempt on the part of the sovereign to induce his people to save their money so that they might be able to help him out financially in times of need'.

Ring brooches, jewellery and social ostentation

'In a courtly world it was important to be seen to be richly accoutred' (Hinton 1993, 328). The following comments of Sir John Fortescue, the tutor of Henry VI's son, in the fifteenth century indicate that lavish display was not just important but was an 'essential attribute of kingship' (Scarisbrick 1994, 3):

> 'It shall need be that the King have such treasure as he . . . may buy him rich clothes, rich stones, and other jewels and ornaments convenient to his state royal . . . For if a King did not do so, he lived then not like his estate, but rather in misery and more in subjection than doth a private person'.

A perceived necessity for such ostentatious extravagance might explain the often huge expenditure on jewels of successive generations of the English aristocracy. Hinton cites a number of examples: in 1355 the Black Prince incurred a debt for jewels to a single merchant of £1459 15s. 8d., while between 1351 and 1355 he spent £1575 5s. 5d. on building Kennington Palace. Similarly, in 1501 Henry VII paid £14,000 to French jewellers when his heir's marriage was to be celebrated; in comparison he spent £20,000 between 1502 and 1509 on his chapel at Westminster Abbey (Hinton 1993, 327). The aristocracy were not the only consumers who used clothing and jewellery to proclaim rank and wealth (Lightbown 1992, 79). Clothing was such 'an important expression of social rank' in the Middle Ages (Dyer 1989, 88) that it constituted 'a way of ordering human relations' (Hughes 1983, 88).

In the thirteenth, fourteenth and fifteenth centuries a series of sumptuary laws were enacted throughout Europe which formally restricted the wearing of clothing and jewellery. This legislation attempted to preserve the hierarchy of feudal society by preventing members of the lower orders from dressing above their station. It was desired that any stranger should be able to tell merely by looking at one's dress to what rank in society one belonged (Baldwin 1926, 10). Such laws were often specifically aimed at the increasingly wealthy urban merchants. With their greater spending power, wealthy members of the bourgeoisie occasionally 'behaved like aristocratic consumers' in displaying and storing their wealth by buying plate and jewels (Dyer 1989, 205–7). The English sumptuary legislation of 1363 decreed that craftsmen and yeomen 'were forbidden to wear precious stones, cloth of silver, silk, girdles, knives, buttons, rings, brooches, chains etc of gold or silver' (Baldwin 1926, 46–8). Hinton (1982, 21) suggests that these attempts to restrict the lesser knights and the bourgeoisie might also reflect the insecurity of the aristocracy, which was not always certain of its own tenure. In contrast, many Italian sumptuary laws have 'an anti-aristocratic flavour' and were used to promote 'republican virtue' (Hughes 1983, 74). While it is unclear how successful either of these attempts were, they illustrate medieval society's perception of the use of jewellery and clothing 'as a social mechanism for maintaining rank' (Hinton 1993, 328).

Those who had aspirations towards nobility, and who could afford to, often imitated expensive jewellery with 'gold-coloured' copper alloys and glass stones. In the Irish corpus there are a number of copper-alloy ring brooches identical in design to gold and silver ring brooches, e.g. compare the copper-alloy brooch from Kilkenny, RB 89, with RB 91, a silver brooch from Killeigh, Co. Offaly, and the unprovenanced silver brooches RB 97 and RB 101. These are all Class 3a brooches with identical decoration—half their frames have a twisted square cross-section with beading along the spiralling bands. Similarly, compare the unprovenanced copper-alloy brooch RB 113 with the gold brooch from Marlboro Street, RB 110, and the two unprovenanced silver brooches RB 112 and RB 115. These are all Class 6a brooches with identical decoration in the form of multiple high collets alternating with bosses decorated with beading. They may have been produced to imitate expensive jewellery for bourgeois consumers who could not quite afford precious metal or were forbidden by law to wear it.

A thirteenth-century French poem, the *Dit du Mercier,* illustrates how the use of ring brooches, in the form of cheap imitations, 'had reached a class that could not afford to

Fig. 24—Late thirteenth-century stone sculpture of a young male musician, Maison des Musiciens, Rheims, France (after Musée du Louvre 1968).

have them of gold' (Evans 1952, 17). The poem is written as 'the sales-talk of a wandering pedlar', who describes the goods he carries in his basket (Lightbown 1992, 53):

> 'J'ai fermaillez d'archal dorez
> Et de laiton sorgentez
> Et tant les aim cux de laiton
> Sovent por argent le met on',

which translates essentially as 'I have little brooches of gilt brass, and of silvered latten, and so fond are folk of latten, that often it is valued as silver' (*ibid.*). A number of manuscript illustrations show craftworkers, including young apprentices, wearing ring brooches (Pls 32 and 33). Similarly, stone sculptures such as those from the Maison des Musiciens, Rheims, France, depict young musicians wearing ring brooches to fasten the slit in the neck of their garments (Figs 24 and 25). Such examples from contemporary literature and art emphasise that ring brooches were indeed worn by all levels of society.

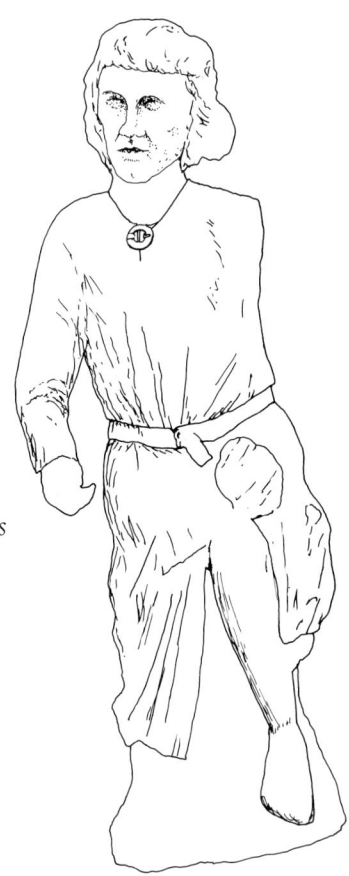

Fig. 25—Late thirteenth-century stone sculpture of a young male harper, Maison des Musiciens, Rheims, France (after Evans 1952).

Other copper-alloy brooches appear to be deliberately simplified versions rather than imitations of gold and silver brooches: e.g. compare the copper-alloy brooches RB 114 from 'the midlands' and RB 111 from County Westmeath with the other Class 6a brooches, RB 110, 112, 113 and 115, discussed above. These brooches have similar multiple high collets which would have been set with glass stones, but if they have bosses they are more subtle. Despite these similarities, they are much more restrained in size and form than RB 110, 112, 113 and 115. It may be that such brooches represent the taste of a more conservative element in society who disapproved of extravagance in jewellery and dress, 'encouraged by medieval religious sentiment' which condemned vanity and ostentation, particularly in women (Lightbown 1992, 79). Indeed, many sumptuary laws were probably partly motivated by 'sheer conservatism' and the belief 'that luxury and extravagance were in themselves wicked and harmful to the morals of the people' (Baldwin 1926, 10).

Ring brooches and jewellery as gifts

Jewellery and clothes were often given as gifts by royalty and wealthy nobles to their supporters. In the thirteenth-century French romance *The Romance of the Rose* or *Guillaume de Dole* by Jean Renart, the emperor frequently rewards his knights with jewels and expensive clothing. Renart comments that 'an emperor so generous with his treasures will have no lack of noble knights' (Terry and Durling 1993, 20, 41). In this tale the frequent and often extravagant gifting of jewellery by the three principal characters signals their nobility to the other characters in the story and of course to the medieval reader. Renart further comments that 'unexpected gifts are best and reflect great honour upon the giver' (Terry and Durling 1993, 44). The wearing of such gifts indicated where one's loyalty and allegiance lay. The often large retinues of aristocratic households wore badges and liveries which identified their affiliation to a particular lord (Dyer 1989, 53). The expense of employing and maintaining men, including many 'for whom there were no specific tasks', was justified by the benefits to the lord's image and standing of being surrounded by 'elegant companions' (*ibid.*). Particular symbols or devices usually worn in the form of badges were frequently also incorporated into other items of jewellery, including ring brooches. Such devices identified 'the spiritual, political or social allegiances or affiliations of the wearer' (Lightbown 1992, 188). A gold ring brooch from Manchester is decorated with open broom-pod motifs. Broom was used as a device by various French nobles, including Geoffrey of Anjou, the father of Henry II (Cherry 1983, 78).

In the light of the attitudes explicit in sumptuary laws, the giving of presents of expensive jewellery could be viewed as 'acknowledgement of the recipients' status' by their aristocratic donors (Hinton 1993, 328). The wider implications of sumptuary laws, which were designed, among other reasons, to prevent the lower orders from wearing 'outrageous and excessive apparel' (Baldwin 1926, 47), were that 'the higher aristocracy ought to wear such things' (Dyer 1989, 88–9). Another important aspect of medieval gift-giving was the concept of reciprocity, in that it was accepted as being an incurred debt, to be requited with allegiance or a service (Hinton 1993, 328). A possible Irish example of this use of jewellery is recorded in the *Calendar of justiciary rolls of Ireland* for 1302. Isabella Cadel and Fynewell Seyuyn, her maid, were arrested and brought to gaol in Kildare for coming from the felons, the Gaelic Irish, of the mountains. Isabella admitted that she had been sent by her lord, Dermot Odymsi, to the mountains to speak with certain friends and confederates of his, and that she had brought with her from the mountains certain jewels sent as a gift to him. Their goods were confiscated, including a 'silver brooch of the weight and value of one penny' (Mills 1905, 368).

Ring brooches in betrothal and love

Gifts of jewellery also played an important part in the highly ritualised *l'amour courtois* (courtly love). Again Jean Renart's *The Romance of the Rose* or *Guillaume de Dole* provides us with an example of the use of jewellery in affairs of the heart. The gift of a brooch, an embroidered cloth belt and a little purse containing a beautiful emerald ring are used to convince a suitor that the woman who has recently refused his advances now regrets her decision and has changed her mind (Terry and Durling 1993, 76). Ring brooches with a frame in the form of a heart are quite common throughout western Europe, although there are no examples in the Irish corpus. The inscriptions decorating many circular ring brooches show that they too were commonly gifts between lovers. Four of the Irish ring brooches bear inscriptions which speak of love. An unprovenanced silver brooch, RB 85, is inscribed 'AMOR VINCIT OMNIA' ('Love conquers all'). The prioress in Geoffrey Chaucer's Prologue to *The Canterbury Tales*, written in the fourteenth century, also wore:

> '. . . a broche of gold ful shene,
> On which was first i-writ a crowned A,
> And after, amor vincit omnia'.

Such love inscriptions in Latin were common, but they were more frequently written in French. This does not necessarily imply a French origin for such brooches as French was accepted as the language of chivalric love and gentility in medieval Europe. An unprovenanced gold brooch, RB 86, is inscribed 'PAR AMUR FIN SUI DUNE' ('I am a gift for fine love'?: J. Cherry, pers. comm.), and the gold brooch from Enniscorthy, Co. Wexford, RB 118, is inscribed 'AMES AMIE; AVES M PAR CES PRESET' ('By this gift you have the friend you love'?). A gold brooch from Trim, Co. Meath, RB 123, is inscribed 'AMEI AMEA' and 'SUI X E X EM ILI DAM', which Cherry (1988, 147) has interpreted as possibly a corruption of 'IE SUIS EN LIEU D'UN AMI' ('I am in place of a friend you love'), which would again appear to indicate the gift of a lover.

The giving of jewellery to a bride on betrothal and marriage was an established custom throughout western Europe in the Middle Ages (Lightbown 1992, 72). These gifts most often took the form of finger-rings and ring brooches. The exchange of gifts symbolised 'a pledge of conjugal affection' and fidelity on betrothal and marriage (*ibid.*, 183). The strong desire of suitors for fidelity in women can be seen in the following testimonies. In 1184 the poet Johannes de Hauville wrote in his *Archithrenius* (*ibid.*, 138):

> 'My bride shall wear a brooch—a witness to her modesty and a proof that hers will be a chaste bed. It will shut up her breast and thrust back any intruder, preventing its closed approach from gaping open and the entrance to her bosom from being cheapened by becoming a beaten path for any traveller, and an adulterous eye from tasting what delights the honourable caresses of a husband.'

That the role of the brooch was to ensure chastity by shutting up the breast is also conveyed by the thirteenth-century French poet Robert de Blois in his poem of advice to women, *Le Chastisment des Dames* (Lightbown 1992, 138):

> 'Take care that you allow no man to put his hand into your bosom, save he who has the right to do so; know that he who first invented the brooch made it for this reason, that no man should put his hand into a woman's bosom if he has no right and she is not married to him.'

A similar sentiment is proclaimed by the inscription on a thirteenth-century gold brooch from Writtle, Essex:

> 'JEO SUI FERMAIL PUR GARDER SEIN
> KE NUS VILEIN N'I METTE MEIN'

—essentially 'I am the brooch to guard the breast that no knave may put his hand thereon' (Cherry 1976, 140). A pledge of unbroken faith was also signified by the incorporation of two pairs of clasped hands into the already symbolic unbroken circle of the frame of the ring brooch (Lightbown 1992). Clasped-hands brooches were common in northern Europe, particularly in Germany, where they were known as *hanntruwebrazen*, 'betrothal brooches' (for examples see Lightbown 1992, figs 86–91; Steen Jensen *et al.* 1992, 175).

This tradition is also represented by a number of the Irish brooches. A gold ring brooch from Trim, RB 123, has one pair of clasped hands incorporated into the top of its frame. The French inscription on the frame, which translates as 'I am in place of the friend you love', shows that it was certainly a lover's gift. Unlike any of the other European examples, this brooch also has a pair of joined hands clasping a collet projecting from the frame. It is unclear whether the projecting joined hands, represented in the Irish Class 7 brooches RB 121–8, shared the same symbolism as the clasped hands of these betrothal brooches. However, the combination of both the projecting joined hands and the clasped hands on RB 123 may suggest that they also signified eternal troth. An unprovenanced Irish silver brooch, RB 99, has a highly stylised pair of joined, rather than clasped, hands incorporated into its frame. The hands join under the pin tip rather than at the top and bottom of the frame, as in the clasped-hands brooches, or at the bottom, as in the projecting-hands brooches. The remainder of the frame, however, represents stylised sleeves as seen on many German *hanntruwebrazen*.

Ring brooches and gender

Despite the common exchange of ring brooches as betrothal gifts, it would be erroneous to assume that ring brooches were worn predominantly by women. To a certain extent contemporary depictions on memorial effigies may appear to confirm this opinion, but this is because women are usually depicted wearing clothes similar to their everyday attire while men are invariably depicted in their knight's armour. While a woman might legitimately be shown wearing a ring brooch to fasten her garment at the neck, a ring brooch was less likely to have been worn on a suit of armour. There are a few exceptions, including a small copper-alloy sculpture of a knight wearing a ring brooch, from Iraq, in the collection of the National Museum of Ireland (M. Dunlevy, pers. comm.). However, this misconception also stems from a misunderstanding of the primary role of ring brooches (which was for fastening clothing), coupled with a modern western cultural viewpoint that women usually wear more jewellery than men. But in the twelfth and thirteenth centuries, as has been discussed above, there was very little difference in the everyday clothing of men and women, apart from when men were hunting and at war (Gardner 1935, pl. 265).

Both men and women wore jewellery, mainly consisting of a girdle buckle, finger-rings and a ring brooch. Members of the aristocracy also often wore crowns to indicate their status, and from the early fourteenth century aristocratic women frequently wore elaborate jewellery in their hair. In many respects the simple undecorated ring brooches (Class 1) have more in common with a button and eyelet or even the modern safety pin than with a modern decorative brooch. Even the most elaborately decorative ring brooches were also functional dress-fasteners and are shown performing this dual role on many contemporary depictions. Some of the smallest ring brooches may have been worn by children. Certainly the pedlar in the French poem *Dit du Mercier* speaks of pewter brooches for children, and there are contemporary references to children wearing clothes and jewellery that were miniature versions of those of their parents (Lightbown 1992, 90). However, contemporary depictions also show adults wearing quite small ring brooches (for examples see Tudor-Craig 1975, pl. 1/4/122; Swaan 1982, 168).

Ring brooches and jewellery with amuletic and talismanic properties

In the Middle Ages precious gemstones were highly valued for their perceived amuletic properties as well as for their beauty and rarity. These beliefs were not the prerogative of the uneducated superstitious masses but were also entertained by the learned. Numerous medieval lapidaries (texts on gemstones), such as the *Book of Minerals* by the thirteenth-century philosopher Albertus Magnus, dwelt mainly on the virtues of gems. The primary source for the medieval lore of precious stones was the eleventh-century poem *Liber Lapidum* ('Book of Stones') by Bishop Marbode of Rennes, which was heavily based on similar work by classical writers such as Damigeron, Pliny and St Isidore (Evans and Serjeantson 1933, xi; Armstrong 1973, 12). Gems valued for their amuletic qualities could be kept in special purses and worn on the dress. These were usually attached with brooches, just as the money-purse is attached to the tunic of *Covoitise* (Pl. 31). However, medieval sources specifically state that stones mounted to be worn as charms were to be mounted in finger-rings, bracelets or as pendants. There is little evidence to show that gems were mounted for 'magical' reasons in other forms of jewellery, including brooches (Lightbown 1992, 96).

Prophylactic inscriptions designed to ward off harm were very common on medieval jewellery. These were usually in the form of religious names or formulae. In the thirteenth century, St Thomas Aquinas debated in his *Summa Theologica* whether it was appropriate for people to wear the words of the Gospels, as he feared that they were worn because of a belief in their magical rather than spiritual power. Such formulae often occurred in a bewilderingly abbreviated form. It is possible that many variations occur because of illiteracy on the part of the engraver. Some inscriptions, however, appear to be deliberately cryptic. This may have been intentional, to make inscriptions more mysterious, thus increasing their 'magical qualities' in the superstitious medieval mind.

The gold projecting-hands brooch, RB 124, bears an example of what is probably a deliberately cryptic inscription. The bifaceted front face is divided into four sections. The inscription occurs alternately on the inner and outer facet around the frame. Although the letters on each of the four facets face alternately inwards and outwards, they must be read clockwise, beginning at the sign of the cross, even if upside down, for the inscription to make sense. Thus it reads '+AVEIMARIAG'. Similarly, the inscription on the unprovenanced RB 83, 'ENYNAICARGAIRAMEVA+', is actually '+AVE MARIA GRACIA NYNE' when read backwards.

The Angelic Salutation, 'Ave Maria Gratia Plena' ('Hail Mary full of grace'), was often used to invoke the protection of the Virgin. By the twelfth century veneration of the Virgin Mary had developed into a cult in the western Church, a cult powerful enough to inspire a wave of church- and cathedral-building right across Europe (Frayling 1995, 57). A similar veneration of the Virgin in medieval Ireland is indicated by the common use of devotional phrases on the inscribed brooches. A silver brooch from Carrickfergus, RB 79, is inscribed with what has been interpreted as 'AVE MARIA GxP III', the last three letters indicating that the salutation should be repeated thrice (Anon. 1857). In other brooches the Salutation is varied somewhat. An unprovenanced silver brooch, RB 84, is inscribed '+AVE(G?)V+AVEX'. An unprovenanced gold brooch, RB 85, is inscribed 'ISEUS MA(I?)RE HV'.

The titulus 'IHESUS NAZARENUS REX IUDAEORUM' ('Jesus of Nazareth, King of the Jews') is a very common inscription on medieval ring brooches (Anon. 1860, 166), often occurring in an abbreviated or blundered form (Callender 1924, fig. 3). The invocation of the cross was believed to be a defence against violent death or sudden harm (Saunders 1983, 146). The silver brooch from Trim, Co. Meath, RB 80, is inscribed on the front face with 'ihc n r i'. An abbreviation of the titulus, '+IHSENAOIIP'CI', occurs within the inscription on a gold ring brooch, RB 81, from County Monaghan, although the remainder of the inscription is unintelligible.

The names of the Magi (Wise Men) from the Orient do not occur in the story prophesied by Isaiah and told by Matthew in the Gospels. It was only in the early Middle Ages that they were named 'Caspar, Melchior and Balthasar' (Schiller 1971, 94-6). Throughout medieval Europe the veneration of the three so-called kings was believed to give protection from a number of illnesses, especially 'the falling sickness' (epilepsy), headache and fevers. They were also believed to protect one from the dangers of the road, sudden death and sorcery, and to assist in recovering lost property (Evans 1922, 125-6). This tradition can also be traced in the Irish ring brooches. The reverse face of the silver brooch from Trim, RB 80, is inscribed with a version of the names of the three Magi, 'IACPAR: MELCHAR: BALTICAR'. In the medieval Corpus Christi pageant in Dublin, the goldsmiths acted as the three kings of Cologne, 'riding worshipfully, with the offering and a star before them' (Clark and Refaussé 1993, 21).

Conclusion

Ring brooches were worn by men, women and children, from almost every class of society, in many countries across Europe throughout the Middle Ages. At their most elemental they were dress accessories, in the form of simple and adaptable clothes-fasteners. They were also jewellery worn for personal adornment. However, the materials they were made from, their decoration and inscriptions, and contemporary accounts all indicate the variety of symbolic values that they could be seen as expressing. Certain types would have been perceived as having amuletic qualities and were therefore worn to promote the wearer's health. As jewellery made of precious materials, ring brooches would have served as financial assets which could be realised in time of need. The wearing of ring brooches must also be viewed in the light of the chivalric ideals of European medieval society. Both the financial capacity to acquire and the legal permission to wear jewellery of precious materials would have been important signifiers of wealth and rank. Imitative brooches of non-precious metals would have expressed a desire to rise in the social hierarchy. Brooches also served as symbols of personal social relations, either secretly in the context of courtly love or more openly between brides and grooms-to-be. Ring brooches which combined the roles of dress-fastener and jewellery with that of the badge blazoned political loyalties and allegiances. Among other things, these insights clearly indicate that some elements of medieval Irish society saw themselves as being part of a wider European tradition.

REFERENCES

Abbreviations

Anon.	Anonymous
CBA	Council for British Archaeology
HMSO	Her Majesty's Stationery Office
JKAS	*Journal of the Kildare Archaeological Society*
JRSAI	*Journal of the Royal Society of Antiquaries of Ireland*
PRIA	*Proceedings of the Royal Irish Academy*
PSAL	*Proceedings of the Society of Antiquaries of London*
PSAS	*Proceedings of the Society of Antiquaries of Scotland*

Alexander, J. and Binski, P. (eds) 1987 *Age of chivalry: art in Plantagenet England 1200–1400*. Royal Academy of Arts, London.

Anon. 1808 Appendix. *Archaeologia* **14**, 275.

Anon. 1846 Several curious specimens of the ring shaped brooch. *Archaeological Journal* **3**, 76–8.

Anon. 1852 Antiquities and works of art exhibited. *Archaeological Journal* **9**, 106–10.

Anon. 1853 Antiquities and works of art exhibited. *Archaeological Journal* **10**, 246–54.

Anon. 1854 Antiquities and works of art exhibited. *Archaeological Journal* **11**, 283–8.

Anon. 1857 Fibula with inscription. *Ulster Journal of Archaeology* **5**, 249.

Anon. 1859 Antiquities and works of art exhibited. *Archaeological Journal* **16**, 179–83.

Anon. 1860 Antiquities and works of art exhibited. *Archaeological Journal* **17**, 164–7.

Anon. 1862 Proceedings of the Royal Historical and Archaeological Association of Ireland. *JRSAI* **7**, 230–4.

Anon. 1864 Proceedings of the Royal Irish Academy. *PRIA* **8**, 219.

Anon. 1874 Proceedings of the Royal Historical and Archaeological Association of Ireland. *JRSAI* **12** (1872–3), 79–82.

Anon. 1878 Antiquities and works of art exhibited. *PSAL* **7**, 76.

Anon. 1879 Antiquities and works of art exhibited. *Archaeological Journal* **36**, 387–8.

Anon. 1880 Antiquities and works of art exhibited. *Archaeological Journal* **37**, 206–9.

Anon. 1913 *Catalogue of the important collection of Irish antiquities in stone, bronze, gold and silver etc formed by Robert Day esq. FSA MRIA of Cork (19–22 May 1913)*. Sotheby, Wilkinson and Hodge, London.

Anon. 1937 Medieval treasure trove. *Antiquaries Journal* **17**, 440–1.

Armstrong, E.C.R. 1913 A note on four armorial pendants in the Academy's collection. *PRIA* **30**, 191–4.

Armstrong, E.C.R. 1915 Catalogue of the silver and ecclesiastical antiquities in the collection of the Royal Irish Academy, by the late Sir William Wilde. *PRIA* **32C**, 287–312.

Armstrong, N. 1973 *Jewellery: an historical survey of British styles and jewels*. Lutterworth

Press, Guildford and London.

Aubert, M. 1926 *La sculpture française du Moyen Age et de la Renaissance*. Librairie Nationale d'art et d'histoire, Paris.

Backhouse, J. 1989 *The Luttrell Psalter*. British Library, London.

Backhouse, J. 1990 *The Bedford Hours*. British Library, London.

Baker, C. 1994 Irish finger rings 1200–1700 AD. Unpublished M.A. thesis, University College Dublin.

Baker, D., Baker, E., Hassall, J. and Simco, A. 1979 Objects of copper alloy. In *ibid.*, 'Excavations in Bedford 1967–79', 278–80. *Bedfordshire Archaeological Journal* **13**, 278–80.

Baldwin, F.E. 1926 *Sumptuary legislation and personal regulation in England*. John Hopkins University, Baltimore.

Barry, T. 1987 *The archaeology of medieval Ireland*. Routledge, London.

Barton, K.J. and Holden, E.W. 1977 Excavations at Bramber Castle, Sussex, 1966–67. *Archaeological Journal* **134**, 11–79.

Basing, P. 1990 *Trades and crafts in medieval manuscripts*. British Library, London.

Bayley, J. 1991 Alloy nomenclature. In G. Egan and F. Pritchard (eds), *Dress accessories: medieval finds from excavations in London*, 13–17. Museum of London, London.

Beresford, G. 1977 Excavation of a moated house at Wintringham in Huntingdonshire. *Archaeological Journal* **134**, 194–286.

Berry, H.F. 1898 *Register of wills and inventories of the diocese of Dublin in the time of Archbishops Tregury and Walton 1457–1483*. Royal Society of Antiquaries of Ireland, Dublin.

Biddle, M. (ed.) 1990 *Object and economy in medieval Winchester, Vol. 2*. Winchester Studies 7.2. Clarendon Press, Oxford.

Biddle, M. and Hinton, D.A. 1990 Annular and other brooches. In M. Biddle (ed.), *Object and economy in medieval Winchester, Vol. 2*, 639–42. Winchester Studies 7.2. Clarendon Press, Oxford.

Binski, P. 1986 *The painted chamber of Westminster*. Occasional Paper (New Series) 9. Society of Antiquaries of London, London.

Binski, P. 1991 *Painters*. Medieval Craftsmen Series. British Museum Press, London.

Blair, C. and Blair, J. 1991 Copper alloys. In J. Blair and N. Ramsay (eds), *English mediaeval industries: craftsmen, techniques, products*, 81–106. Hambleton Press, London.

Bliss, A. and Long, J. 1993 Literature in Norman French and English to 1534. In A. Cosgrove (ed.), *A new history of Ireland, vol. II. Medieval Ireland 1169–1534*, 708–35. Clarendon Press, Oxford.

Bogdan, N.Q. and Wordsworth, J.W. 1978 *The medieval excavations at the High Street, Perth 1975–6*. Perth High Street Archaeological Excavation Committee, Perth.

Bradley, J. 1985 The medieval tombs of St Canice's. In A. Empey (ed.), *A worthy foundation: the cathedral church of St Canice, Kilkenny*, 49–103. The Dolmen Press, Portlaoise.

Bradley, J. 1991 Anglo-Norman towns. In M. Ryan (ed.), *The illustrated archaeology of Ireland*, 177–9. Country House, Dublin.

Bradley, J. 1995 *Walled towns in Ireland*. Country House, Dublin.

Brewis, P. 1930 Six silver ring brooches of the fourteenth century. *Archaeologia Aeliana*

(4th ser.) **7**, 104–8.

Brindley, A. 1986 *Archaeological Inventory of County Monaghan*. The Stationery Office, Dublin.

Brooke, I. 1972 *A history of English costume*. Eyre Methuen, London.

Brooks, E. St.J. (ed.) 1936 *The register of the hospital of St. John the Baptist without the New Gate*. Irish Manuscripts Commission, Dublin.

Brown, D. 1977 The significance of the Londesborough ring brooch. *Antiquaries Journal* **57**, 95–7.

Cahill, M. 1994 Mr Anthony's bog oak case of gold antiquities. *PRIA* **94C**, 53–109.

Callender, J.G. 1924 Fourteenth century brooches in the National Museum of Antiquities of Scotland. *PSAS* **58** (1923–4), 160–84.

Campbell, M. 1991 Gold, silver and precious stones. In J. Blair and N. Ramsay (eds), *English mediaeval industries: craftsmen, techniques, products*, 107–66. Hambleton Press, London.

Cherry, J. 1969 A ring brooch from Waterlooville, Hants. *Medieval Archaeology* **13**, 224–6.

Cherry, J. 1973 The medieval jewellery from the Fishpool, Nottinghamshire hoard. *Archaeologia* **104**, 307–21.

Cherry, J. 1976 Medieval jewellery. In H. Tait (ed.), *Jewellery through seven thousand years*, 138–40. British Museum, London.

Cherry, J. 1981 A silver ring brooch from Cliffe Hill, Lewes. *Sussex Archaeological Collections* **119**, 221–2.

Cherry, J. 1983 A medieval gold brooch found in Manchester. In M. Morris (ed.), *Medieval Manchester*, 77–8. Greater Manchester Archaeological Unit, Manchester.

Cherry, J. 1985 The medieval brooches. In R. Shoesmith (ed.), *Hereford City excavations 3: the finds*, 21–4. Research Report 56. CBA, London.

Cherry, J. 1987 Jewellery. In J. Alexander and P. Binski (eds), *Age of chivalry: art in Plantagenet England 1200–1400*, 176–8. Royal Academy of Arts, London.

Cherry, J. 1988 Medieval jewellery from Ireland: a preliminary survey. In G. Mac Niocaill and P. Wallace (eds), *Keimelia: studies in medieval archaeology and history in memory of Tom Delaney*, 143–61. Galway University Press, Galway.

Cherry, J. 1992 *Goldsmiths*. British Museum Press, London.

Cherry, J. 1994 *The Middleham jewel and ring*. Yorkshire Museum, York.

Clark, M. and Refaussé, R. 1993 *Directory of historic Dublin guilds*. Dublin Public Libraries, Dublin.

Collins, M. and Davies, V. 1991 *A medieval book of seasons*. Sidgwick and Jackson, London.

Connolly, P. and Martin, G. 1992 *The Dublin guild merchant roll, c. 1190–1265*. Dublin Corporation, Dublin.

Coutil, L. 1938 Broches du Musée d'Antiquités de Rouen. *Bulletin de la Société Préhistorique Française* **35**, 105–8.

Cowen, J.D. 1937 An English inscribed brooch of the 14th century. *Proceedings of the Society of Newcastle Upon Tyne* **7**, 203–6.

Cowman, D. 1988 The silvermines—sporadic working: 1289–1874. *Tipperary Historical Journal* (1988), 96–113.

Craddock, P.T. 1990 Metalworking techniques. In S. Youngs (ed.), *'The work of angels':*

masterpieces of Celtic metalwork, 6th–9th centuries AD, 170–213. British Museum Publications, University of Texas Press, Austin.

Crofton Rotheram, E. 1898 The moat of Patrickstown. *JRSAI* **28**, 62–3.

Cuming, S. 1862 On the Norman fermail. *Journal of the British Archaeological Association* **18**, 227–31.

Cunnington, C. and Cunnington, P. 1969 *Handbook of English medieval costume*. Faber and Faber, London.

Curtis, E. 1932 *Calendar of Ormond deeds, 1172–1350*. Irish Manuscripts Commission, Dublin.

Cutts, E.L. 1849 *A manual for the study of the sepulchral slabs and crosses of the Middle Ages*. John Henry Parker, London.

Davison, B.K. 1961–2 Excavations at Ballynarry Rath, Co. Down. *Ulster Journal of Archaeology* **24–5**, 39–87.

Deevy, M. 1996 Ring-brooches in medieval Ireland. *Archaeology Ireland* **36**, 8–10.

Deputy Keeper of Ireland 1903 *Pipe rolls of Ireland for the year 1220*. HMSO, Dublin.

Dickinson, C.W. and Waterman, D.M. 1960 Excavations at Castle Skreen, Co. Down. *Ulster Journal of Archaeology* **23**, 63–77.

Down, K. 1993 Colonial society and economy. In A. Cosgrove (ed.), *A new history of Ireland, vol. II. Medieval Ireland 1169–1534*, 439–90. Clarendon Press, Oxford.

Dunlevy, M. 1989 *Dress in Ireland*. Batsford, London.

Du Noyer, G.V. 1845 Notice on the cross-legged sepulchral effigies existing at Cashel. *Archaeological Journal* **2**, 125–7.

Dyer, C. 1989 *Standards of living in the Middle Ages: social change in England c. 1200–1520*. Cambridge University Press, Cambridge.

Eco, U. 1986 *Art and beauty in the Middle Ages*. Yale University Press, London.

Egan, G. 1991a The metal dress accessories—some observations. In G. Egan and F. Pritchard (eds), *Dress accessories: medieval finds from excavations in London*, 18–34. Museum of London, London.

Egan, G. 1991b Buckles. In G. Egan and F. Pritchard (eds), *Dress accessories: medieval finds from excavations in London*, 50–123. Museum of London, London.

Egan, G. 1991c Brooches. In G. Egan and F. Pritchard (eds), *Dress accessories: medieval finds from excavations in London*, 247–71. Museum of London, London.

Egan, G. and Pritchard, F. (eds) 1991 *Dress accessories: medieval finds from excavations in London*. Museum of London, London.

Ellis, H.D. 1916 An antique silver brooch inscribed in twelfth century northern French. *Archaeological Journal* **73**, 299–301.

Eogan, G. 1984 *Excavations at Knowth 1*. Royal Irish Academy, Dublin.

Eogan, G. 1994 *The accomplished art: gold and gold-working in Britain and Ireland during the Bronze Age*. Monograph 42. Oxbow, Oxford.

Evans, J. 1922 *Magical jewels*. Clarendon Press, Oxford.

Evans, J. 1952 *Dress in medieval France*. Clarendon Press, Oxford.

Evans, J. 1970 *A history of jewellery 1100–1870*. Faber and Faber, London.

Evans, J. and Serjeantson, M.S. 1933 *English medieval lapidaries*. Early English Texts Society, London.

Fanning, T. 1994 *Viking Age ringed pins from Dublin*. Royal Irish Academy, Dublin.

Fitzgerald, W. 1902 New Abbey of Kilcullen. *JKAS* **3**, 301–6.

Foley, C. 1989 Excavation at a medieval settlement site in Jerpointchurch townland, County Kilkenny. *PRIA* **89C**, 71–126.

Ford, B. 1987 Copper alloy objects. In P. Holdsworth (ed.), *Excavations in the medieval burgh of Perth 1979–1981*, 121–30. Monograph Series no. 5. Society of Antiquaries of Scotland, Edinburgh.

Frayling, C. 1995 *Strange landscape: a journey through the Middle Ages*. BBC Books, London.

Gardner, A. 1935 *English medieval sculpture*. Hacker Art Books, New York.

Glasscock, R.E. 1993 Land and people, *c.* 1300. In A. Cosgrove (ed.), *A new history of Ireland, vol. II. Medieval Ireland 1169–1534*, 205–39. Clarendon Press, Oxford.

Gleeson, D.F. 1937 The silver mines of Ormond. *JRSAI* **67**, 101–16.

Goodall, A.R. 1981 The medieval bronzesmith and his products. In D.W. Crossley (ed.), *Medieval industry*, 63–71. Research Report 40. CBA, London.

Goodall, A.R. 1982 Copper alloy objects. In H.K. Murray, J.C. Murray *et al.*, *Excavations in the medieval burgh of Aberdeen 1973–81*, 186–9. Monograph Series no. 2. Society of Antiquaries of Scotland, Edinburgh.

Goodall, A.R. 1984 Objects of non-ferrous metal. In J.P. Allan (ed.), *Medieval and post-medieval finds from Exeter, 1971–1980*, 337–47. Exeter Archaeological Report: Vol. 3. Exeter City Council and the University of Exeter, Exeter.

Goodall, A.R. 1991 Copper-alloy objects. In T.G. Hassall, C.E. Halpin and M. Mellor (eds), 'Excavations in St. Ebbe's, Oxford, 1967–1976: Part 1: Late Saxon and medieval domestic occupation and tenements, and the medieval Greyfriars', 223–6. *Oxoniensia* **54** (1989), 71–277.

Goodall, A.R. 1993 Copper alloy objects. In H.K. Murray and J.C. Murray (eds), 'Excavations at Rattray, Aberdeenshire: a Scottish deserted burgh', 188–94. *Medieval Archaeology* **37**, 109–218.

Grant King, D. 1969 A medieval brooch from Little Avebury. *Wiltshire Archaeological and Natural History Magazine* **64**, 118.

Gresham, C.A. 1968 *Medieval stone carving in North Wales: sepulchral slabs and effigies of the thirteenth and fourteenth centuries*. University of Wales Press, Cardiff.

Harbison, P. 1970 *Guide to the National Monuments in the Republic of Ireland*. Gill and MacMillan, Dublin.

Harbison, P. 1971–6 The Castledillon stone. *JKAS* **14**, 136–40.

Hardiman, J. (ed.) 1843 *Tracts relating to Ireland: a statute of the 40th year of King Edward III, enacted in a parliament held in Kilkenny 1367*. Irish Archaeological Society, Dublin.

Harvey, J. 1975 *Medieval craftsmen*. Batsford, London and Sydney.

Hassall, M. and Rhodes, J. 1974 Excavations at the New Market Hall, Gloucestershire, 1966–67. *Transactions of the Bristol and Gloucestershire Archaeological Society* **93**, 66–7.

Hattatt, R. 1985 *Iron age and Roman brooches: a second selection from the author's collection*. Oxbow Books, Oxford.

Hattatt, R. 1987 *Brooches of antiquity: a third selection of brooches from the author's collection*. Oxbow Books, Oxford.

Hawthorne, J.G. and Stanley Smith, C. 1979 *Theophilus: On divers arts*. Dover Publications,

New York.

Hayden, A. 1992 Cornmarket/Francis St./Lamb Alley, Dublin. In I. Bennet (ed.), *Excavations 1992*, 20–1. Organisation of Irish Archaeologists, Dublin.

Hayden, A. (forthcoming) Archaeological excavations at Cornmarket and Francis Street, Anglo-Norman ditch.

Héjj-Détári, A. 1965 *Old Hungarian jewelry*. Corvina Press, Budapest.

Higgins, J. 1995 The medieval font from Kilballyowen, Co. Clare. *The Other Clare* **19**, 29–32.

Higgins, J. (forthcoming a) Medieval and late medieval funerary monuments at Kilferagh, Co. Kilkenny. *Old Kilkenny Review*.

Higgins, J. (forthcoming b) *The medieval sculpture of the Franciscan graveyard, Galway*. Crow's Rock Press, Galway.

Higgins, J. and Heringklee, S. 1992 *Monuments of St. Nicholas' and Collegiate Church, Galway: A historical, genealogical and archaeological record*. Galway.

Hinton, D. 1982 *Medieval jewellery*. Shire Archaeology No. 21. Shire Books, Princes Risborough.

Hinton, D. 1990 Buckles and buckle-plates. In M. Biddle (ed.), *Object and economy in medieval Winchester, Vol. 2*, 506–25. Winchester Studies 7.2. Clarendon Press, Oxford.

Hinton, D. 1993 Reviews. *Medieval Archaeology* **37**, 327–9.

Hirst, S.M. 1985 *An Anglo-Saxon inhumation cemetery at Sewerby, East Yorkshire*. York University Archaeological Publications 4.

Hodkinson, B. 1992 St. Mary's Cathedral, Limerick. In I. Bennett (ed.), *Excavations 1992*, 42–3. Organisation of Irish Archaeologists, Dublin.

Hodkinson, B. (forthcoming) Archaeological excavations at St. Mary's Cathedral, Limerick. *North Munster Archaeological Journal*.

Holmes, U.T. 1964 *Daily living in the twelfth century; based on observations of Alexander Neckham in London and Paris* (3rd edn). University of Wisconsin Press, Madison.

Homer, R.F. 1991 Tin, lead and pewter. In J. Blair and N. Ramsay (eds), *English mediaeval industries: craftsmen, techniques, products*, 57–80. Hambleton Press, London.

Hughes, D.O. 1983 Sumptuary law and social relations in Renaissance Italy. In J. Bossy (ed.), *Disputes and settlements; law and human relations in the west*, 69–99. Cambridge University Press, Cambridge.

Hunt, J. 1946 Clonroad More, Ennis. *JRSAI* **76**, 195–209.

Hunt, J. 1974 *Irish medieval figure sculpture, 1200–1600*. Irish University Press, Dublin.

Hurley, M.F. 1990 Excavations at Grand Parade, Cork, II (Part 2). *Journal of the Cork Historical and Archaeological Society* **95**, 64–87.

Hurley, M.F., Scully, O.M.B. and McCutcheon, S.W.J. (eds) 1997 *Late Viking Age and medieval Waterford excavations 1986–1992*. Waterford Corporation, Waterford.

Hurst, J.G. 1988 Medieval pottery imported into Ireland. In G. Mac Niocaill and P. Wallace (eds), *Keimelia: studies in medieval archaeology and history in memory of Tom Delaney*, 229–53. Galway University Press, Galway.

Ivens, R.J. 1987 The Early Christian monastic enclosure at Tullylish, Co. Down. *Ulster Journal of Archaeology* **50**, 55–121.

Jackson, J.S. 1980 Bronze Age copper mining in counties Cork and Kerry, Ireland. In P.T.

Craddock (ed.), *Scientific studies in early metallurgy I*, 9–30. Occasional Paper 20. British Museum, London.

James, T. (forthcoming) Excavations at Carmarthen Greyfriars.

Johnson, C. 1995 The small finds. In L. Simpson, *Excavations at Essex Street West, Dublin*, 74–103. Temple Bar Archaeological Report No. 2. Dublin.

Jope, E.M., Jope, H.M., Stewart, I.H. and Thompson, J.D.A. 1960 A hoard of fifteenth-century coins from Glenluce sand-dunes and their context. *Medieval Archaeology* **3** (1959), 259–79.

Karklins, K. 1992 *Trade ornament usage among the native peoples of Canada, a source book*. Studies in Archaeology, Architecture and History. National Historic Sites and Parks Services, Environment Canada, Ottawa.

Kelly, E.P. 1991 Crannogs. In M. Ryan (ed.), *The illustrated archaeology of Ireland*, 120–3. Country House, Dublin.

Kelly, F. 1895 Some old Galway laws. *JRASI* **25**, 382–3.

Kelly, F.M. and Schwabe, R. 1931 *A short history of costume and armour: chiefly in England, 1066–1800*. Batsford, London.

Lacy, B. 1983 *Archaeological survey of County Donegal*. Donegal County Council, Lifford.

La Niece, S. 1983 Niello: an historical and technical survey. *Antiquaries' Journal* **63**, 279–95.

Larking, L.B. 1858 Inventory of the effects of Roger de Mortimer at Wigmore Castle and Abbey, Herdfordshire, dated 15 Edward II, A. D. 1322. *Archaeological Journal* **15**, 361.

Lawlor, H.L. 1925 *Monastery of Saint Mochaoi of Nendrum*. Belfast.

Lewis, J.M. 1966 Post-Roman finds from the Caerleon fortress baths excavation. *Monmouthshire Antiquary* **2**, 105–19.

Lewis, J.M. 1982 A medieval ring brooch from Oxwich Castle, West Glamorgan. *Antiquaries' Journal* **62**, 126–31.

Lewis, S. 1840 *Topographical dictionary of Ireland*. London.

Lightbown, R.W. 1978 *Secular goldsmith's work in medieval France: a history*. Research Report 36. Society of Antiquaries, London.

Lightbown, R.W. 1992 *Medieval European jewellery: with a catalogue of the collection in the Victoria and Albert Museum*. Victoria and Albert Museum, London.

Lightbown, R.W. 1997 The jewellery. In M.F. Hurley, O.M.B. Scully and S.W.J. McCutcheon (eds), *Late Viking Age and medieval Waterford excavations 1986–1992*, 518–23. Waterford Corporation, Waterford.

Lightfoot, K.W.B. 1992 Rumney Castle, a ringwork and manorial centre in South Glamorgan. *Medieval Archaeology* **36**, 96–154.

Lins, P.A. and Oddy, W.A. 1975 The origins of mercury gilding. *Journal of Archaeological Science* **2**, 365–73.

Lydon, J.F. 1972 *The lordship of Ireland in the Middle Ages*. Gill and Macmillan, Dublin.

Lydon, J.F. 1984 *The English in medieval Ireland*. Royal Irish Academy, Dublin.

Lydon, J.F. 1993 A land of war. In A. Cosgrove (ed.), *A new history of Ireland, vol. II. Medieval Ireland 1169–1534*, 240–74. Clarendon Press, Oxford.

Lyford, C.A. 1945 *Iroquois crafts*. Iroqrafts Ltd, Ontario.

Lynch, A. (forthcoming) Archaeological excavations at Tintern Abbey, Co. Wexford.

McClintock, H.F. 1950 *Old Irish and highland dress*. Dundalgan Press, Dundalk.

McCormick, F. 1995 False Bay, Co. Galway, in the Bronze Age. *Archaeology Ireland* **9** (1), 12–13.

McCutcheon, C. 1995 Medieval and post-medieval pottery. In L. Simpson, *Excavations at Essex Street West, Dublin*, 40–67. Temple Bar Archaeological Report No. 2, Dublin.

Maclagan, E. and Oman, C.C. 1936 An English gold rosary of about 1500. *Archaeologia* **85**, 13–22.

MacLeod, C. 1945 Mediaeval wooden figure sculptures in Ireland: the Kilcorban St. Catherine and Calvary figures. *JRSAI* **75**, 195–203.

Mac Niocaill, G. 1964 *The Red Book of the earls of Kildare*. Irish Manuscripts Commission, Dublin.

Mahr, A. 1976 *Christian art in ancient Ireland; selected objects illustrated and described* (2 vols). Hacker Art Books, New York.

Margeson, S. 1985 The small finds. In M. Atkin, A. Carter and D.H. Evans (eds), *Excavations in Norwich 1971–1978, Part 2*, 201–13. East Anglian Archaeological Report 26. Norwich Survey, Centre of East Anglian Studies, University of East Anglia, Norwich.

Maryon, H. 1971 *Metalwork and enamelling*. Dover Publications, New York.

Millar, E.G. 1932 *The Luttrell Psalter*. Trustees of the British Museum, London.

Mills, J. 1891 *Account roll of the priory of the Holy Trinity, Dublin, 1337–1346*. RSAI, Dublin.

Mills, J. 1905 *Calendar of justiciary rolls of Ireland, 1295–1303*. HMSO, Dublin.

Mills, J. 1914 *Calendar of justiciary rolls of Ireland, 1304–1307*. HMSO, Dublin.

Murdoch, T. 1991 *Treasures and trinkets: jewellery in London from pre-Roman times to the 1930s*. Museum of London, London.

Musée du Louvre 1968 *L'Europe Gothique: XIIe–XIVe siècles: douzième exposition du Conseil de L'Europe*. Ministère d'État Affaires Culturelles, Paris.

Musty, J., Algar, D.J. and Ewence, P.F. 1969 The medieval pottery kilns at Laverstock, near Salisbury, Wiltshire. *Archaeologia* **102**, 83–150.

Nicholls, K.W. 1993 Gaelic society and economy. In A. Cosgrove (ed.), *A new history of Ireland, vol. II. Medieval Ireland 1169–1534*, 397–435. Clarendon Press, Oxford.

NMAS 1892 *Catalogue of the National Museum of Scotland*. Society of Antiquaries of Scotland, Edinburgh.

NMAS 1979 *Brooches in Scotland*. National Museum of Antiquities of Scotland, Edinburgh.

NMAS 1982 *Angels, nobles and unicorns: art and patronage in medieval Scotland*. National Museum of Antiquities of Scotland, Edinburgh.

NMI 1961 Archaeological acquisitions in the year 1959. *JRSAI* **91**, 43–107.

O'Brien, A.F. 1994 Economy, growth and settlement in medieval Ireland. *Irish Historic Settlement Newsletter* **3**, 4–6.

O'Dwyer, M. (no date) *St. Patrick's, Kilkenny: gravestone inscriptions, with historical notes on the parish*. Kilkenny Archaeological Society, Kilkenny.

Ó Floinn, R. 1983 The Norman Conquest and the Later Middle Ages 1169 A.D. – ca. 1500 A.D. In M. Ryan (ed.), *Treasures of Ireland: Irish art 3000 B.C. – 1500 A.D.*, 70–3. Royal Irish Academy, Dublin.

Ó Floinn, R. 1991 The eleventh/twelfth century renaissance in metalwork. In M. Ryan (ed.), *The illustrated archaeology of Ireland*, 163–6. Country House, Dublin.

Ó Floinn, R. 1996 Sandhills, silver and shrines: fine metalwork of the medieval period from Donegal. In W. Nolan *et al.* (eds), *Donegal: history and society,* 85–148. Geography Publications, Lifford.

O'Kelly, C. 1978 *Illustrated guide to Newgrange and the other Boyne monuments*. Privately published, Cork.

O'Meara, J.J. 1982 *Topographia Hibernica: The History and Topography of Ireland by Gerald of Wales*. Penguin, Harmondsworth.

Omurethi 1911 Castledillon in the Barony of South Salt. *JKAS* **6** (1909–11), 207–13.

O'Neill, T. 1987 *Merchants and mariners*. Irish Academic Press, Dublin.

Ó Ríordáin, B. 1971 Excavations at High Street and Winetavern Street, Dublin. *Medieval Archaeology* **15**, 73–8.

Oswald, A. and Taylor, G. 1964 Durrance Moat, Upton Warren, Worcester. *Transactions of the Birmingham and Warwickshire Archaeological Society* **79**, 61–75.

Otway-Ruthven, A.J. 1993 *A history of medieval Ireland*. Barnes and Nobles Books, New York.

Palmer, N. 1981 A beaker burial and medieval tenements in the Hamel, Oxford. *Oxoniensia* **45** (1980), 124–234.

Pritchard, F. 1991 Hair accessories. In G. Egan and F. Pritchard (eds), *Dress accessories: medieval finds from excavations in London,* 291–6. Museum of London, London.

Pryor, F. 1976 A descriptive catalogue of some ancient Irish metalwork in the collections of the Royal Ontario Museum, Toronto. *JRSAI* **106**, 73–88.

Rae, E.C. 1970 Irish sepulchral monuments of the later Middle Ages; Part 1. The Ormond group. *JRSAI* **100**, 1–38.

Rae, E.C. 1971 Irish sepulchral monuments of the later Middle Ages; Part 2. The O'Tunney atelier. *JRSAI* **101**, 1–39.

Redknap, M. 1996 Some medieval brooches, pendants and moulds from Wales: a short survey. *Archaeologia Cambrensis* **143** (1994), 92–138.

Reynolds Brown, K. 1992 Six gothic brooches at The Cloisters. In E. C. Parker and M. B. Shepard (eds), *The Cloisters: studies in honor of the fiftieth anniversary*, 409–19. Metropolitan Museum of Art in association with the International Center of Medieval Art, New York.

Richardson, K.M. 1961 Excavations in Hungate, York. *Archaeological Journal* **116** (1959), 51–114.

Richter, M. 1988 *Medieval Ireland: the enduring tradition*. Gill and MacMillan, Dublin.

Roach Smith, C. (no date) Researches and discoveries: Suffolk. *Collectanea Antiqua* **3**, 253–4. Privately printed, London.

Roach Smith, C. 1857 Medieval brooches. *Collectanea Antiqua* **4**, 108–11. Privately printed, London.

Roe, H. 1968 *Medieval fonts of Meath*. Meath Archaeological and Historical Society, Longford.

Roe, H. and Prendergast, E. 1946 Excavation of a mound at Blessington, Co. Wicklow. *JRSAI* **76**, 1–5.

Ryan, M. (ed.) 1983 *Treasures of Ireland: Irish art 3000 B.C.–1500 A.D.* Royal Irish Academy, Dublin.

Ryan, M. (ed.) 1991 *The illustrated archaeology of Ireland*. Country House, Dublin.

Saul, N. 1992 *Age of chivalry: art and society in late medieval England*. Collins and Brown, London.

Saunders, P.R. 1983 An inscribed medieval brooch from Amesbury. *Wiltshire Archaeological and Natural History Magazine* (1983), 146–7.

Scarisbrick, D. 1994 *Jewellery in Britain 1066–1837: a documentary, social, literary and artistic survey*. Michael Russell, Norwich.

Schiller, G. 1971 *Iconography of Christian art*. Lund Humphries, London.

Scott, A.B. and Martin, F.X. 1978 *Expugnatio Hibernica: The Conquest of Ireland by Giraldus Cambrensis*. Royal Irish Academy, Dublin.

Scully, O.M.B. 1998 Ferrous and non-ferrous artefacts. In R.M. Cleary, M.F. Hurley and E. Shee-Twohig (eds), *Excavations at Skiddy's Castle and Christ Church, Cork, 1974–77, by D. C. Twohig*, 165–190. Cork Corporation, Cork.

Simpson, M.L. and Brannon, N. 1988 Uncovering the past in a busy town. In A. Hamlin and C. Lynn (eds), *Pieces of the past*, 64–6. HMSO, Belfast.

Simpson, M.L. and Dickson, A. 1981 Excavations in Carrickfergus, Co. Antrim, 1972–79: a summary report on the excavations directed by the late T.G. Delaney. *Medieval Archaeology* **25**, 79–89.

Smith, C. 1909 *Jewellery*. Methuen, London.

Spencer, B. 1968 Small finds, Appendix II. In A.C. Harrison and C. Flight (eds), 'The Roman and medieval defences of Rochester in the light of recent excavations', 102–3. *Archaeologia Cantiana* **83**, 55–104.

Steen Jensen, J., Bendixen, K., Liebgott, N.-K. and Lindahl, F. 1992 *Danmarks middelalderlige skattefund c. 1050–c. 1550*. Kongeleig Norid Oldskrifselska, København.

Steingraber, E. 1957 *Antique jewellery: its history in Europe from 800 to 1900*. Thames and Hudson, London.

Stone, L. 1955 *Sculpture in Britain: the Middle Ages*. The Pelican History of Art, Penguin.

Stothard, C.A. (ed.) 1876 *The monumental effigies of Great Britain*. London.

Swaan, W. 1982 *The Gothic cathedral*. Elek, London.

Sweetman, H.S. 1880 *Calendar of documents relating to Ireland 1285–1292*, vol. 3. Longman, London.

Sweetman, H.S. 1881 *Calendar of documents relating to Ireland 1293–1301*, vol. 4. Longman, London.

Sweetman, H.S. and Handcock, G.F. 1886 *Calendar of documents relating to Ireland 1302–1307*, vol. 5. Public Record Office, London.

Sweetman, P.D. 1979 Archaeological excavations at Ferns Castle, County Wexford. *PRIA* **79C**, 217–45.

Sweetman, P.D. 1991 Anglo-Norman fortresses. In M. Ryan (ed.), *The illustrated archaeology of Ireland*, 183–8. Country House, Dublin.

Sweetman, P.D. 1995 *Irish castles and fortified houses*. Country House, Dublin.

Taburet-Delahaye, E. 1989 *L'Orfevrerie gothique au Musée de Cluny*. Ministère de la culture, de la communication, des grands travaux et du bicentenaire, Editions de la reunion des musées nationaux, Paris.

Terry, P. and Durling, N.V. 1993 *The Romance of the Rose or Guillaume de Dole by Jean Renart.* University of Pennsylvania Press, Philadelphia.

Thompson, J.D.A. 1956 *Inventory of British coin hoards, A.D. 600–1500.* Special Publications No. 1. Royal Numismatic Society, Oxford.

Tudor-Craig, P. 1975 *Wells: west front, central section: cathedrals and monastic buildings in the British Isles, Archive 1, Part 4.* Harvey Miller and the Courtauld Institute of Art, University of London.

Tummers, H.A. 1980 *Early secular effigies in England: the thirteenth century.* E.J. Brill, Leiden.

Tylecote, R.F. 1962 *Metallurgy in archaeology.* Edward Arnold, London.

Unger, R.W. 1991 *The art of medieval technology.* Rutgers University Press, New Brunswick.

Vitry, P. 1973 *French sculpture during the reign of Saint Louis, 1226–1270.* Hacker Art Books, New York.

Wallace, P. 1985 The archaeology of Anglo-Norman Ireland. In H. Clarke and A. Simms (eds), *The comparative history of urban origins in non-Roman Europe*, 379–410. British Archaeological Reports, International Series 255 (ii), Oxford.

Walsh, C. (forthcoming) *Archaeological excavations at Ross Road/Christchurch Place, Dublin.*

Ward-Perkins, J.B. 1940 Circular brooches. In *ibid., London Museum medieval catalogue*, 273–6. HMSO, London.

Watt, J. 1972 *The church in medieval Ireland.* Gill and MacMillan, Dublin.

Welch, M.G. 1989 A ring brooch and penannular brooch pin from Kelvedon, Essex. *Medieval Archaeology* **33**, 151–3.

Welch, R. 1902 Rosguil and the old kingdom of Fanad: the country of Mac Swyne-na-doe and Mac Swyne-na-Fanait. *JRSAI* **32**, 225–8.

Whitfield, N. 1993 The sources of gold in Early Christian Ireland. *Archaeology Ireland* **7** (4), 21–3.

Wilde, W. 1862 *A descriptive catalogue of the antiquities of gold in the museum of the Royal Irish Academy.* Royal Irish Academy, Dublin.

Wilson, P. 1995 Sand dunes and archaeology. *Archaeology Ireland* **9** (2), 24–6.

Wincott Hecket, E. 1991 Textiles in archaeology. *Archaeology Ireland* **5** (2), 11–13.

Youngs, S. (ed.) 1990 *'The work of angels': masterpieces of Celtic metalwork, 6th–9th centuries AD.* British Museum Publications, University of Texas Press, Austin.

THE CATALOGUE

About the catalogue

The catalogue is organised by class. Within each class the entries are ordered alphabetically by county. Brooches from the same county are ordered alphabetically by site, and those from the same site are ordered by registration number. The provenanced examples are followed by the unprovenanced brooches, listed alphabetically by the collection in which they are presently located.

A standard layout has been adopted for each entry. The unique number for each brooch (prefixed by the letters RB, denoting 'ring brooch') is followed by the county provenance, where known. The collection in which the brooch is presently located is presented in abbreviated form (a list of these abbreviations is provided at the beginning of the catalogue), followed by the museum registration number of the brooch. The lack of a collection abbreviation indicates that the brooch was recovered by recent excavation and is presently in the care of the archaeologist responsible. In this case the excavation registration number of the brooch is given.

The find circumstances are then detailed. If the brooch was excavated, the name of the site is noted, along with a summary of contextual and dating information. Some brooches are stray finds or were recovered by metal-detecting. The find circumstances of many nineteenth-century stray finds were not recorded, and these are described as 'unknown'. If the locality of the brooch is known, the OS 6-inch sheet details are given.

The succeeding lines contain a description of the brooch—metallurgical identification, shape, decoration, etc. Any possibly contemporary distortion of the brooch is recorded here, along with details of its present condition (i.e. any damage that may have occurred over time, before its recovery).

The description is followed by the dimensions, listed in abbreviated form (a list of abbreviations is given at the beginning of the catalogue). These include the external diameter, the thickness of the frame and the height of the frame (Fig. 1). When a brooch has a frame with an oval outline, its dimensions are given as maximum length by width. A brooch with a lozenge-shaped outline has both the length by width measurements and its 'diameter', taken perpendicular to the axis of the pin. The weight of each brooch is noted, when available.

Finally, any references to previously published, unpublished or forthcoming accounts of each brooch are listed.

The catalogue is followed by an appendix of artifacts which might possibly be ring brooches. Some may be annular buckles. Others are known only from nineteenth-century literature and sales catalogues, and in the absence of illustrations cannot be confirmed as ring brooches.

Illustrations are at 1:1 except where indicated.

Abbreviations

Collections

coll.	collection
BM	British Museum, London
CPM	Cork Public Museum
DM	Downpatrick Museum
LCM	Limerick City Museum
NMI	National Museum of Ireland, Dublin
PRO	Pitt Rivers Museum, Oxford
ex RIA	Previously in the collection of the Royal Irish Academy
ROM	Royal Ontario Museum
RSAI	Previously in the collection of the Royal Society of Antiquaries of Ireland
UM	Ulster Museum, Belfast
WHC	Waterford Heritage Centre

Measurements

D	External diameter of frame
L	Length of frame
W	Width of frame
T	Thickness of frame
Ht	Height of frame
CH	Collet height
Wt	Weight of brooch

CLASS 1: undecorated ring brooches

RB 1. County Antrim   NMI 1897:186 (ex Milligan coll.)
Find circumstances unknown.
Copper-alloy circular frame with a flat rectangular cross-section. The frame is undecorated. The pin is composed of a length of iron wire with a simple crude loop: it may be a replacement of a broken copper-alloy pin.
D 45mm, T 8mm, Ht 1.9mm, Wt 16.41g.

RB 2. County Clare   NMI A24
Excavated at Clonroad More, Ennis (OS 6" sheet 33). Unstratified.
Copper-alloy circular frame with a square cross-section. The frame is undecorated. The pin has a plano-convex cross-section and a simple loop. Both the frame and the pin are patinated. A small arrow-shaped piece of metal is inserted between the pin loop and the frame. It may be that the constriction was insufficient to hold the pin in position on the frame, necessitating the insertion of the wedge.
D 32.5mm, T 2.3mm, Ht 1.7mm, Wt 3.15g.
Hunt 1946.

RB 3. County Down   UM A1925.1001, on loan to DM (not illustrated)
Excavated at the monastery of St Mochaoi, Nendrum (OS 6" sheet 17). Unstratified.
Copper-alloy circular frame with a flat rectangular cross-section. The frame is undecorated. The pin has a flat rectangular cross-section and a simple loop.
Dimensions unavailable.
Lawlor 1925, pl. 11, no. 85.

RB 4. County Dublin   NMI E71:1827
Excavated at High Street, Dublin (OS 6" sheet 18). The stratigraphic sequence of this site has not yet been fully resolved. Provisional dating: thirteenth century.
Copper-alloy circular frame with an angled cross-section. The frame is undecorated. The pin is narrow with a plano-convex cross-section and a simple loop. It is attached through a small circular hole in the frame

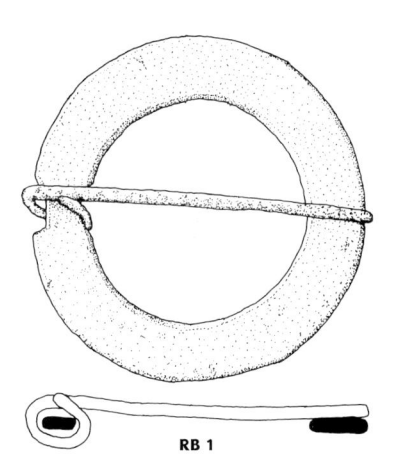

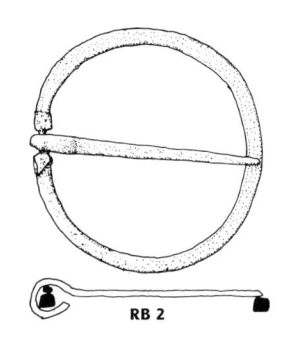

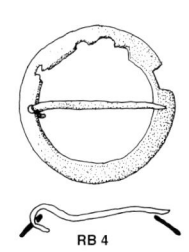

instead of the more common constriction. The frame is very flimsy and has partly corroded away. The pin is quite bent and damaged.
D 18.5mm, T 2mm, Ht 2.5mm, Wt 0.44g.

RB 5. County Dublin   NMI E71:4019
Excavated at High Street, Dublin (OS 6" sheet 18). The stratigraphic sequence for this site has not yet been fully resolved. Provisional dating: probably late twelfth/thirteenth century.
Copper-alloy circular frame with a circular cross-section. The frame is undecorated. The pin has a rectangular cross-section, a simple loop and a bevelled shaft. The frame is possibly plated with a white metal such as tin (P. Mullarky, pers. comm.).
D 20.5mm, T 2.2mm, Ht 2.2mm, Wt 2.37g.

RB 6. County Dublin   NMI E71:19702
Excavated at High Street, Dublin (OS 6" sheet 18). Unstratified.
Copper-alloy, slightly distorted circular frame with a circular cross-section. The frame is undecorated. The pin has a plano-convex cross-section, a simple loop, a transverse ridge and a shallow depression on the head.
D *c.* 22mm, T 3mm, Ht 3mm, Wt 3.73g.

RB 7. County Dublin   93E10:594:4
Excavated at Ross Road/Christchurch Place, Dublin (OS 6" sheet 18). Contextually dated to between 1200 and 1225 (C. Walsh, pers. comm.).
Copper-alloy circular frame with a circular cross-section. The frame is undecorated. The pin is missing. The frame is broken at the constriction.
D 22mm, T 2mm, Ht 2mm, Wt unavailable.
Walsh, forthcoming.

RB 8. County Dublin   NMI E132:24686, on loan to 'Dublinia'
Excavated at Wood Quay, Dublin (OS 6" sheet 18). Precise contextual details are not available at present. Provisional dating: thirteenth century.
Copper-alloy and lead-alloy circular frame with a plano-convex cross-section. This is a composite frame, combining an upper ring of sheet copper alloy which has been shaped to provide a convex cross-section with a lower flat ring of lead. The frame is undecorated. The pin is a very narrow simple strip of

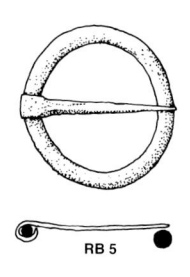

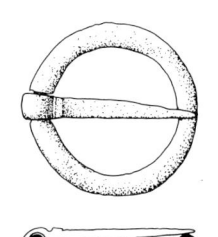

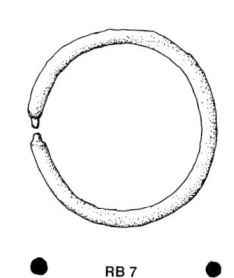

copper alloy with a simple loop and a transverse ridge. The hollow space within the frame (now visible because the lower part of the frame has come loose) is filled with a white powdery substance which has been identified as lead corrosion (P. Mullarky, pers. comm.). The pin is very bent out of shape, as one might expect from a pin so narrow and thin. It also appears to have been replaced upside down. It may be that the lead element of the frame was intended to lend the brooch some of the weight associated with precious metal.
D 30mm, T 6mm, Ht 3.5mm, Wt 5.91g.

RB 9. County Dublin   NMI E132:96537, on loan to 'Dublinia'
Excavated at Wood Quay, Dublin (OS 6" sheet 18). Precise contextual details are not available at present.
Provisional dating: thirteenth century.
Copper-alloy circular frame with a circular cross-section. The frame is undecorated. The pin has a plano-convex cross-section and a simple loop. Its shaft is bent down in the middle, probably as a result of the weight of the cloth on the pin when worn.
D 14mm, T 1.5mm, Ht 1.5mm, Wt 0.82g.

RB 10. County Leitrim   NMI, not registered yet
Found by metal-detector at a crannog on Lake McHugh.
Silver circular frame with a lozenge cross-section. The frame is undecorated. The pin has a circular cross-section, a simple loop and a collar. The pin head is decorated with one faint longitudinal line.
D 12mm, T 1.5mm, Ht 1.5mm, Wt unavailable.

RB 11. County Meath   NMI, not registered yet
Found by metal-detector at a crannog on Lake Ervey (OS 6" sheet 2).
Silver circular frame with a lozenge-like cross-section. The outer edges are slightly concave and the inner edges slightly convex. The frame is undecorated. The pin has a circular cross-section, a pincer loop, a biconical collar and a circular cross-section. The pin tip is broken.
D 14.5mm, T 2mm, Ht 2mm, Wt unavailable.

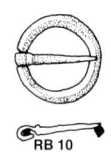

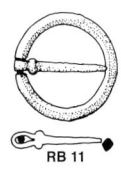

RB 12. County Waterford   E435:228:B118:1
Excavated at Bakehouse Lane, Waterford (OS 6" sheet 9).
Recovered from graveyard soil, burial period III,
contextually dated to the mid-thirteenth–early
seventeenth century.
Copper-alloy, slightly distorted circular frame with a
circular cross-section. The frame is undecorated. The pin
has a circular cross-section, a simple loop and three
transverse grooves under the head.
D 18.5mm, T 2mm, Ht 2mm, Wt unavailable.
Lightbown 1997, 522.

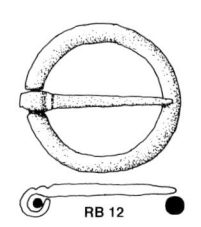

RB 13. County Westmeath   NMI E499:380
Found by metal-detector at Ballymore, Loughsewdy (OS 6"
sheet 23/24).
Silver circular frame with a lozenge cross-section. The
frame is undecorated. The pin has a rectangular cross-
section, a simple loop and a flanged transverse ridge,
decorated with a row of beading within two transverse
raised lines. The pin is slightly bent upwards.
D 16mm, T 2mm, Ht 2mm, Wt 1.2g.

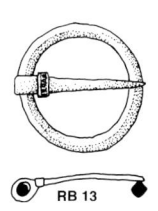

RB 14. County Westmeath   NMI E621:47
Found by metal-detector at Portloman Abbey, Lough Owel
(OS 6" sheet 11).
Copper-alloy circular frame with a circular cross-section.
The frame is undecorated. The pin has a circular cross-
section, a pincer loop and a circular collar.
D 17mm, T 2mm, Ht 2mm, Wt 1.86g.

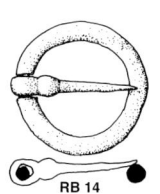

RB 15. Ireland   NMI 23.W.5. (ex RIA)
Find circumstances unknown.
Silver circular frame with a narrow plano-convex cross-
section. The frame is undecorated. The pin has a plano-
convex cross-section, a simple loop and a ridge along the
underside of the shaft.
D 24mm, T 2.5mm, Ht 0.7mm, Wt 1.55g.
 Armstrong 1915, 294.

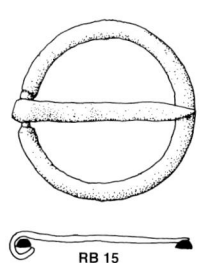

RB 16. Ireland NMI 34.W.6. (ex RIA) (Pl. 2)
Find circumstances unknown.
Silver circular frame with a narrow plano-convex cross-section. The frame is undecorated. The pin has a plano-convex cross-section, a simple loop and a ridge along the underside of the shaft.
D 23.5mm, T 2.5mm, Ht 0.7mm, Wt 1.54g.
Armstrong 1915, 294–5.

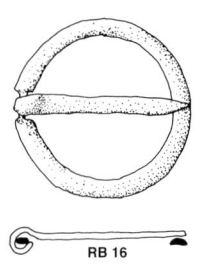

RB 17. Ireland NMI 24.W.7 (ex RIA)
Find circumstances unknown.
Silver circular frame formed by a ring of sheet metal of convex cross-section. The frame is undecorated. The pin is formed of narrow wire and has a simple loop. A small circular hole in the frame takes the place of the usual type of constriction.
D 24mm, T 3.5mm, Ht 1mm, Wt 1.08g.
Armstrong 1915, 295.

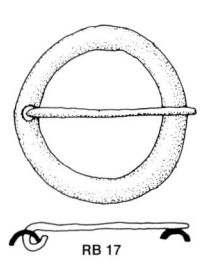

RB 18. Ireland NMI 25.W.8 (ex RIA)
Find circumstances unknown.
Silver circular frame formed by a ring of sheet metal of convex cross-section. The frame is undecorated. The pin is formed of narrow wire and has a simple loop. A small circular hole in the frame takes the place of the usual type of constriction.
D 24mm, T 3.5mm, Ht 1.1mm, Wt 1.07g.
Armstrong 1915, 295.

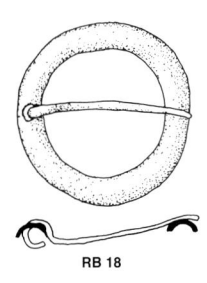

RB 19. Ireland NMI 26.W.9 (ex RIA)
Find circumstances unknown.
Silver circular frame formed by a ring of sheet metal of convex cross-section. The frame is undecorated. The pin is formed of narrow wire and has a simple loop. A small circular hole in the frame takes the place of the usual type of constriction. The pin is quite bent.
D 23.5mm, T 2.5mm, Ht 1mm, Wt 1.05g.
Armstrong 1915, 295.

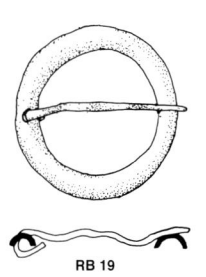

RB 20. Ireland NMI 27.W.10 (ex RIA)
Find circumstances unknown.
Silver circular frame formed by a ring of sheet metal of convex cross-section. The frame is undecorated. The pin is formed of narrow wire and is looped upside down through a small circular hole in the frame which takes the place of the usual type of constriction.
D 23.5mm, T 2.5mm, Ht 1mm, Wt 1.01g.
Armstrong 1915, 295.

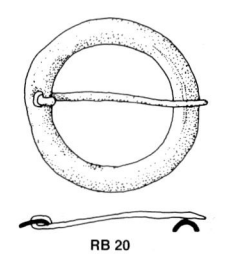

RB 21. Ireland NMI 1.W.11 (ex RIA)
Find circumstances unknown.
Silver circular frame with a curved, angled cross-section. The frame is undecorated. The pin is quite robust with a triangular cross-section, and is incised longitudinally along the shaft. It is attached through a D-shaped hole in the frame instead of the more common constriction.
D 25mm, T 4mm, Ht 4.5mm, Wt 2.57g.
Armstrong 1915, 295.

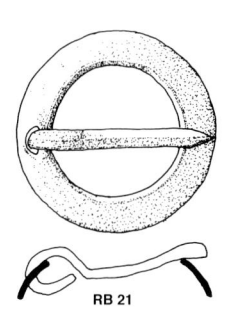

RB 22. Ireland NMI 21.W.14 (ex RIA) (Pl. 2)
Find circumstances unknown.
Silver circular frame with a narrow plano-convex cross-section. The frame is undecorated. The pin has a plano-convex cross-section and a simple loop, and its shaft is slightly bent.
D 23.5mm, T 2mm, Ht 0.7mm, Wt 1.31g.
Armstrong 1915, 295.

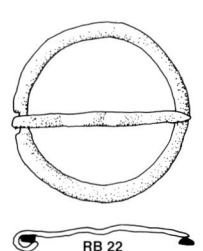

RB 23. Ireland NMI 39.1886:15 (ex RIA)
Find circumstances unknown.
Silver circular frame with a circular cross-section. The frame is undecorated. The pin has a plano-convex cross-section and a simple loop.
D 21.5mm, T 2.5mm, Ht 2.5mm, Wt 3.47g.

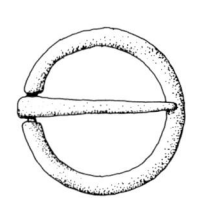

RB 24. Ireland NMI '35' (ex RIA)
Find circumstances unknown.
Silver circular frame with a plano-convex cross-section. The frame is undecorated. The pin has a plano-convex cross-section, a simple loop and a ridge along its underside.
D 22.5mm, T 3mm, Ht 0.8mm, Wt 1.88g.

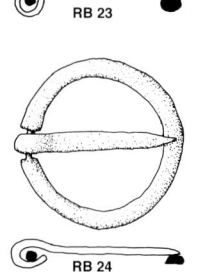

RB 25. Ireland   NMI RSAI 44 (Pl. 1)
Find circumstances unknown.
Copper-alloy circular frame with a circular cross-section. The frame is undecorated. The pin has a circular cross-section, a pincer loop and a biconical collar. The pin tip is bent upwards, probably as a result of the weight of the cloth when worn. The frame and the pin have a dark patination.
D 25.5mm, T 3mm, Ht 3mm, Wt 4.41g.

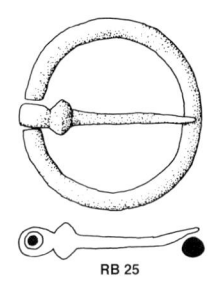

RB 26. Ireland   NMI P1135 (ex RIA)
Find circumstances unknown.
Copper-alloy, crudely shaped circular frame with a flat rectangular cross-section. The frame is undecorated. The pin has a flat rectangular cross-section and a simple loop.
D 24.5mm, T 4mm, Ht 0.6mm, Wt 1.83g.

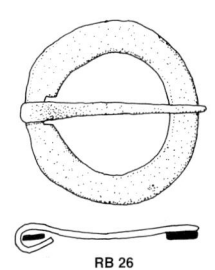

RB 27. Ireland   NMI 22:R4062 (ex RIA) (Pl. 2)
Find circumstances unknown.
Silver circular frame with a narrow plano-convex cross-section. The frame is undecorated. The pin has a plano-convex cross-section and a simple loop.
D 21.5mm, T 2.5mm, Ht 1mm, Wt 0.99g.

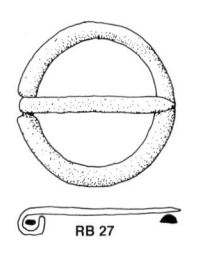

RB 28. Ireland   PRO 1884.79.24
Find circumstances unknown.
Silver circular frame with a plano-convex cross-section. The inner edge of the frame is slightly bevelled. The frame is undecorated, although the letter 'K' is crudely inscribed on the reverse. The pin has a flat rectangular cross-section and a simple loop; its shaft is decorated with a rocked tracer motif. The pin tip is bent sideways.
D 21.5mm, T 3.5mm, Ht 1mm, Wt unavailable.

RB 29. Ireland   UM A137:1974
Find circumstances unknown.
Copper-alloy circular frame with a lozenge cross-section. The frame is undecorated. The pin has a square cross-section, a simple loop and flat transverse flanges.
D 24mm, T 2mm, Ht 2mm, Wt unavailable.

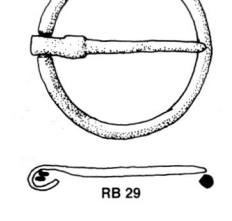

CLASS 2: ring brooches with engraved and/or false relief decoration

Class 2a

RB 30. County Antrim   CF II 197
Excavated at High Street, Carrickfergus (OS 6" sheet 52). Contextually dated to the sixteenth century (Lesley Simpson, pers. comm.).
Copper-alloy circular frame with a flat rectangular cross-section. The front face is decorated with seven groups of two-three radial grooves. The frame has open and overlapping ends through which the constriction is cut. The pin has a rectangular cross-section, a simple loop and two transverse grooves under the head.
D 43mm, T 5.5mm, Ht 2.5mm, Wt unavailable.
Cherry 1988, 147–61.

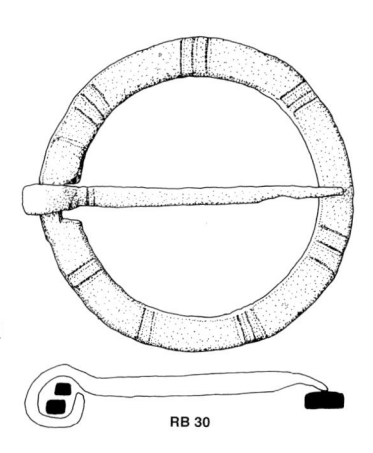

RB 31. County Antrim   CF III 655
Excavated at Joymount, Carrickfergus (OS 6" sheet 52). Contextually dated to the early thirteenth century (Lesley Simpson, pers. comm.).
Lead-alloy(?) circular frame with an angled plano-convex cross-section. The front face is decorated with nine quatrefoils, each surrounded by diamond-shaped incised lines, with the intervening spaces filled with incised triangles. The pin has a plano-convex cross-section, a simple loop and a flanged transverse ridge.
D 16.5mm, T 3mm, Ht 1mm, Wt unavailable.
Cherry 1988, 147–61.

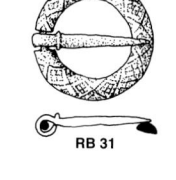

RB 32. County Cork   CPM E146, no finds number available
Excavated at Christchurch, Cork (OS 6" sheet 74). Unstratified.
Copper-alloy circular frame with a lozenge cross-section. All four facets are decorated with double rows of a continuous zigzag motif which sometimes degenerates into a straight line. There is a biconical shoulder on one side of the frame constriction. The pin has a rectangular cross-section and a simple loop.
D 22.5mm, T 3mm, Ht 2.5mm, Wt unavailable.
Scully 1997.

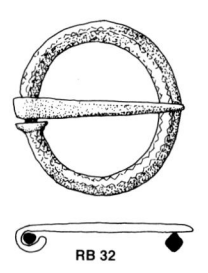

RB 33. County Donegal   NMI 1944:241
Stray find from sandhill midden, Clondahorky Parish, Dunfanaghy Townland (OS 6" sheet 15).
Copper-alloy circular frame which swells slightly at the point where the pin tip rests and has a flat rectangular cross-section. It is decorated on the front face with a crudely executed chevron motif. A radial groove on the frame serves as a pin notch. The slender pin has a plano-convex cross-section and a simple loop, and is decorated with two parallel transverse grooves under the head.
D 26mm, T 3mm, Ht 1.2mm, Wt 2.47g.

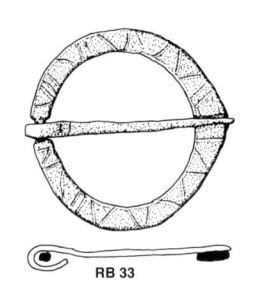

RB 34. County Donegal   NMI 1959:212 (ex Major Nesbit coll.) (Pl. 3)
Stray find, possibly from a midden at Magheramore, near Ardara (OS 6" sheet 73).
Copper-alloy circular frame with a flat rectangular cross-section. The front face is decorated with a continuous chevron motif in which the outer triangles are filled with concentric grooves. The frame has open, overlapping ends at the constriction. The pin has a curved rectangular cross-section and a simple loop.
D 32mm, T 5.5mm, Ht 1mm, Wt 5.26g.
Ó Floinn 1996; NMI 1961, 102.

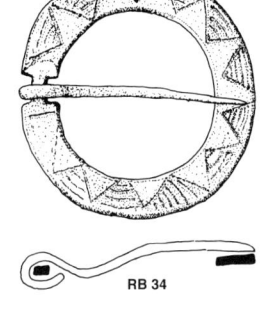

RB 35. County Donegal   Present location unknown
Stray find in a shell midden at Rosapenna, on the Rosguil Peninsula (OS 6" sheet 16).
Copper-alloy circular frame with a lozenge cross-section. All four facets are decorated with a variety of continuous zigzag motifs. The pin has a simple loop and is decorated along the shaft with a chevron motif.
D *c.* 22mm.
Welch 1902.

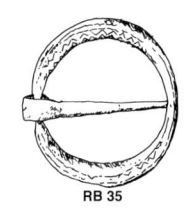

RB 36. County Down   NMI RSAI 74
'Said to have been found within the walls of Castleskreen castle, in the Parish of Dunsfort, Co. Down in 1836' (OS 6" sheet 37/44).
Copper-alloy circular frame with a flat rectangular cross-section. The front face is decorated with a very faintly punched continuous chevron motif. There is a notch on the frame to accommodate the pin tip, with a decorative groove at either side. The frame has open, overlapping

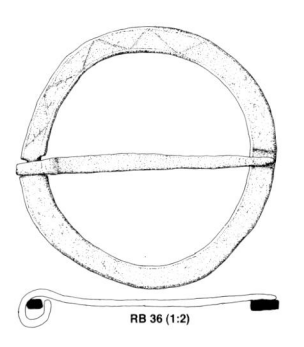

ends. The pin has a rectangular cross-section, a simple loop and four transverse grooves under the head.
D 67mm, T 6mm, Ht 2.5mm, Wt 28.16g.
Anon. 1862, 233.

RB 37. County Dublin   NMI E71:2236
Excavated at High Street, Dublin (OS 6" sheet 18).
Unstratified.
Copper-alloy circular frame with a horizontal oval cross-section. One half of the frame is decorated with a deeply engraved continuous chevron motif. The pin is missing.
D 23mm, T 3mm, Ht 2mm, Wt 1.86g.

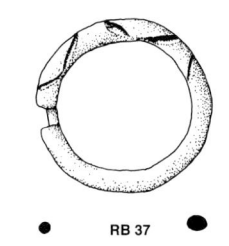

RB 38. County Dublin   NMI E71:2277
Excavated at High Street, Dublin (OS 6" sheet 18). The stratigraphic sequence for this site has not yet been fully resolved. Provisional dating: mid-twelfth to early fourteenth century.
Copper-alloy circular frame with a lozenge cross-section. All four facets are decorated with double rows of concentric continuous zigzag motifs which sometimes degenerate into a straight line. The pin has a flat rectangular cross-section and a simple loop.
 D 22.5mm, T 4mm, Ht 3mm, Wt 2.29g.

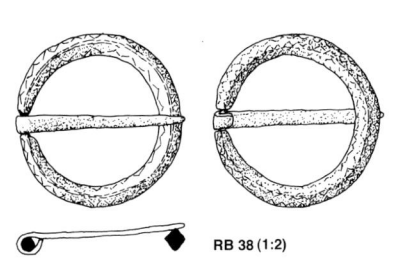

RB 39. County Dublin   NMI E71:3370
Excavated at High Street, Dublin (OS 6" sheet 18). The stratigraphic sequence of this site has not yet been fully resolved. Provisional dating: mid-twelfth to early fourteenth century.
Copper-alloy, thin circular frame with a circular cross-section. The front face is decorated with shallow oblique grooves. The pin is missing.
D 17.5mm, T 1.5mm, Ht 1.5mm, Wt 0.86g.

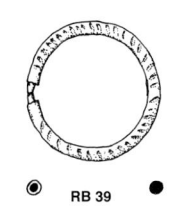

RB 40. County Dublin   NMI E71:3488
Excavated at High Street, Dublin (OS 6" sheet 18).
Unstratified.
Copper-alloy circular frame with a plano-convex cross-section. The front face is decorated with eight shallow swellings, four of which are alternately decorated with punched circles. The pin has a plano-convex cross-section, a simple loop and a double-moulding transverse ridge.
D 14.5mm, T 2mm, Ht 1.5mm, Wt 1.18g.

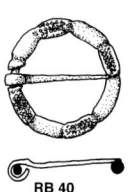

RB 41. County Dublin   NMI E71:16155
Excavated at High Street, Dublin (OS 6" sheet 18). The stratigraphic sequence for this site has not yet been fully resolved. Provisional dating: late twelfth/early thirteenth century.
Copper-alloy circular frame with a subtriangular cross-section with raised inner and outer edges. The inner surfaces of the raised edges are decorated with faint diagonal grooves. The two facets of the front face are decorated with a faint alternating chevron pattern in which the inner spaces are filled with radial grooves. The pin has a plano-convex cross-section and a simple loop.
D 20mm, T 3mm, Ht 2mm, Wt 2.03g.

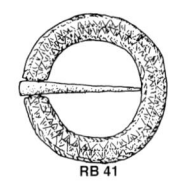

RB 42. County Dublin   NMI E81:582
Excavated at Winetavern Street, Dublin (OS 6" sheet 18). Unstratified.
Copper-alloy circular frame with a flat rectangular cross-section. Only slightly more than a third of the frame survives and the constriction is missing. The front face is decorated with a continuous chevron pattern in which the outer triangles are filled with deep, punched, concentric lines. The pin is missing.
D *c.* 38mm, T 5mm, Ht 1mm, Wt 1.58g.

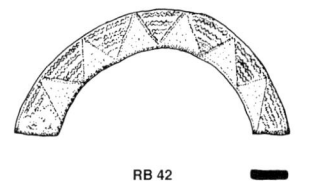

RB 43. County Dublin   NMI E132:36634
Excavated at Wood Quay, Dublin (OS 6" sheet 18). Precise contextual details are not available at present. Provisional dating: thirteenth century.
Copper-alloy circular frame; subsquare cross-section with a curved upper surface. The front face is decorated with sixteen shallow swellings. The pin has a plano-convex cross-section and a simple loop, and is decorated with two parallel transverse grooves under the head. Corrosion has caused the pin to remain stuck open. The gold-coloured substance on the surface of the brooch was identified as a form of corrosion rather than gilding (P. Mullarky, pers. comm.).
D 29mm, T 3.5mm, Ht 4.6mm, Wt 7.11g.

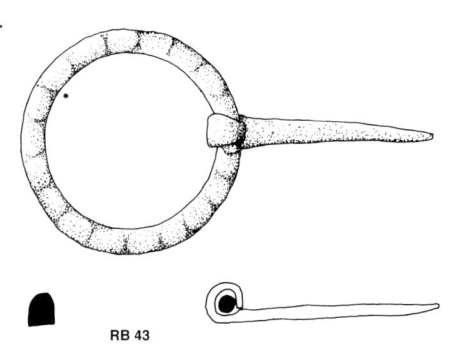

RB 44. County Dublin   NMI E132:52167, on loan to 'Dublinia'
Excavated at Wood Quay, Dublin (OS 6" sheet 18). Precise contextual details are not available at present. Provisional dating: thirteenth century.
Silver circular frame with a horizontal oval cross-section. One half of the front face is decorated with a deeply engraved continuous chevron pattern. The intervening spaces are filled with parallel concentric rows of punched square dots. The pin is missing. There is a ridge along the casting seam around the inner and outer edges of the frame.
D 23.5mm, T 3mm, Ht 2mm, Wt 1.72g.

RB 45. County Kildare   E179:34
Excavated at nos 14–16 Main Street North, Naas (OS 6" sheet 19/24). Unstratified (K. Campbell, pers. comm.).
Copper-alloy circular frame with a flat rectangular cross-section. The frame is decorated on the front face with eight pairs of unevenly spaced radial grooves. The pin is missing. The frame is broken at the constriction.
D 24mm, T 4mm, Ht 1.5mm, Wt unavailable.

RB 46. County Kilkenny   NMI E123:3644
Excavated at a medieval settlement site in Jerpointchurch townland (OS 6" sheet 28/32). Unstratified.
Copper-alloy circular frame with a circular cross-section. The front face is decorated with six evenly spaced groups of between three and six radial grooves. The pin has a flat rectangular cross-section, a simple loop and a narrow head decorated with one longitudinal groove. There are also traces of a dark patination on the frame and pin. There is no pin constriction.
D 35mm, T 3mm, Ht 3mm, Wt 6.78g.
Foley 1989, 95–6.

RB 47. County Limerick   LCM 92E75:2381
Excavated at St Mary's Cathedral, Limerick (OS 6" sheet 5). Contextually dated to the mid–late thirteenth century.
Copper-alloy circular frame with a rectangular cross-section. The front face is decorated with an octagonal cusped-edged outline which has been left in relief with the background cut away. The outer spaces are decorated with radial grooves. The inner space is filled with a band

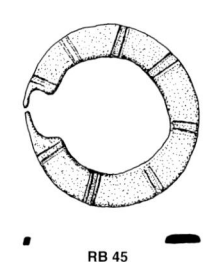

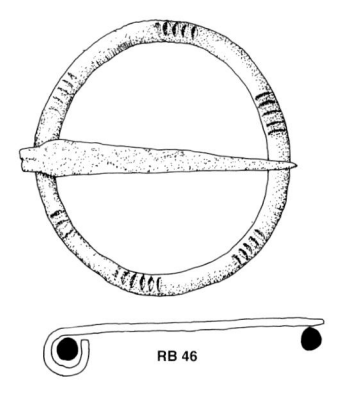

of a red enamel *en champlevé*. The pin has a narrow plano-convex cross-section and a simple loop, and is quite bent out of shape. The tip is broken.
D 14.5mm, T 3–3.5mm, Ht 1.1mm, Wt unavailable.
 Hodkinson, forthcoming; 1992.

RB 48. County Meath   K 72 Br. 15   (Pl. 5)
Excavated at Knowth (OS 6" sheet 19). Unstratified (H. Roche, pers. comm.).
Copper-alloy circular frame with a flat rectangular cross-section. The overlapping soldered frame ends are visible on the reverse. The front face of the frame is decorated with a continuous chevron pattern in which the six inner triangles are decorated with a short triangular groove. The outer spaces are filled with rows of rocked tracer ornament. The pin has a rectangular cross-section and a simple loop. The frame and pin have a green patination.
D 27mm, T 5.5mm, Ht 0.7mm, Wt unavailable.

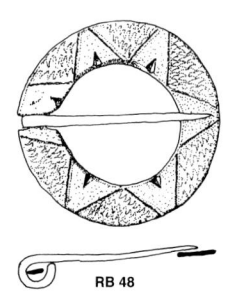

RB 49. County Meath   NMI 1862:709 (ex Rev. Richard Butler coll.)
Found near 'Piggotstown' (OS 6" sheet 15/22).
Copper-alloy, crude circular frame with a flat rectangular cross-section. The frame is formed of a flat strip of metal of uneven width with open and overlapping ends. There are faint traces of a continuous chevron motif on the front face. The pin has a plano-convex cross-section and a simple loop. There are traces of patination on the frame and the pin is highly patinated, though chipped around the head and tip.
D 18.5mm, T 3mm, Ht 0.8mm, Wt 1.11g.
Anon. 1864.

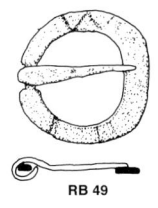

RB 50. County Tyrone   UM A5382
Found by metal-detector at Dantusk, River Blackwater.
Copper-alloy circular frame with a circular cross-section. The front face is decorated with alternating radial and oblique grooves. The pin is narrow, with a plano-convex cross-section and a low transverse ridge. There are patches of a gold-coloured substance on the frame and pin which may be corrosion.
D 17.5mm, T 2mm, Ht 2mm, Wt unavailable.

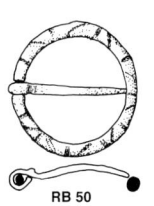

RB 51. Counties Tyrone/Armagh   Private coll., RS 1993.143   (not illustrated)
Found by metal-detector at the River Blackwater, Cos Tyrone/Armagh (?) (C. Bourke, pers. comm.).
Copper-alloy circular frame with a rectangular cross-section. The front face is decorated with shallow swellings. The pin has a rectangular cross-section and a simple loop.
D 24mm; other dimensions unavailable.

RB 52. County Waterford   E435:228:B128:8
Excavated at Bakehouse Lane, Waterford (OS 6" sheet 9). Recovered from graveyard soil, burial period III, contextually dated to the mid-thirteenth to early seventeenth century.
Copper-alloy circular frame with a circular cross-section. The front face of the frame is decorated with a number of evenly spaced radial grooves. The pin is missing. The constriction is missing and the frame is open-ended with uneven edges.
D 14mm, T 1.5mm, Ht 1.5mm, Wt unavailable.
Lightbown 1997, 523.

RB 53. County Westmeath   NMI 19
Found by metal-detector at Newtownlow crannog (OS 6" sheet 38).
Copper-alloy circular frame with a flat rectangular cross-section. The front face is decorated with a simple continuous chevron motif, partly obscured by corrosion. The pin has a rectangular cross-section and a flanged transverse ridge decorated with a herring-bone motif. The pin is also corroded and bent. Both frame and pin have traces of a green patination.
D 32.5mm, T 3mm, Ht 1.5mm, Wt 4.28g.

RB 54. Ireland   NMI '18' (ex RIA)
Find circumstances unknown.
Silver circular frame with a plano-convex cross-section. The front face is decorated with shallow depressions alternating with pairs of radial grooves. The pin has a plano-convex cross-section and a simple loop, and is decorated with a pair of transverse grooves under the head.
D 19mm, T 2mm, Ht 0.9mm, Wt 1.35g.

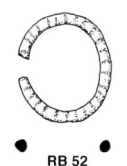

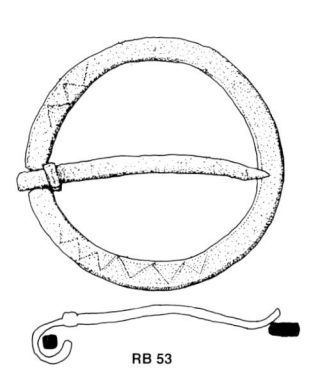

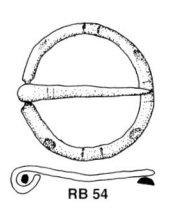

RB 55. Ireland   NMI 17 R4058 (ex RIA)
Find circumstances unknown.
Silver circular frame with a narrow plano-convex cross-section. The front face is decorated in three areas with a short radial groove on either side of a shallow depression. There is also one radial groove at either side of the constriction. The pin has a flat rectangular cross-section and a simple loop, and is decorated with two transverse grooves under the head.
D 20mm, T 2mm, Ht 0.8mm, Wt 1.44g.

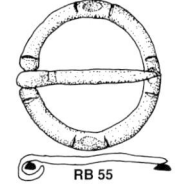

RB 56. Ireland   NMI 19:R4060 (ex RIA)
Find circumstances unknown.
Silver circular frame with a circular cross-section. One half of the front face is decorated with a simple continuous chevron motif. The pin has a circular cross-section, a simple loop and transverse ridge.
D 19mm, T 2mm, Ht 2mm, Wt 2.19g.

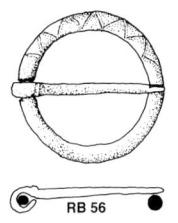

RB 57. Ireland   NMI 30:R4061 (ex RIA)
Find circumstances unknown.
Silver circular frame with a rectangular cross-section. The front face is decorated with a band of quatrefoils. The reverse face is decorated with a continuous chevron motif in which the inner triangles are cross-hatched. The pin has a plano-convex cross-section, a pincer loop and a flanged transverse ridge with double moulding.
D 23mm, T 4.5mm, Ht 0.6mm, Wt 2.14g.

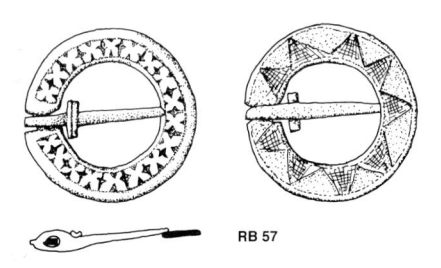

RB 58. Ireland   NMI 16 R5051 (ex RIA)
Find circumstances unknown.
Silver circular frame with a narrow plano-convex cross-section. The front face is decorated with two shallow depressions, each with a radial groove at either side. There is also a shallow depression at either side of the constriction and three radial grooves under the pin tip. The pin has a plano-convex cross-section and a simple loop.
D 22mm, T 2mm, Ht 1.2mm, Wt 1.87g.

RB 59. Ireland   NMI 7.W.1 (ex RIA)
Find circumstances unknown.
Silver circular frame with a rectangular cross-section. The front face is decorated on one half with widely spaced, punched radial lines and on the other half with a punched chevron pattern. The reverse face is also decorated with a chevron pattern. The pin has a flat rectangular cross-section, a simple loop and a thin, flanged, transverse ridge. It is also decorated with a chevron pattern on its shaft.
D 21mm, T 3mm, Ht 1.2mm, Wt 2.5g.
Armstrong 1915, 294.

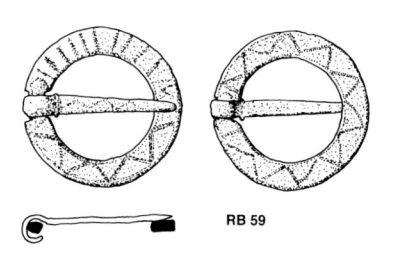

RB 60. Ireland   NMI 10.W.2 (ex RIA) (Pl. 3)
Find circumstances unknown.
Silver circular frame with a slightly angled, flat, rectangular cross-section. The frame is decorated on the front face with an incised continuous chevron motif in which the inner triangles are filled with concentrically incised lines. The pin has a plano-convex cross-section and a simple loop, and is decorated with two tiny raised dots at the base of the head.
D 19mm, T 4mm, Ht 1mm, Wt 1.05g.
Armstrong 1915, 294.

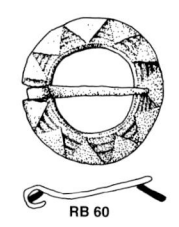

RB 61. Ireland   NMI W.3 (ex RIA)
Find circumstances unknown.
Silver circular frame with a flat rectangular cross-section. One half of the front face is decorated with a chevron pattern in which the outer triangles have been filled with concentric grooves and the other half is decorated with radial grooves, within a band formed by inner and outer concentric circles. The pin has a flat rectangular cross-section, a simple loop and a transverse ridge. It is also decorated with a chevron motif on the shaft.
D 18mm, T 2mm, Ht 0.6mm, Wt 0.92g.
Armstrong 1915, 294.

RB 62. Ireland   NMI 4.W.4 (ex RIA)
Find circumstances unknown.
Silver circular frame with a flat rectangular cross-section. The front face is decorated on one half with punched thin radial lines and on the other half with a punched continuous chevron motif, both within a band formed by inner and

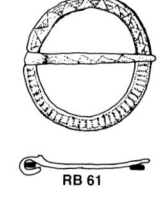

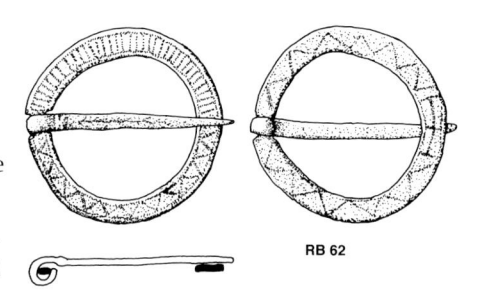

outer concentrically incised lines. The reverse face is decorated with
a crudely executed continuous chevron motif and a cross motif positioned opposite the constriction. The pin has a plano-convex cross-section, a simple loop, and a transverse ridge with a double moulding. It is also decorated with a herring-bone motif on the shaft.
D 26mm, T 3mm, Ht 0.8mm, Wt 2.61g.
Armstrong 1915, 294.

RB 63. Ireland   NMI 11.W.13 (ex RIA)
Find circumstances unknown.
Silver circular frame with a flat rectangular cross-section and a step on the external edge of one face. This face is decorated with a step motif and the cutaway area surrounding it is inlaid with niello. The other face is decorated with a continuous chevron motif in which the outer triangles are inlaid with niello. The pin has a circular cross-section, a pincer loop and a transverse ridge on both sides.
D 16.5mm, T 4mm, Ht 1mm, Wt 1.51g.
Armstrong 1915, 295.

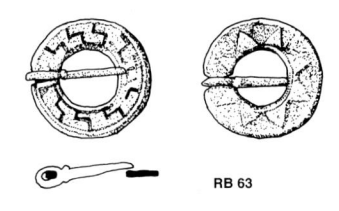

RB 64. Ireland   NMI 32.W.15 (ex RIA)
Find circumstances unknown.
Silver circular frame with a wide, flat, rectangular cross-section. The front face of the frame is decorated with rosettes and the reverse face is decorated with quatrefoils and three-leafed foliage. All the decoration is very faint. The pin has a horizontal oval cross-section and a simple loop.
D 27mm, T 6mm, Ht 1mm, Wt 4.09g.
Armstrong 1915, 295.

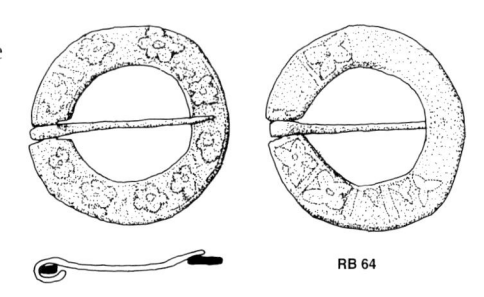

RB 65. Ireland   NMI 31.W.16 (ex RIA) (Pl. 4)
Find circumstances unknown.
Silver circular frame with a rectangular cross-section. The front face is decorated with a raised outline of five inward-facing semicircles. The inner and outer edges of the frame are also raised. The resulting inner semicircular spaces are incised with foliage motifs and the outer spaces are cross-hatched. The pin has an oval cross-section, a pincer loop and a transverse ridge with a double moulding.
D 23mm, T 5mm, Ht 1mm, Wt 3.73g.
Cherry 1988, 161; Armstrong 1915, 295.

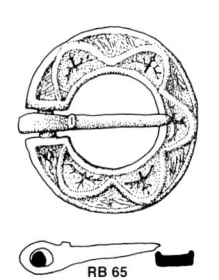

RB 66. Ireland   NMI 8.W.19 (ex RIA)
Find circumstances unknown.
Silver circular frame with a narrow, flat, rectangular cross-section. The front face of the frame is decorated with a punched continuous chevron design in which the outer triangles have been filled with two or three radial grooves. The pin has a plano-convex cross-section, a simple loop and a transverse ridge.
D 22mm, T 2mm, Ht 0.6mm, Wt 1.18g.
Armstrong 1915, 295.

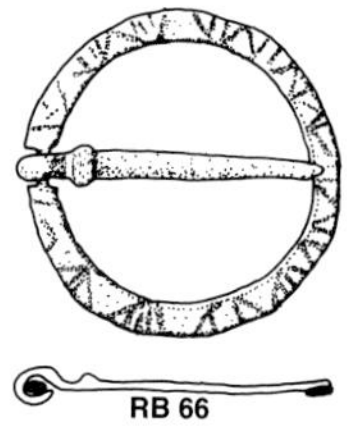

RB 67. Ireland   NMI 5.W.20 (ex RIA)
Find circumstances unknown.
Silver circular frame with a flat rectangular cross-section. The front face is decorated with a punched continuous chevron design in which the outer triangles have been filled with two or three concentric grooves. The pin has a plano-convex cross-section, a simple loop and a transverse ridge, and is decorated with a wavy chevron motif on the shaft.
D 25mm, T 3mm, Ht 0.9mm, Wt 2.77g.
Armstrong 1915, 295.

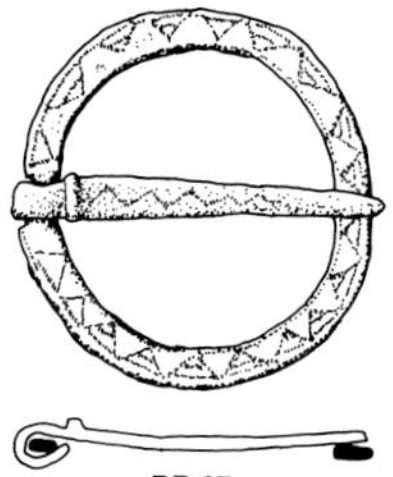

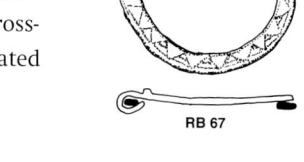

RB 68. Ireland   NMI 6.W.23 (ex RIA)
Find circumstances unknown.
Silver circular frame with a wide rectangular cross-section. The front face is decorated with a continuous chevron motif, with one radial line within each triangle. The outer edge is bevelled and is decorated with punched circles. The reverse face is decorated with a continuous chevron motif in which the inner triangles have been filled with crude cross-hatching. The pin has a curved square cross-section, a pincer loop and a flanged transverse ridge decorated with four punched circles. There is also one punched circle on the head of the pin.
D 23mm, T 4.5mm, Ht 1mm, Wt 2.81g.
Armstrong 1915, 295.

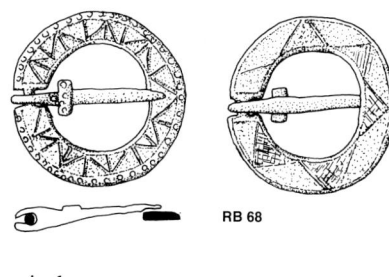

RB 69. Ireland   NMI P1136 (ex RIA)
Find circumstances unknown.
Copper-alloy circular frame with a square cross-section. The front face is decorated with closely spaced radial grooves. The pin has a flat rectangular cross-section and a simple loop. It is decorated with alternating transverse and diagonal grooves along the shaft.
D 19mm, T 2mm, Ht 2mm, Wt 2.02g.

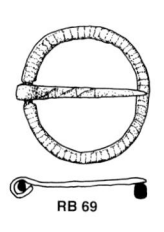

RB 70. Ireland   NMI P1137 (ex RIA)
Find circumstances unknown.
Copper-alloy circular frame with a rectangular cross-section. The front face is decorated with an elegantly executed, deeply engraved chevron motif in which each triangle is filled with one short radial groove. All the grooves of the design are filled with a white powdery substance. The pin has a plano-convex cross-section, a simple loop and a flanged transverse ridge. Both the frame and the pin are patinated and badly chipped.
D 24.5mm, T 3mm, Ht 1.2mm, Wt 2.35g.

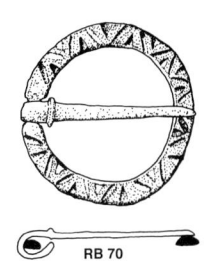

RB 71. Ireland   NMI 363-1920 (ex Killua Castle coll.)
Find circumstances unknown.
Copper-alloy circular frame with curved square cross-section. It is decorated on the front face with two concentric rows of loosely spaced beading. There is an additional row of beading around the outer edge of the frame. The pin has a a plano-convex cross-section and a simple loop. It is quite crude, with a wide head narrowing sharply to a narrow shaft. It is broken and falls short of the opposite side of the frame.
D 19mm, T 2mm, Ht 2mm, Wt 1.9g.

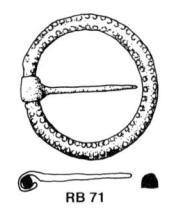

RB 72. Ireland   NMI W.455 (ex RIA)
Find circumstances unknown.
Copper-alloy circular frame with a rectangular cross-section. The front face is decorated with two unevenly punched concentric lines. There is also an incised line on the inner edge of the frame. The pin has a plano-convex cross-section and a simple loop. Both the frame and the pin are patinated.
D 21mm, T 3.5mm, Ht 1.5mm, Wt 2.87g.

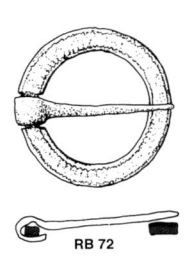

RB 73. Ireland   NMI W.457 (ex RIA)
Find circumstances unknown.
Copper-alloy circular frame with an angled, robust cross-section so that the front face is bevelled. The inner facet is decorated with a wavy line, with one short concentric groove in each curve. The outer facet is decorated with a broken step motif. The pin has a plano-convex cross-section, a simple loop and a transverse ridge. It is also decorated on the head with one longitudinal line. The frame has a notch, whose function is unclear, on its

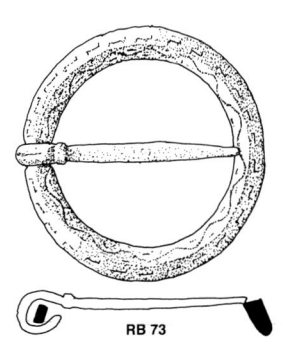

underside, beneath where the pin tip rests on the front face of the frame.
D 32.5mm, T 4mm, Ht 4.5mm, Wt 9.99g.

RB 74. Ireland   NMI W.458 (ex RIA)
Find circumstances unknown.
Copper-alloy circular frame with a wide, flat, rectangular cross-section. The front face is decorated with a double-edged squarish shape within a circle. The intervening spaces are filled with groups of radial lines. The pin is missing.
D 44mm, T 8mm, Ht 1mm, Wt 8.39g.

RB 75. Ireland   PRO 1884.79.11
Find circumstances unknown.
Copper-alloy circular frame with a horizontal oval cross-section. The front face is decorated with raised diamonds and triangles in the intervening spaces, and three pairs of oblique raised flame-shapes. The pin has a plano-convex cross-section and a simple loop, and appears to be slightly too short for the frame. It may be that too much of the pin was incorporated into the loop, causing it to fall short of the necessary length.
D 27mm, T 5.5mm, Ht 3.5mm, Wt unavailable.

RB 76. Ireland   PRO 1884.79.23
Find circumstances unknown.
Silver circular frame with a circular cross-section. Both faces are decorated on one half with ten widely spaced radial grooves inlaid with niello. The pin has a circular cross-section, a pincer loop and a conical collar, decorated with loosely spaced punched circles.
D 16mm, T 2mm, Ht 2mm, Wt unavailable.

RB 77. Ireland   UM A197:1966
Find circumstances unknown.
Copper-alloy circular frame with a plano-concave cross-section. The flat front face is undecorated. The curved reverse face is decorated with nine groups of paired, widely spaced radial grooves. The pin has a plano-convex cross-section, a simple loop and transverse flanges decorated with four transverse grooves. There is a notch in the

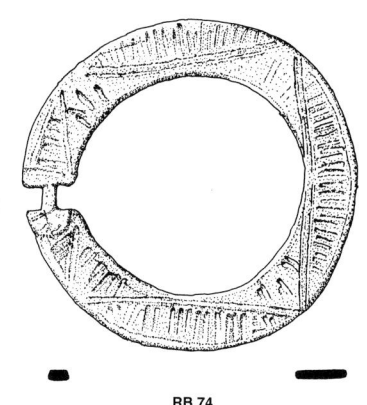

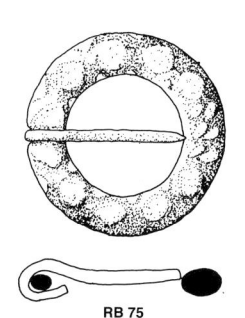

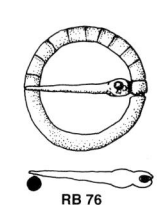

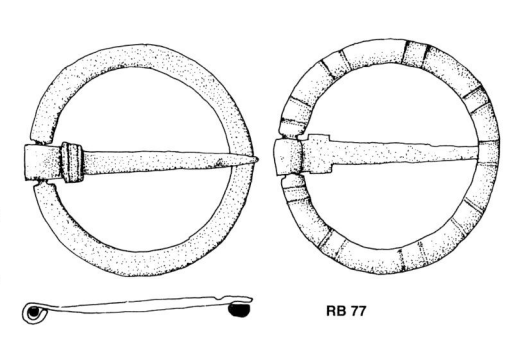

upper surface of the pin near the tip. There is a break in the constriction.
D 30.5mm, T 3mm, Ht 1.5mm, Wt unavailable.

RB 78. Ireland   UM AWM 7700 (ex Welcombe coll.)
Find circumstances unknown.
Copper-alloy circular frame with a flat rectangular cross-section. The inner and outer edges of the frame are scalloped. The front face is decorated with unevenly spaced radial grooves, which do not always respect the shapes formed by the scalloping. The pin is very slender, with a circular cross-section, a simple loop and two transverse grooves under the head.
D 34.5mm, T 5mm, Ht 1mm, Wt unavailable.

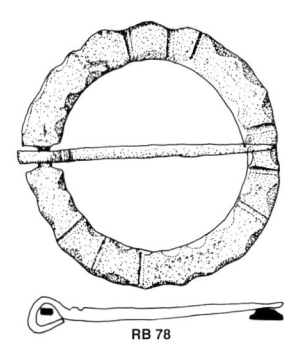

Class 2b

RB 79. County Antrim   Present location unknown
'Found near Carrickfergus Castle' (OS 6" sheet 52).
Silver circular frame with a flat rectangular cross-section. One face is decorated with the Lombardic inscription 'AVE MARIA GxP III'. The other face is decorated with the same inscription in reverse, 'IIIPxG AIRAM EVA'. The pin has a pincer loop and a collar. The inscription on the front face has been interpreted as 'Ave Maria, Gratiae Plena (Ter)', i.e. the Angelic Salutation, 'Hail Mary, full of grace (thrice)', repeated on the other face in reverse.
D 25mm.
Cherry 1988, 148; Anon. 1857.

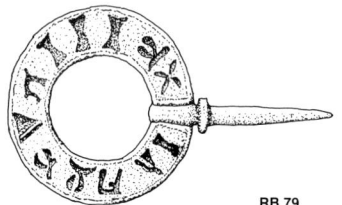

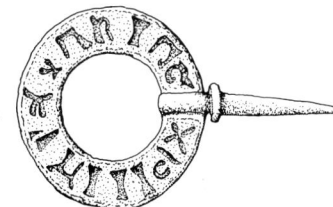

RB 80. County Meath   NMI R4002 (ex RIA) (Pls 6 and 7)
Found at Trim, details unknown (OS 6" sheet 36). The use of Black Letter script indicates a fourteenth–fifteenth-century date for this brooch.
Silver circular frame with a wide

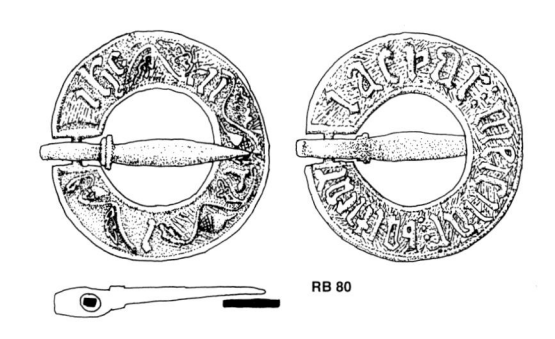

rectangular cross-section. The front face is decorated in relief with the Black Letter inscription 'ihc n r i' interwined with a foliage scroll of oak leaves and acorns. The reverse is decorated with the Black Letter inscription 'IACPAR:MELCHAR:BALTICAR'. The intervening areas on both faces are cross-hatched. The pin has a plano-convex cross-section, a pincer loop and a flanged transverse ridge with double moulding. The inscription on the front is an abbreviated version of the titulus and that on the reverse is a version of the names of the three Magi—Caspar, Melchior and Balthasar.
D 29.5mm, T 7mm, Ht 1mm, Wt 6.63g.
Cherry 1988, 147–61.

RB 81. County Monaghan   Present location unknown
'Found near the ruins of Donaghmoyne or Mannin Castle in Ulster, the ancient head of the Barony of Farney' (OS 6" sheet 28/31).
Gold circular frame with a flat rectangular cross-section. The front face is decorated with the Lombardic inscription '+IHSENAOIIP'CI'. The pin has a flanged transverse ridge with a transverse groove, leaving two ridges in relief. It may have a pincer loop. The meaning of the inscription is obscure and not readily translatable; however, the first three letters preceded by a cross are probably an abbreviation of the titulus.
Wt 1.18g; other dimensions unavailable.
Cherry 1988, 147–61; Anon. 1854, 285.

RB 82. Ireland   NMI '15' (ex RIA)
Find circumstances unknown.
Silver circular frame with a plano-concave cross-section. The front face is decorated with the Lombardic inscription 'AMOR:VINCIT OMNIA', which translates as 'Love conquers all'. The pin is missing.
D 19.5mm, T 3mm, Ht 1.5mm, Wt 2.19g.

RB 83. Ireland   NMI 13.W.17 (ex RIA)
Find circumstances unknown.
Silver circular frame with a flat rectangular cross-section. The front face is decorated with the Lombardic inscription 'ENYNAICARGAIRAMEVA+'. The pin has a plano-convex cross-section, a simple loop and a flanged transverse ridge decorated with four longitudinal grooves. The shaft is also

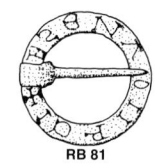

decorated with a chevron and dot design. When read backwards, the inscription translates as the Angelic Salutation, 'Hail Mary full of grace, nine', indicating that it should be repeated nine times.
D 26mm, T 3mm, Ht 0.8mm, Wt 2.71g.
Armstrong 1915, 295.

RB 84. Ireland   NMI 14.W.18 (ex RIA)
Find circumstances unknown.
Silver circular frame with a flat rectangular cross-section. The front face is decorated with the Lombardic inscription '+AVE(?)(?)+AVEX'. The pin has a plano-convex cross-section, a simple loop and a flanged transverse ridge. The frame is broken. The inscription is probably a version of the Angelic Salutation.
D 21mm, T 3mm, Ht 0.6mm, Wt 1.58g.
Armstrong 1915, 295.

RB 85. Ireland   NMI W.85 (ex RIA)   (Pl. 8)
Find circumstances unknown.
Gold circular frame with a plano-concave cross-section. The flat face is decorated with the Lombardic inscription '+IESUS MAIRE HV'. The pin has a plano-concave cross-section, a pincer loop and a six-faceted collar.
D 19mm, T 2.5mm, Ht 0.8mm, Wt 1.47g.
Cherry 1988, 147–61; Wilde 1862, 44.

RB 86. Ireland   NMI W.86 (ex RIA) (Pl. 8)
Find circumstances unknown.
Gold circular frame with a plano-concave cross-section. The frame is decorated on the flat face with the Lombardic inscription '+PAR+AMUR+FIN+SUI DVNE', which may translate as 'I am a gift for fine love' (J. Cherry, pers. comm.). The curved face is decorated with a row of arrows alternating with double rows of punched circles. The pin has a circular cross-section, a pincer loop and a rectangular collar with a double moulding.
D 29mm, T 3.5mm, Ht 2mm, Wt 7.99g.
Cherry 1988, 147–61; Wilde 1862, 44.

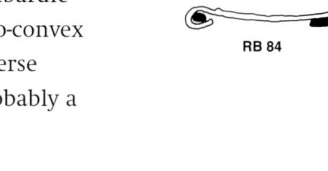

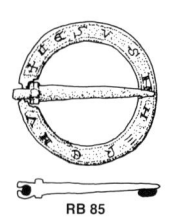

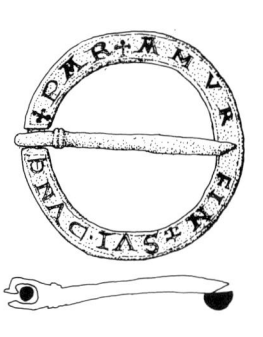

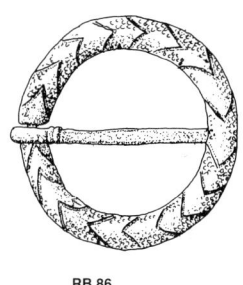

CLASS 3: ring brooches with cable decoration

Class 3a

RB 87. County Dublin   92E109:72:53
Excavated at Cornmarket/Francis Street, Dublin (OS 6" sheet 18). Recovered from ditch fill. Contextually dated to the later thirteenth century.
Copper-alloy circular frame with a circular cross-section. The frame is tightly twisted and has the appearance of 'ribbing'. The pin is missing. The frame is broken at the constriction.
D 38mm, T 2.5mm, Ht 2.5mm, Wt unavailable.
Hayden, forthcoming.

RB 88. County Dublin   NMI E132:18299, on loan to 'Dublinia'
Excavated at Wood Quay, Dublin (OS 6" sheet 18). Precise contextual details are not available at present. Provisional dating: thirteenth century.
Lead-alloy circular frame with a plano-convex cross-section. One half of the front face is decorated with pairs of raised, curved diagonal lines forming bands filled with rilling, alternating with bands of beading. The pin is missing. The constriction is shouldered and would appear to be strengthened by the addition of a ridge on its underside.
D 17mm, T 3mm, Ht 0.5mm, Wt 0.63g.

RB 89. County Kilkenny   NMI 1959:759
Found in a field at the old Kilkenny College, Kilkenny (OS 6" sheet 24).
Copper-alloy circular frame. One half of the frame has a circular cross-section and the other half has a square profile which is twisted to form four spiralling bands decorated with deeply punched circles. The pin has a curved rectangular cross-section, a simple loop and a flanged transverse ridge.
D 23mm, T 3mm, Ht 3mm, Wt 4.07g.
NMI 1961, 101, fig. 23:e.

RB 90. County Meath   Present location unknown
(not illustrated)
Found during an 'excavation of a moat' (motte) at Patrickstown (OS 6" sheet 9/15).

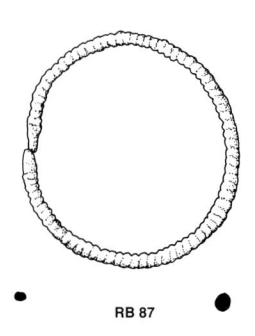

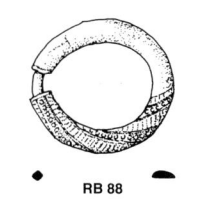

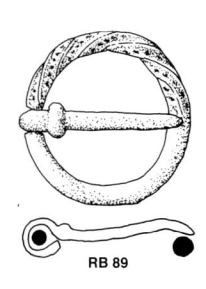

Silver circular frame. One half of the frame has a circular cross-section and the other half appears to have a square profile twisted to give spiralling bands decorated with beading. The pin appears to have a cylindrical collar.
D 22.5mm; other dimensions unavailable.
Cherry 1988, 148–61; Crofton Rotheram 1898.

RB 91. County Offaly   NMI RSAI 48   (Pl. 9)
Found by Mr William Stanley at Killeigh (OS 6" sheet 25).
Silver circular frame. One half of the frame has a circular cross-section and the other half has a square profile and is twisted to form four spiralling bands decorated with beading. The pin has a circular cross-section, a pincer loop and a biconical collar. The pin head and the collar are decorated with randomly placed punched circles.
D 19.5mm, T 2mm, Ht 2mm, Wt 2.48g.
Cherry 1988, 156–61; Anon. 1874, 81–2.

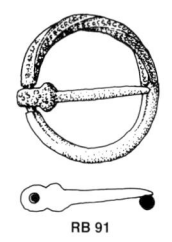

RB 92. County Roscommon   NMI E621:48   (Pl. 9)
Found by metal-detector at a crannog in Lough na hIncha.
Copper-alloy circular frame. One half of the frame has a circular cross-section and the other half has six spiralling bands filled with 'rilling'. There is a ridge, probably a casting seam, along the inner and outer edges of the frame. The pin is missing.
D 23mm, T 2.5mm, Ht 2.5mm, Wt 1.97g.

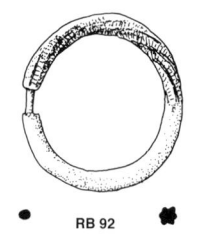

RB 93. County Waterford   E527:196:52
Excavated at Arundel Square, Waterford (OS 6" sheet 9).
Contextually dated to the thirteenth century.
Copper-alloy circular frame with a twisted square cross-section. The frame is formed of a square-sectioned bar, twisted and then bent into a circular shape. The pin is missing. The constriction is missing and the frame is open-ended and uneven.
D 26mm, T 2.5mm, Ht 2.5mm, Wt unavailable.
Lightbown 1997, 523.

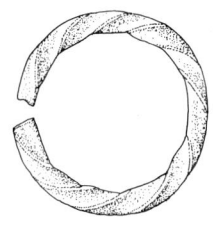

RB 94. County Waterford   E527:1510:6
Excavated at Arundel Square, Waterford (OS 6" sheet 9).
Contextually dated to the mid-twelfth century.
Lead-alloy circular frame with a vertical oval cross-section. Both faces are decorated with cast oblique ridges and

grooves imitating a twisted bar. There is a ridge, a casting seam, along the inner and outer edges. The pin is missing.
D 24.5mm, T 2.5mm, Ht 3mm, Wt unavailable.
Lightbown 1997, 522.

RB 95. County Waterford   E435:230:39
Excavated at Bakehouse Lane, Waterford (OS 6" sheet 9). Recovered from graveyard introduced soil, period III, and contextually dated to the mid-thirteenth century. Copper-alloy circular frame, decorated with oblique grooves giving the appearance of a twisted bar. The pin is missing; a piece of metal corroded onto the frame may be the remains of the pin head.
D 19mm, T 2mm, Ht 2mm, Wt unavailable.
Lightbown 1997, 523.

RB 96. County Wexford   E237:1089
Excavated at Tintern Abbey (OS 6" sheet 45). Recovered from a monastic drain which served the rear dortor, found in drain fill F677. Contextually dated to between 1250 and 1300.
Silver circular frame with a circular cross-section. One half of the frame is decorated with a cable motif. The pin has a curved rectangular cross-section and a pincer loop. It also has an applied collar decorated with tiny incised grooves at the sides. The pin head was bent around to form the loop and the excess length was then soldered to the underside of the shaft. The collar was soldered on around this join.
D 39mm, T 2.5mm, Ht 2.5mm, Wt unavailable.
Lynch, forthcoming.

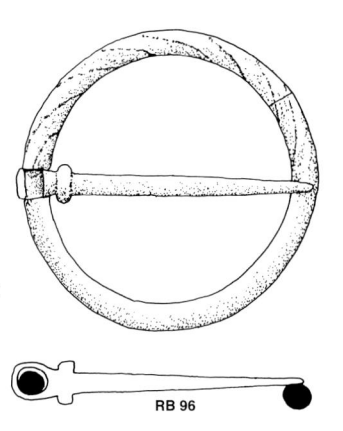

RB 97. Ireland   NMI 20.W.22 (ex RIA)   (Pl. 9)
Find circumstances unknown.
Silver circular frame. One half of the frame has a circular cross-section and the other half has a square profile and is twisted to form four spiralling bands decorated with beading. The pin has a circular cross-section, a simple loop and a transverse ridge.
D 19mm, W 2mm, Ht 2mm, Wt 2.3g.
Cherry 1988, 148–61; Armstrong 1915, 295.

RB 98. Ireland NMI '33' (ex RIA) (Pl. 10)
Find circumstances unknown.
Silver circular frame with a circular cross-section. One half of the front face is decorated with a simple, faintly engraved cable design. The pin has a circular cross-section, a pincer loop and a collar. The pin tip is missing.
D 27mm, T 2mm, Ht 2mm, Wt 3.31g.

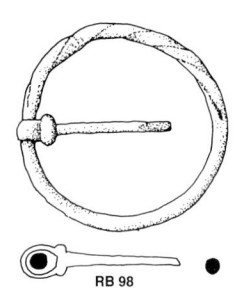

RB 99. Ireland NMI '36' (ex RIA)
Find circumstances unknown.
Silver circular frame with a plano-convex cross-section. The front face is decorated with curved, diagonally incised lines forming bands alternating with curved diagonal rows of beading. This decoration imitates the twisted decoration of Class 3a brooches. The decoration on this brooch also represents two sleeved arms with joined hands meeting opposite the constriction, providing a notch for the pin tip. The pin has a plano-convex cross-section, a simple loop and a tiny transverse ridge decorated with tiny, deeply punched circles.
D 15.5mm, T 2.5mm, Ht 1mm, Wt 1.05g.

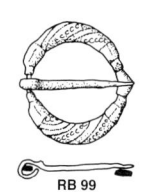

RB 100. Ireland NMI number unavailable
Find circumstances unknown.
Silver circular frame with a circular cross-section. The frame is 'ribbed', decorated with a series of transverse ridges which travel all the way round the circular profile of the frame. The pin has a curved rectangular cross-section, a simple loop and a transverse ridge with double moulding.
D 15.5mm, T 2mm, Ht 2mm, Wt 1.31g.

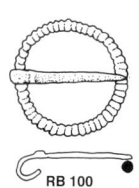

RB 101. Ireland PRO 1884,79.22
Find circumstances unknown.
Silver, slightly distorted, circular frame. One half of the frame has a circular cross-section; the other half has a square cross-section and is twisted to form four spiralling raised lines alternating with bands of punched circles. The lower half of the front face is decorated with three groups of beading alternating with three groups of radial grooves inlaid with niello. The pin has a circular cross-section, a pincer loop, and a conical collar decorated with beading.
D 21mm, T 2.5mm, Ht 2.5mm, Wt unavailable.

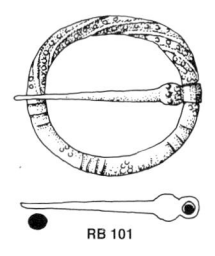

RB 102. Ireland   ROM 926.26.12
Find circumstances unknown. Bought from G.F. Lawrence (London), 29 September 1926.
Copper-alloy circular frame. One half of the frame has a circular cross-section and the other half has a twisted square profile. The pin has a circular cross-section, a pincer loop and a collar. It is badly bent at the tip.
D 30mm; other dimensions unavailable.
Pryor 1976, 88, fig. 33:84.

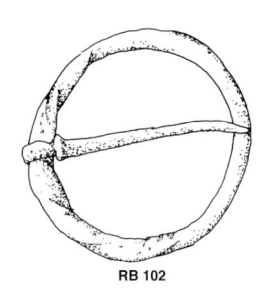

Class 3b

RB 103. County Meath NMI R4003 (ex RIA) (Pl. 11)
Found at Trim, details unknown (OS 6" sheet 36).
Silver circular frame with a rectangular cross-section. The front face is decorated as a 'laurel wreath'. The frame is formed of two twisted rings attached to each other, with the twists facing in opposite directions. These are attached to a plain flat base. A central 'stalk' is incorporated between the 'leaves' of the 'laurel'. The pin has a plano-convex cross-section, a simple loop and a flanged transverse ridge with a double moulding.
D 27mm, T 3mm, Ht 1.6mm, Wt 3.83g.
Cherry 1988, 161.

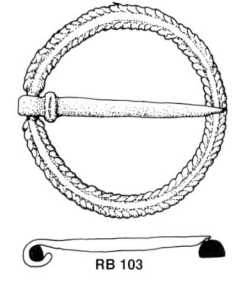

RB 104. Ireland   NMI 1862:710 (ex. Rev. Richard Butler coll.) (Pl. 11)
Find circumstances unknown.
Silver circular frame with a subtriangular cross-section. The frame is decorated as a 'laurel wreath'. It is formed of two twisted rings attached to each other, with the twists facing in opposite directions. A central 'stalk' is attached onto one side of the 'laurel' so that the frame takes on an almost triangular cross-section. The pin has a plano-convex cross-section, a simple loop and a flanged transverse ridge.
D 14mm, T 2mm, Ht 1.2mm, Wt 0.91g.
Anon. 1864.

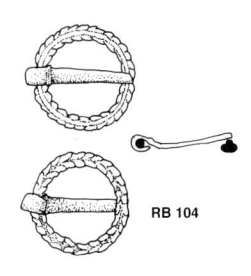

CLASS 4: ring brooches with applied plates

RB 105. County Dublin   93E191:42:1
Excavated at Essex Street West, Dublin (OS 6" sheet 18). Recovered from a reclamation layer. It was stratigraphically sealed between layers containing pottery with a date range from the twelfth to the fourteenth century, but the vast majority of examples were dated to the thirteenth century (McCutcheon 1995, 64; Linzi Simpson, pers. comm.).
Copper-alloy circular frame with a circular cross-section. The front face is decorated with an applied, thin triangular plate decorated with rocked tracer work. Traces of solder on the frame indicate that it would originally have been quartered by four applied triangles. The pin has a simple loop and is not decorated.
D 32mm, T 2.5mm, Ht 2.5m, Wt unavailable.
Johnson 1995, 75.

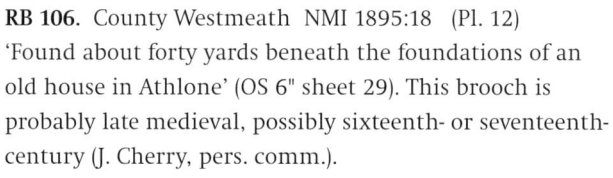

RB 106. County Westmeath NMI 1895:18 (Pl. 12)
'Found about forty yards beneath the foundations of an old house in Athlone' (OS 6" sheet 29). This brooch is probably late medieval, possibly sixteenth- or seventeenth-century (J. Cherry, pers. comm.).
Silver circular frame with a circular cross-section. The frame is composed of a ribbed wire ring to which are attached two lozenge-shaped plates, each decorated with an engraved lattice design. These alternate with two elongated hourglass-shaped plaques. Each plaque depicts two human heads with scroll and dot motifs. One of the plaques is cut through to provide a constriction for the pin. The pin has a flat rectangular cross-section and a simple loop. It appears to have a different metal content to the frame.
D 34mm, T 2.5mm, Ht 2.5mm, Wt 10.38g.

CLASS 5: composite ring brooches with projecting elements

RB 107. County Down   UM A9550
Excavated at Ballynarry Rath. Unstratified.
Silver circular frame composed of three rings, a ribbed ring between two cylindrical rings, arranged on top of each other at an oblique angle. Four cylindrical collets set

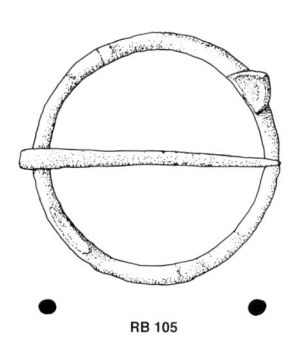

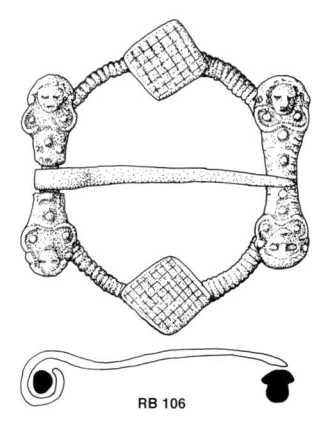

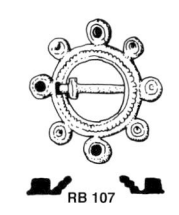

with red glass alternating with four conical cups set with metal studs project from the lower edge of the frame. The pin has a flat rectangular cross-section, a simple loop and a flanged transverse ridge decorated with a transverse groove. A rectangular piece removed from the central ring in the frame forms a constriction for the pin.
D 12.5mm; other dimensions unavailable.
Cherry 1988, 147–61; Davison 1961–2, 62, 71.

RB 108. County Westmeath NMI 1984:16 (Pl..13)
Found by metal-detector at Dysart (OS 6" sheet 13/25). Silver circular frame composed of three rings, one ribbed ring between two cylindrical rings, arranged on top of each other at an oblique angle. A flat, outward-projecting ring with scalloped edges is attached to the lower ring, which has been cut to create twenty individual projections, each decorated with three punched circles and dots. The pin has a plano-convex cross-section, a simple loop and a flanged transverse ridge. A rectangular piece removed from the central ring in the frame forms a constriction for the pin.
D 35mm, T 1.5mm, Ht 4.mm, Wt 6.56g.

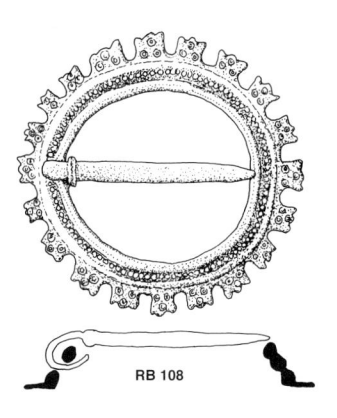

RB 109. Ireland   NMI 2.W.135 (ex RIA)
Find circumstances unknown.
Silver circular frame composed of three rings, a ribbed ring between two cylindrical rings, arranged on top of each other at an oblique angle. Three joined knobs project from the lower edge of the frame under the pin tip. The pin has a plano-convex cross-section, a simple loop and a flanged transverse ridge decorated with a transverse groove at either side of a row of squared beading. A rectangular piece removed from the central ring in the frame forms a constriction for the pin.
D 16mm, T 1mm, Ht 3mm, Wt 1.72g.

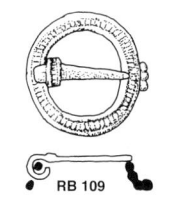

CLASS 6: ring brooches with multiple collets

Class 6a

RB 110. County Dublin   NMI 1897:26, on loan to 'Dublinia' (Pl. 14)
Found in May 1879 at the lower end of Marlboro Street, Dublin, during 'excavation' of the main sewer (OS 6" sheet 18).

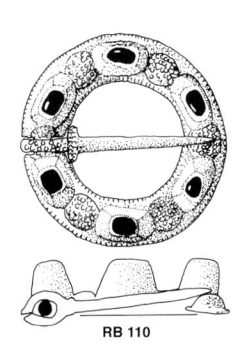

Gold circular frame. The front face is decorated with six high, tapering collets set with alternating blue and pink gemstones. These collets alternate with six bosses, each decorated with rows of punched circles. One boss narrows to a cylindrical bar to form a constriction for the pin; however, the pin head mimics the shape and decoration of the boss. The upper surfaces of the inner and outer edges of the frame are serrated. The pin has a pincer loop, a curved head decorated with punched circles, and a flanged transverse ridge decorated with deeply punched circles. There is a notch on the upper surface of the pin near the tip.
D 26.5mm, T 5.5mm, Ht 3mm, Wt 8.41g.
Cherry 1988, 146–61.

RB 111. County Westmeath   NMI E499:375
Found by metal-detector at Lough Ree.
Copper-alloy circular frame. The front face is decorated with six high, tapering collets (now empty) which slope slightly outwards. The intervening spaces are plain. The outer edges of the frame are serrated. The pin is very thin, with a circular cross-section and a simple loop. There is a small pin notch on the frame.
D 28.5mm, T 5mm, Ht 2.5mm, Wt 7.88g.

RB 112. Ireland   NMI 42.W.12 (ex RIA)   (Pl. 15)
Find circumstances unknown.
Silver circular frame. The front face is decorated with ten high, tapering collets (now empty) alternating with ten bosses, one of which has been partly cut away to create a constriction for the pin. The bosses are decorated with oblique bands of punched circles. The pin has a plano-convex cross-section, a simple loop, and a flanged transverse ridge with a double moulding. A small rectangular collet is positioned halfway down the shaft, and the remainder of the shaft is decorated with a chevron and dot motif.
D 47.5mm, T 7mm, CH 9.3mm, Wt 18.45g.
Cherry 1988, 161; Armstrong 1915, 295.

RB 113. Ireland   NMI number unavailable
Find circumstances unknown.
Copper-alloy circular frame. The front face is decorated with eight high, tapering collets (now empty) alternating with eight bosses, each covered with

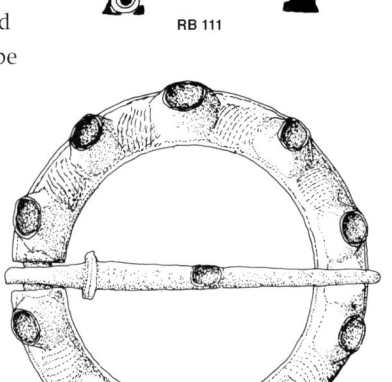

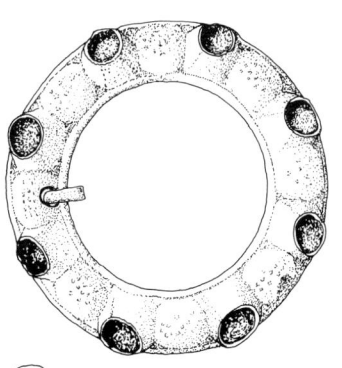

punched circles. The pin has a simple loop and is broken, only the head and loop remaining. The pin head is decorated with two parallel transverse grooves.
D 41.5mm, T 8mm, CH 7.8mm, Wt 28.22g.

RB 114. Ireland   NMI, not registered yet
Found by metal-detector at an unspecified location in the 'midlands'.
Copper-alloy circular frame decorated with six tapering, outward-slanting collets alternating with six bosses. Two collets are set with green glass 'stones', three have traces of the original fill, and one is empty. The pin is missing. There is a break in the frame through one of the bosses which was probably the position of a constriction for the pin.
D 26mm, T 2.5mm, Ht 3.5mm, CH 6.5mm, Wt unavailable.

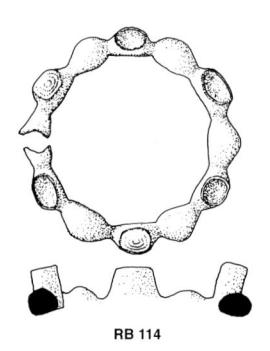

RB 115. Ireland   BM MLA 93,6-18,28
Find circumstances unknown.
Silver circular frame composed of a flat base set with four bosses alternating originally with four high, tapering collets, only one of which remains. The bosses are decorated with radial grooves alternating with radial rows of beading. The collet, now empty, is decorated with six double incised lines. There are clusters of three tiny knobs between each boss and collet. The reverse is decorated with a continuous chevron motif in which the inner triangles are cross-hatched. The pin has a curved square cross-section and a pincer loop; the head is decorated to imitate the boss, which has been cut through to form a constriction for the pin.
D 27.5mm, T 6mm, Ht 0.2mm, Wt unavailable.
Cherry 1988.

Class 6b

RB 116. County Dublin   92E109:75:28   (Pl. 16)
Excavated at Cornmarket/Francis Street, Dublin (OS 6" sheet 18). Recovered from ditch fill. Contextually dated to the later thirteenth century.
Copper-alloy lozenge-shaped frame. The front face is decorated with four pairs of tubular collets alternating with three groups of three blind holes in each corner (except for the remaining corner, at which there is only one hole,

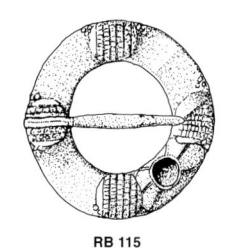

through which the pin is attached). Each of the corners is also decorated with short grooves. The pin has a triangular cross-section and a simple loop. Three of the collets are completely empty, but a white powdery residue in five of them may be the remains of the paste that glued the original 'stones' in position.
Max. 37mm x 37mm, T 7mm, Ht 2.5mm, CH 5mm, Wt unavailable.
Hayden, forthcoming; 1992.

RB 117. County Waterford   WHC E435:1013:3   (Pl. 17)
Excavated at Bakehouse Lane, Waterford (OS 6" sheet 9). Recovered from an ash/charcoal layer associated with a hearth/oven, and contextually dated to the mid–late thirteenth century.
Gold circular frame composed of a wide, flat ring decorated with four tubular collets, each set with alternating blue and green glass 'stones'. The inner and outer edges are each decorated with an applied concentric ring of beaded wire. The frame between each collet is decorated with filigree in the form of thin bands of gold curved into spirals and applied on edge, with curled-up ends. The curled ends are each set with a tiny granule of gold. Thin beaded wire is attached to the top edge of each of the curved bands. The pin has a plano-convex cross-section, a simple loop and a flanged transverse ridge decorated with rows of beading. The pin is attached to the frame through a D-shaped hole in the frame.
D 26.5mm, T 6mm, Ht 1.5mm, Wt unavailable.
Lightbown 1992, 147, pl. 28; 1997, 519–20, pl. 44B.

RB 118. County Wexford   BM MLA 1849,3-1,32 (ex Redmond Anthony coll.)   (Pl. 18)
Found in the remains of the Franciscan friary at Enniscorthy (OS 6" sheet 20/26).
Gold, slightly subcircular frame. The front face is decorated with two oval, tapering collets, set with rubies *en cabochon*, positioned opposite each other at the top and bottom of the frame. The bases of the collets project slightly outside the frame outline. There are also two pairs of small cylindrical collets set with faceted emeralds positioned at either end of the pin. John Cherry (pers. comm.) has suggested that these emeralds are probably replacements. The bifaceted frame is decorated with the

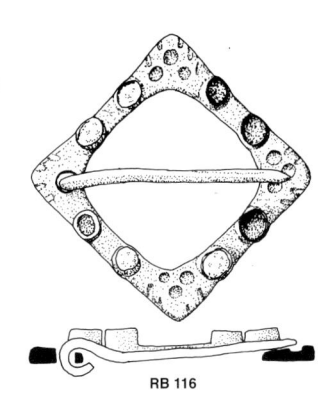

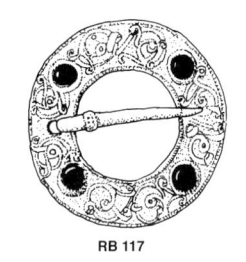

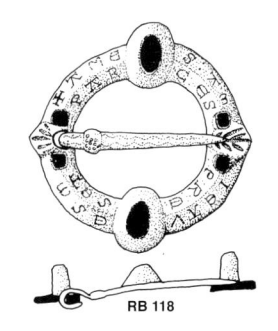

Lombardic inscription '+AMES:AMIE:AVES M PAR CES PRESET', which translates as 'By this gift you have the friend you love' (Cherry 1988). The frame swells out slightly behind the pin head and under the pin tip, and these areas are decorated with foliate ornament. The pin has a plano-convex cross-section, a simple loop and a flanged transverse ridge with punched circles. The pin head and shaft are decorated along their length with wavy lines and dots. A semicircular hole in the frame provides a pin constriction.
D 29mm, T 8.5mm, Ht 1mm, Wt unavailable.
Cahill 1994, 102; Cherry 1988; Smith 1909, pl. 20, no. 5; S. Lewis 1840, 604.

RB 119. County Wexford   BM MLA 1849,3-1,34
(ex Redmond Anthony coll.)
Find circumstances unknown.
Gold circular frame composed of sixteen semicircular hollow cups, each with one tiny tubular collet set with tiny emeralds *en cabochon*. A tiny rivet is visible on the underside of each cup where the collets are joined to the cups. The pin is looped around a hinge soldered onto the underside of the frame. It has a plano-convex cross-section, a simple loop, three transverse ridges and a notch on the upper surface near the tip. The tip rests on a catch in the shape of an acanthus leaf soldered onto the frame.
D 26mm, T 3mm, Ht 1mm, Wt unavailable.
Cahill 1994, 98–102; Cherry 1988.

RB 120. Ireland   NMI C373 (ex RIA)
Find circumstances unknown.
Gold circular frame. The front face is decorated with four high, tapering collets alternating with three small rosettes and a shouldered constriction for the pin. Each collet is supported by two raised diagonal struts adorned with leafy ornamentation. The collets are now empty and the pin is missing.
D 26mm, T 3mm, Ht 1mm, CH 8mm, Wt 8.11g.

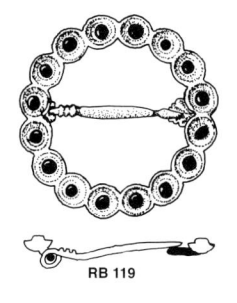

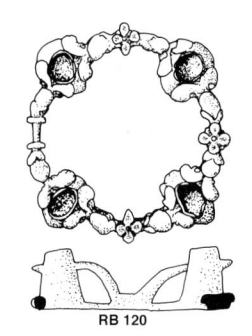

CLASS 7: ring brooches with projecting hands

RB 121. County Cork   NMI 1956:7   (Pl. 19)
Found in an open field in Carrigaline Parish, Ballinrea Townland (OS 6" sheet 86/87).
Gold pointed-oval frame with a triangular cross-section. A pair of joined hands project from the frame. The bifaceted frame is decorated with a chevron and short concentric groove motif. There are two rosette plates attached to the frame. There are raised shoulders at each side of the constriction, each decorated with one radial groove. The pin is attached on the right-hand side of the frame. It has a triangular cross-section, a simple loop and a flanged transverse ridge in the form of a rosette. The shaft is decorated with a chevron motif similar to that on the frame. There is also a notch on the shaft near the tip.
L 25mm, W 15.5mm, T 2mm, Ht 1.5mm, Wt 3.74g.
Cherry 1988, 161.

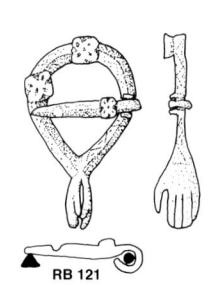

RB 122. County Kilkenny   NMI 1881:113 (ex William Perry coll.; previously mislabelled W87)   (Pl. 19)
Find circumstances unknown.
Gold pointed-oval frame with a triangular cross-section. A pair of joined hands project from the frame. The bifaceted frame is decorated with unintelligible, probably pseudo-, inscriptions. It is also decorated with a high, tapering collet (now empty) and two rosettes, through one of which the pin is attached. There is an empty space between the projecting hands which may once have held a stone. The pin has a plano-convex cross-section, a simple loop and a flanged transverse ridge decorated with beading. There is a notch on its upper surface near the tip.
L 25.5mm, W 17mm, T 2.5mm, CH 6.5mm, Wt 2.9g.
Cherry 1988, 147–61.

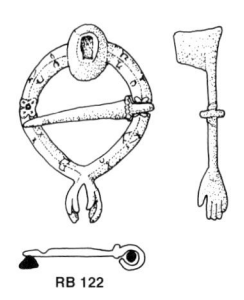

RB 123. County Meath   NMI R4001   (ex RIA)   (Pl. 19)
Found at Trim, details unknown (OS 6" sheet 36).
Gold circular frame with a rectangular cross-section. A pair of hands holding a collet (now empty) project from the frame. Another pair of clasped hands are incorporated into the frame. The frame is decorated with the Lombardic inscriptions 'SUIXEXEMILIDAM' on the front face and

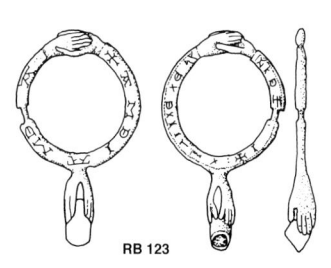

'+AMEIAMEA' on the reverse. Cherry has interpreted the inscription on the front face as a corruption of the medieval French love inscription 'IE SUIS EN LIEU D'UN AMI', which translates as 'I am here in place of the friend you love'. The pin is missing but would have been attached at the right-hand side of the frame.
L 28mm, D 17mm, T 2mm, Ht 0.8mm, Wt 1.95g.
Cherry 1988, 147–61.

RB 124. Ireland   BM MLA 1849,3-1,33 (ex Redmond Anthony coll.)   (Pl. 20)
Find circumstances unknown.
Gold pointed-oval frame with an uneven-sided triangular cross-section. The frame is divided into four quadrants in which the wider facet is alternately on the inner and outer edge. The wider facet is decorated with the Lombardic inscription '+AVE I MARIA G', an abbreviated version of the Angelic Salutation, 'Hail Mary full of grace'. The narrower facet is decorated with a row of beading. A pair of joined hands clasping an opal projects from the frame. John Cherry (pers. comm.) has suggested that the opal is probably a replacement. The front face of the frame is decorated with a high biconical collet set with a small ruby *en cabochon* and three lozenge-shaped plates depicting rosettes, through one of which the pin is attached. The rosette motif is incorporated into the pin head. The pin has a plano-convex cross-section, a simple loop and a flanged transverse ridge with beading. The shaft narrows under the transverse ridge and bears a notch near the tip.
 L 26mm, W 18mm, T 3mm, CH 7mm, Wt unavailable.
Cahill 1994, 98–102; Cherry 1988.

RB 125. Ireland   NMI W87 (ex RIA; previously mislabelled W88)   (Pl. 19)
Find circumstances unknown.
Gold pointed-oval frame with a triangular cross-section. A pair of joined hands project from the frame. Three rosettes, through one of which the pin is attached, decorate the frame. The bifaceted frame bears two Lombardic inscriptions, 'RU/SUI/SUI/SUI/RUI' on the inner facet and '+IO/+IO/DED/DCD+IO' on the outer facet. The meaning is obscure and not readily translatable. The pin is attached on the right-hand side of the frame. It has a plano-convex cross-section, a simple loop and a flanged transverse ridge

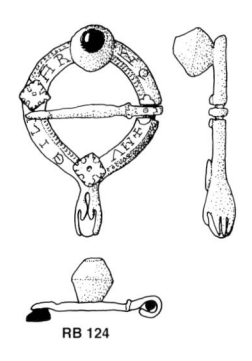

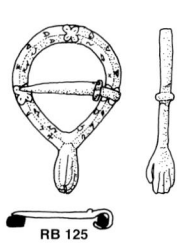

decorated with a row of beading. It is bent sideways.
L 22mm, W 14mm, T 2mm, Ht 1.5mm, Wt 1.92g.
Cherry 1988, 145–61; Wilde 1862, 44.

RB 126. Ireland   NMI 43.W.21 (ex RIA)
Find circumstances unknown.
Silver pointed-oval frame with a flat rectangular cross-section. A pair of joined hands project from the frame. The front face of the frame is decorated with a punched wavy zigzag motif and a low cylindrical collet, now empty. The pin is attached at the right-hand side of the frame. It has a triangular cross-section, a simple loop and a transverse ridge with two transverse grooves. A white powdery residue in the base of the collet may be the remains of the paste which glued the original stone in position.
L 33.5mm, W 19mm, T 2mm, Ht 1mm, CH 4.8mm, Wt 2.6g.
Armstrong 1915, 295.

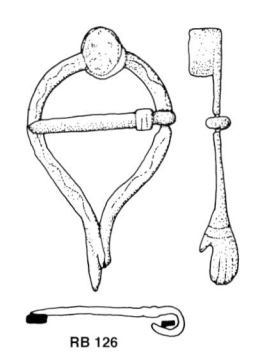

RB 127. Ireland   PRO 1884.79.20
Find circumstances unknown.
Gold pointed-oval frame with a triangular cross-section. A pair of joined hands clasping a 'pink' stone project from the frame. There is a collar at the 'wrists' of the projecting hands. The bifaceted frame is decorated with a loosely punched continuous chevron motif, and in the external facet each intervening space in the chevron motif is filled with one radial groove. Two four-petalled rosettes are punched into the frame at the top and under the pin tip. The pin has a plano-convex cross-section, a simple loop and flanges decorated with two punched transverse grooves. It is attached on the right-hand side of the frame and the constriction is shouldered.
L 19mm, W 10mm, T 2.5mm, Ht 1mm, Wt unavailable.

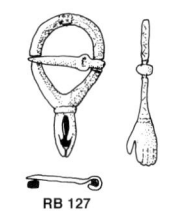

RB 128. Ireland   PRO 1884.79.21
Find circumstances unknown.
Silver-gilt circular frame with a flat rectangular cross-section. The frame has projecting ends which hold a cylindrical collet set with tiny, faceted pink stones. The collet is held in place by a tiny metal dowel. A cylindrical bar is crudely bent around the junction between the frame and the projection. The front face is decorated with abstract markings. The pin has a plano-convex cross-section, a simple loop and a flanged transverse ridge with

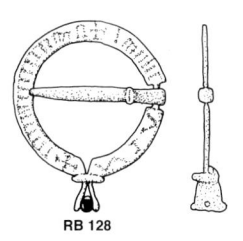

one narrow transverse groove.
L 24mm, W 20mm, T 2mm, Ht 0.6mm, Wt unavailable.

CLASS 8: ring brooches with derivative decoration

RB 129. County Dublin   NMI E71:491
Excavated at High Street, Dublin (OS 6" sheet 18).
Unstratified.
Lead-alloy circular frame with a plano-convex cross-section. The front face is decorated with groups of combinations of raised radial lines and raised short concentric lines. The pin is missing.
D 19mm, T 3mm, Ht 0.8mm, Wt 0.94g.

RB 130. County Dublin   NMI E71:2401
Excavated at High Street, Dublin (OS 6" sheet 18). The stratigraphic sequence of this site has not yet been fully resolved. Provisional dating: late twelfth/early thirteenth century.
Copper-alloy, slightly distorted circular frame with a plano-convex cross-section. The front face of the frame is ribbed and decorated with four low collets, now empty. The pin is missing.
D 13mm, T 2mm, Ht 1mm, Wt 0.96g.

RB 131. County Dublin   NMI E71:2818, on loan to 'Dublinia'
Excavated at High Street, Dublin (OS 6" sheet 18). The stratigraphic sequence of this site has not yet been fully resolved. Provisional dating: probably late twelfth/early thirteenth century.
Lead-alloy, slightly distorted circular frame with a horizontal oval cross-section. The frame is decorated on the front face with four evenly spaced knops. The pin is missing. There are casting ridges along the inner and outer edges of the frame.
D 17mm, T 1mm, Ht 1mm, Wt unavailable.

RB 132. County Dublin   NMI E132:33904, on loan to 'Dublinia' (Pl. 21)
Excavated at Wood Quay, Dublin (OS 6" sheet 18). Precise contextual details are not available at present. Provisional dating: thirteenth century.

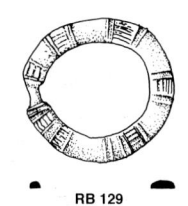

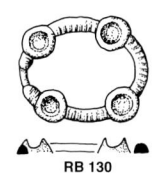

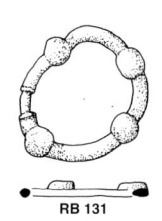

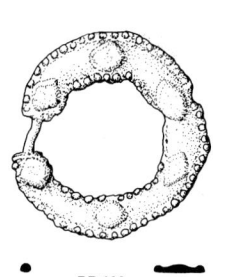

Lead-alloy circular frame with a broadly plano-convex cross-section. The inner and outer edges of the frame are decorated with rows of beading. The frame is also decorated with six evenly spaced, lozenge-shaped bosses. The constriction is shouldered and the pin is missing.
D 25mm, T 4.5mm, Ht 0.9mm, Wt 2.41g.

RB 133. County Dublin   NMI E132:64248
Excavated at Wood Quay, Dublin (OS 6" sheet 18). Precise contextual details are not available at present. Provisional dating: thirteenth century.
Lead-alloy circular frame. The inner and outer edges of the frame are ribbed. Within this band are five raised circular outlines alternating with five lozenge-shaped outlines. Each of these shapes has an internal boss. There are also two smaller bosses between each of these shapes. There is an extra large boss behind a square hole which acts as a constriction for the pin, which is now missing. The remaining spaces on the front face are filled with cross-hatching. On the reverse of the frame are three raised bosses corresponding to the central bosses within three of the five circular shapes, and there were probably two more which are now missing. There is also a small area decorated with thin radial lines, and a short ridge along the inner edge at the constriction.
D 35mm, T 10mm, Ht 2mm, Wt 5.56g.

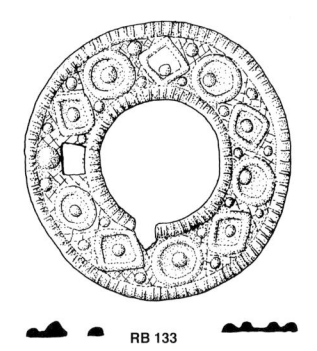

RB 134. County Dublin   NMI E132:1857319, on loan to 'Dublinia'   (Pl. 21)
Excavated at Wood Quay, Dublin (OS 6" sheet 18). Precise contextual details are not available at present. Provisional dating: thirteenth century.
Lead-alloy circular frame. The front face of the frame would originally have been decorated with twelve bosses, ten of which remain. Each boss is surrounded by two semicircular ridges. The outer edge of the frame is bevelled. The undersurface of the frame has what may be a functional concentric ridge. The pin is missing. The frame is incomplete; it may have been broken and soldered in another place, and it is now in a very fragile condition.
D 24mm, T 3.5mm, Ht 0.8mm, Wt 1.14g.

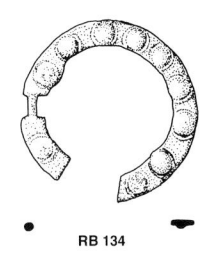

RB 135. Ireland   UM A32:1990 (ex Seaby coll.)
Find circumstances unknown.

Lead-alloy circular frame with a flat rectangular cross-section. The front face of the frame is decorated with a raised continuous chevron motif, with one small raised boss in each of the intervening spaces. The inner and outer edges of the frame have raised borders. The pin is missing. The pin constriction is formed by a small hole in the frame. The frame is quite corroded.
D 37.5mm, T 8mm, Ht 2.5mm, Wt unavailable.

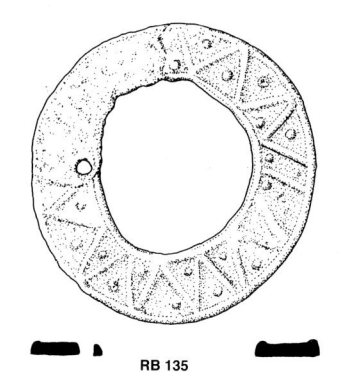

CLASS 9: miscellaneous ring brooches

RB 136. County Antrim   CF VI 277
Excavated at Irish Quarter, Carrickfergus (OS 6" sheet 52). Contextually dated to the early thirteenth century (Lesley Simpson, pers. comm.).
Silver-gilt eight-lobed frame, composed of four oval bosses alternating with four open semicircular rings. The bosses are decorated with closely spaced radial rows of beading and the rings are each decorated with a concentric row of beading. The pin has a plano-convex cross-section, a simple loop and a flanged transverse ridge with a transverse row of beading between two transverse raised lines. The pin head is decorated with two longitudinal grooves, giving three raised ridges.
D 24mm, T 6.5mm and 9mm, Ht 2.5mm and 5.5mm, Wt unavailable.
Cherry 1988; Simpson and Brannon 1988, 65.

RB 137. County Dublin   NMI E71:3918
Excavated at High Street, Dublin (OS 6" sheet 18). The statigraphic sequence of this site has not yet been fully resolved. Provisional dating: late twelfth/early thirteenth century.
Lead-alloy circular frame composed of an outer cylindrical ring and an inner, flat, rectangular-sectioned ring joined by 23 radial cylindrical bars, giving an openwork effect. The outer ring is decorated on the upper surface with diagonal raised lines, and the inner ring with serrated ridges around its inner and outer margins. The pin, of iron, is narrow with a circular cross-section and a simple loop.
D 23mm, T 6mm, Ht 2mm, Wt 1.8 g.

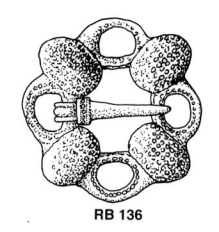

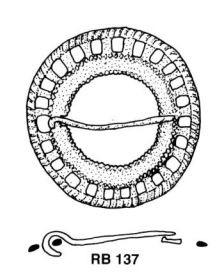

RB 138. Ireland   NMI W.454 (ex RIA)
Find circumstances unknown.
Copper-alloy circular frame with a square cross-section. The frame is divided by five deep radial grooves, which continue down the outer edge of the frame. The front face is decorated with paired concentric lines and tightly packed radial lines. The outer edge of the frame is scored, creating three rows of high-relief 'brambling'. The pin has wide flanges and is decorated with two longitudinal lines on its head.
D 18.5mm, T 4mm, Ht 4.5mm, Wt 6.27g.

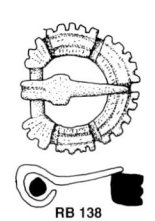

RB 139. Ireland   NMI W.456 (ex RIA)
Find circumstances unknown.
Copper-alloy circular frame with a pronounced plano-convex cross-section. The front face is decorated with three alternating rows of evenly spaced blind holes, composed of an outer and an inner row of nine holes and alternating with these an upper row of ten slightly larger holes. There is also a very faint leafy motif in a diamond shape surrounding each of the holes. The pin has a pincer loop and a square-profiled collar. Unusually, the pin is bent upwards instead of downwards. It may be that it was replaced backwards at some stage, or perhaps the brooch was worn with the decoration facing the body, although this seems unlikely.
D 25mm, T 5mm, Ht 3mm, Wt 5.58g.

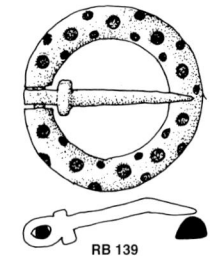

RB 140. Ireland   PRO 1884.79.26   (Pl. 22)
Find circumstances unknown.
Silver sexfoil frame. The front face is decorated with six lion-heads, each with eight or nine petal-shaped depressions surrounding their raised faces. There are twelve holes arranged in pairs around the inner edge of the frame, and the intervening spaces are filled with short, closely spaced radial grooves. The pin has a rectangular cross-section, a simple loop and a pronounced upward curve in profile where its shaft begins. The shaft is decorated along its length with a loose wavy line between two straight lines, and there are tiny oblique grooves within each wave. The overall impression is of an organic, plant-like effect. The pin is slightly bent sideways. One of the circular holes arranged in pairs around the frame has been widened to a rectangle to provide a constriction for the pin.
D 39mm, T 7–12mm, Ht 1–3mm, Wt unavailable.

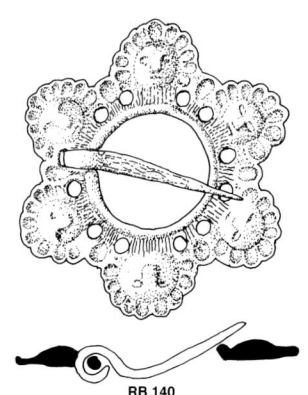

APPENDIX 1

Additional ring brooches, not included in catalogue

95E023:19. Bachelors Lane, Drogheda, Co. Louth. Copper-alloy brooch with a circular frame of triangular cross-section, i.e. the front face is bifaceted. D 27.5mm (K. Campbell, pers. comm.).

E110:9620. Kells Priory, Co. Kilkenny. Copper-alloy brooch with circular frame of subcircular cross-section. The front face is decorated with four groups of radially incised lines. D 28mm.

Ashmolean Museum 1927.6289. Copper-alloy brooch with circular frame of rectangular cross-section. One face is decorated with the raised inscription 'AVE MARIA'. D 31mm. It was found in Ireland in 1872 and was part of the Joan Evans collection presented to the Ashmolean Museum by Arthur Evans in 1927 (J. Cherry, pers. comm.).

Ashmolean Museum 1927.6303. Copper-alloy brooch with circular frame of rectangular cross-section. One face is decorated with a meaningless pattern of lines. No measurements available. It was part of the Joan Evans collection presented to the Ashmolean Museum by Arthur Evans in 1927 (J. Cherry, pers. comm.).

95E77:310:15. Trim Castle, Co. Meath. Recovered from ditch fill in the north-west of the keep; contextually dated to the fourteenth century (A. Hayden, pers. comm.). Silver brooch with a circular frame of flat rectangular cross-section. The front face is decorated with two high tapering collets, divided by the pin and a lozenge-shaped flat plate. One of the collets retains its original enamel(?) inset which is now pink but may originally have been red (S. Kelly, conservator's report). Each collet is supported by two raised diagonal struts adorned with leafy ornamentation. The frame and decoration are forged rather than cast integrally. The pin has a flanged transverse ridge decorated with a single incised transverse line. The frame is badly distorted. This brooch is very similar to RB 120, Class 6b.
Present dimensions 29mm x 17mm, estimated D *c.* 23mm, T 2mm, H 0.5mm, CH 8.5mm (M.B. Deevy, artifact report).

95E77:1251:1. Trim Castle, Co. Meath. Recovered from occupation material in the south tower of the keep; contextually dated to between the fourteenth and sixteenth centuries (A. Hayden, pers. comm.). Copper-alloy brooch with a circular frame of plano-convex cross-section. The brooch would appear to have been reversible as the frame is decorated on both sides. The flat face is inlaid with 'criss-crosses' of lead alloy/(silver?). The intervening spaces are decorated with punching. The other side is divided into approximately twenty shallow swellings, rather crudely executed. The curved areas are also decorated with rows of punched circles. The pin is missing. Ext. D 40mm, T 4mm, H 2–2.5mm (M.B. Deevy, artifact report).

The use of inlaid metal decoration on this ring brooch is the first example from Ireland. A close parallel for the use of inlay is provided by a Welsh brooch found during restoration of Kidwelly Castle, Dyfed (Redknap 1996, 96–7). This slightly smaller brooch (ext. D 33mm) has a reversible gunmetal frame inlaid with silver to form a 'crossed-garter' pattern on half its frame. A similar brooch was recovered in the Swan Lane excavations in Lower Thames Street, London (Egan 1991c, 250). This brooch (ext. D 37mm) has a reversible gunmetal frame decorated with inlaid lead strips. A further similar brooch was recovered from the 1983 Billingsgate lorry park watching brief in London (*ibid.*, 251–2). This slightly larger example (ext. D 45.5mm) again had a reversible gunmetal frame whose decoration included bands of inlaid tin. The Swan Lane brooch is contextually dated to the late thirteenth–early fourteenth century, while the Billingsgate brooch is contextually dated to the late fourteenth century. A smaller fourteenth-century example (ext. D 26mm) from Tanner Street in Winchester has a reversible copper-alloy frame, inlaid with strips of what is possibly silver (Biddle and Hinton 1990, 641–2).

APPENDIX 2

Unlocated ring brooches and artifacts which may be ring brooches

1. 'A small, open, brass buckle with fragmentary remains of the hinge part of an iron tongue [pin]' was amongst the finds from the excavation of a mound at Blessington, Co. Wicklow (Roe and Prendergast 1946, 5).

2. A copper-alloy 'annular brooch' is described as having a flat cross-section and as being undecorated except for two raised ribs on the frame opposite the pin constriction. It is also described as being a 'late and decadent specimen . . . derived from the penannular type with moulded terminals'. It is located in Cambridge University Museum (IDNO1927:702) and is labelled 'Irish buckle, Bateman Sale, Bought from T. Ready'.

3. 'A small garter fibula or brooch of gold, 1 1/16 inches in diameter. Around the two sides is engraved the motto "AVE . MARIA . GRATAIA" — "PLENA . DOMINUS". The field was probably filled in with a soft vitreous enamel. In the centre of the pin are two small supports on which are fixed, one on each side of the pin, the letters "H" and "K". Both were originally surmounted by a crown but that of the first letter alone now remains. There can be little doubt that these letters refer to Henry VIII and Queen Katherine of Aragon rather than Katherine Parr.' Lot 463, Robert Day Sale Catalogue (Anon. 1913).

4. 'An earlier ring brooch in silver 1 5/16 in diameter. On the flat side of the hoop is engraved "+AVE . MARIA . GRACIA . PLENA". English work, late XIIIth century. Bought by Fernardent £9.5.' Lot 464, Robert Day Sale Catalogue (Anon. 1913).

5. 'Two small ring brooches in silver, plain one of very light make from Westmeath and an old Scotch brooch of silver shaped as a crowned heart, from Co. Down.' Bought by Wilson for £2.4. Lot 465, Robert Day Sale Catalogue (Anon. 1913).

6. 'No. 88, another [ring brooch] of the same size [small], but somewhat lighter [than 1 dwt 5gr.], and differently ornamented, Wt., 22gr.' (Wilde 1862, 44). No. 87 has a pair of praying hands and an inscription and is described as being one of a pair, suggesting that no. 88 might also have had 'praying hands' ornamentation. While all other gold objects from the RIA collection are located in the NMI, this artifact is at present unlocated.

7. Copper-alloy ring described as being from a 'small medieval stick-pin brooch'. It was cut from sheet metal and measures 23mm in diameter. The outer edge forms a perfect circle but the inner edge is very uneven. It is decorated with irregular short incised lines. It has a pin constriction but the pin is missing. It is contextually dated to *c.* the fifteenth century (Ivens 1987, 109).

8. NMI, no registration number. Silver artifact formed of conjoined annular rings, i.e. spectacle-shaped. This is not a medieval spectacle buckle as it has two pins attached to the outer edges of each ring and facing inwards. Spectacle buckles are larger and have one pin attached to the central bar. The arrangement of pins is not unique and could have functioned in a similar way to those of a ring brooch. The large medieval Scottish 'Glenlyon brooch' has a circular frame with a fixed central bar and a similar arrangement of pins. A number of Scottish seventeenth- and eighteenth-century ring brooches have a similar arrangements of pins but their frames are quite distinctively shaped in the form of crowned hearts (also known as Luckenbooth brooches).

9. This artifact, E249:4107, was excavated at James Street, Drogheda, Co. Louth (OS 6" sheet 24). It was unstratified (K. Campbell, pers. comm.). It is of copper alloy, with a circular frame and a rectangular cross-section. The front face is decorated with four pairs of notches, one on the inner edge and one on the external edge. There is also one notch at either side of the constriction, which is now broken. The external edge of the frame is serrated. The pin is missing. D 27.5mm, T 3mm, Ht 1.5mm, Wt unavailable.

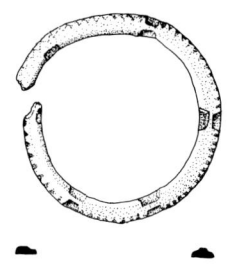

APPENDIX 3

List of ring brooch depictions in Ireland

County Clare—Depiction of John the Baptist wearing a ring brooch to fasten a cloak on his chest, carved on a panel of a limestone baptismal font. Originally in the church of St John the Baptist, Kilballyowen; presently located in the Eamonn de Valera Library and Museum, Ennis.
Higgins 1995.

County Down—Depiction of a woman wearing a ring brooch. Stone-carved recumbent effigy.
Hunt 1974, 133–4, pl. 22; Cherry 1988, 144.

County Dublin—Depiction of a woman wearing a ring brooch. Stone carving on a capital in Christchurch Cathedral.

County Dublin—Depiction of St Paul wearing a ring brooch to fasten a cloak on his chest. Stone carving on the northern side panel of the Purcell double tomb-chest. Originally in the All Hallows monastery; presently located in St Werburgh's.
Hunt 1974, 141–3, pl. 204.

County Galway—Depiction of Christ showing his five wounds, wearing a ring brooch to fasten a cloak on his chest. Stone carving on the southern niche of the Joyce tomb, in the church of St Nicholas of Myra, Galway.
Hunt 1974, 149, pl. 261; Higgins and Heringklee 1992.

County Galway—Depiction of St Catherine wearing a ring brooch to fasten a cloak on her chest (Pl. 30). Wooden sculpture, presently located in the Diocesan Museum in Loughrea.
Mahr 1976, 167; MacLeod 1945, 196.

County Galway—Depiction of a bearded male figure wearing a ring brooch to fasten a cloak on his chest. Stone carving on the side panel of the Sir Peter French tomb-chest, presently located in the graveyard of the Franciscan abbey at Newtownsmith.
Higgins, forthcoming b.

County Kildare—Depiction of a woman wearing a ring brooch to fasten the vent in the neck of her gown. Incised stone slab, originally located in Friarstown churchyard, Castledillon; presently stored by the OPW in the Market House in Kildare town.
Omurethi 1911; Harbison 1971–6; Hunt 1974, 154, pl. 23.

County Kildare—Depiction of St Catherine wearing a ring brooch to fasten a cloak on her chest. Stone carving on the side panel of a tomb-chest, presently located in the graveyard at New Abbey, Kilcullen.
Fitzgerald 1902; Hunt 1974, 159, pl. 216.

County Kildare—Depiction of St Margaret of Antioch wearing a ring brooch to fasten a cloak on her chest. Stone carving on the side panel of a tomb-chest, presently located in the graveyard at New Abbey, Kilcullen.
Fitzgerald 1902; Hunt 1974, 159, pl. 216.

County Kilkenny—Depiction of a woman wearing a ring brooch at her throat. Stone carving on an architectural panel, located over the outside of the north door of St Mary's church, Callan.
Hunt 1974, 165, pl. 174.

County Kilkenny—Depiction of Christ showing the five wounds, wearing a ring brooch to fasten a cloak on his chest. Stone carving on the side panel of a tomb-chest, presently located in the north transept in St Canice's Cathedral, Kilkenny.
Rae 1971; Hunt 1974, 192, pl. 319; Bradley 1985.

County Kilkenny—Depiction of Christ showing the five wounds, wearing a ring brooch to fasten a cloak on his chest. Stone carving on the side panel of a tomb-chest, presently propped against the west wall of the north aisle in St Canice's Cathedral, Kilkenny.
Hunt 1974, 193, pl. 314.

County Kilkenny—Depiction of a man with long hair curled up at the ends, wearing a ring brooch to fasten the vent at the neck of his garment (Pl. 25). Stone carving of a bust acting as a label stop on the entrance to the south porch of St Canice's Cathedral, Kilkenny.

County Kilkenny—Depiction of a man wearing a ring brooch to fasten the vent at the neck of his garment. Stone carving of a bust acting as a label stop on the entrance to the south porch of St Canice's Cathedral, Kilkenny.

County Kilkenny—Depiction of a woman wearing a ring brooch to fasten the vent at the neck of her garment (Pl. 26). Stone carving of a bust acting as a label stop on the entrance to the south porch of St Canice's Cathedral, Kilkenny.

County Kilkenny—Depiction of a man wearing a ring brooch to fasten the vent at the neck of his garment. Stone carving of a bust acting as a label stop on the entrance to the south porch of St Canice's Cathedral, Kilkenny.

County Kilkenny—Depiction of a man wearing a ring brooch to fasten the vent at the neck of his garment. Stone carving of a bust on the outer wall of Gowran church, Gowran.

County Kilkenny—Depiction of Christ showing the five wounds, wearing a ring brooch to fasten a cloak on his chest (Pl. 27). Stone carving on the side panel of the tomb-chest of a Butler knight in Gowran church, Gowran.
Rae 1970; Hunt 1974, 169, pl. 305.

County Kilkenny—Depiction of St Andrew wearing a ring brooch to fasten a cloak on his chest (Pl. 29). Stone carving on the side panel of a tomb-chest, in the northernmost chapel of the north transept of the Jerpoint Abbey church .
Rae 1971; Hunt 1974, 176, pl. 295.

County Kilkenny—Depiction of St Margaret of Antioch wearing a ring brooch to fasten a cloak on her chest (Pl. 28). Stone carving on the side panel of a tomb-chest, in the south chapel of the north transept of the church at Jerpoint Abbey.
Rae 1971; Hunt 1974, 177, pl. 294.

County Kilkenny—Depiction of a woman wearing a ring brooch to fasten the vent at the neck of her garment. Fragment of a recumbent stone effigy, presently set into the wall of the ruined church on the road at the entrance to Kells Priory.
Hunt 1974, 180, pl. 21.

County Kilkenny—The ring brooch is positioned within the lozenge-like space at the junction of the arms and shaft of an incised foliated cross, Kilferagh.
J. Higgins, pers. comm.; Higgins, forthcoming a.

County Kilkenny—The ring brooch is positioned within an octagonal space at the junction of the arms and shaft of an incised eight-point cross with fleur-de-lis terminal. Recovered during restoration and built into the boundary wall of St Patrick's graveyard.
O'Dwyer (no date).

County Louth—Depiction of a ring brooch held in a hand (Pl. 23). Applied decoration on pottery, now only one large sherd remaining.
K. Campbell, pers. comm.; Hurst 1988, 252.

County Louth—Depiction of ring brooch. Applied decoration on pottery, now only one small sherd remaining.
K. Campbell, pers. comm.

County Mayo—Depiction of Christ showing the five wounds, wearing a ring brooch to fasten a cloak on his chest. Stone carving on the side panel of a tomb-chest, presently forming a tomb front on a gabled tomb niche in the church at Strade.
Hunt 1974, 169, pl. 305; Rae 1970.

County Meath—Depiction of Christ showing the five wounds, wearing a ring brooch to fasten a cloak on his chest. Stone carving on a panel of a baptismal font in the church of St Lawrence, Rathmore.
Roe 1968, 92–8.

County Tipperary—Depiction of a woman wearing a ring brooch to fasten the vent in the neck of her gown (Pl. 24). Stone recumbent effigy, presently standing in a niche near the south end of the east wall of the churchyard of St John the Baptist's church, Cashel.
Du Noyer 1845; Cutts 1849, pl. LXXIV; Hunt 1974, 224, pl. 26.

County Tipperary—Depiction of a woman wearing a ring brooch to fasten the vent in the neck of her gown. Stone recumbent effigy, presently standing in a niche in the medieval town wall on the south side of the churchyard of St

John the Baptist's church, Cashel.
Du Noyer 1845; Hunt 1974, 224, pl. 28.

County Tipperary—Depiction of a young man wearing a ring brooch at his neck. Fragment of a recumbent stone effigy (?), presently set high onto the wall of Burke Lane, Cashel.

County Waterford—Depiction of Christ as Judge wearing a ring brooch to fasten a cloak on his chest. Stone carving on the side panel of a tomb-chest, presently set onto a wall foundation of the remains of the Augustinian church at Mothel.
Hunt 1974, 233, pl. 332.

County Wexford—Depiction of a woman, Alis La Kerdif, with a ring brooch at her neck. Stone head slab presently set into the north wall of the chancel of St Mary's church, New Ross.
Hunt 1974, 239, pl. 96.

GLOSSARY

Amulet	A protective charm usually worn on the person.
Annular	In the form of a ring.
Beading	A row of deeply punched circles.
Black Letter	Ornate Gothic lettering, usually lower case, in use in England from the later fourteenth century. Its main characteristic is angularity and verticality of form.
Blind holes	Holes occurring on brooches which were not intended to be filled with stones or enamel and were often arranged in a pattern for decorative effect. They were probably drilled into the frame and by their nature are only suitable for thick, robust brooches.
Book of hours	A form of devotional book developed in the Middle Ages containing prayers and meditations appropriate to seasons, months, days, and hours.
Brambled	Scored in a grid pattern to leave upstanding knobs, somewhat like the surface of a blackberry.
Cabling	Decoration in the form of a twisted bar or imitating a twisted bar or cord.
Cabochon	A precious or semi-precious stone which is polished without being cut into facets.
Champlevé	A technique of enamelling in which the enamel is set in recesses which are cast or gouged out of the surface of the metal. The process required a substantial thickness of metal and was most often used on base metals such as copper alloy.
Collet	A round band of metal that encircles a gemstone and holds it in place.
Engraving	Cutting a design into the surface of metal by removing a thin strip from the surface of the metal.

Epigraphy	The study of inscriptions.
Filigree	A decorative pattern made of fine gold or silver wires, often beaded and twisted and usually soldered onto a metal backing.
Granulation	Decoration consisting of minute spherical grains of gold or silver soldered onto a background.
Incising	Cutting a design into the surface of metal without removing any metal; the metal is merely pushed aside.
Jewel	An item of jewellery made of precious metal and possibly, but not necessarily, incorporating a gemstone.
Label stop	An ornamental, in this case figurative, boss at the beginning and end of a hood-mould (the projecting moulding to throw off rain above an arch, window or doorway).
Lapidary	A medieval book about gems, often primarily concerned with gem lore, i.e. describing the magical properties of various types of gemstones.
Lombardic	Lettering derived from Roman capitals but with a number of curved letter forms; in use until the later fourteenth century, when it was replaced by Black Letter.
Niello	A black compound of metal sulphides, fusible at low temperatures, inlaid into incised decoration in metal, usually silver or gold.
Titulus	'I.N.R.I.', the Latin inscription placed over Christ's head during the Crucifixion, meaning 'Iesus Nazarenus Rex Iudaeorum' ('Jesus of Nazareth, King of the Jews').
Weepers	Small images of mourners on tombs, usually set in arcading along the side of the tomb.